THE MOUNTAIN
AND THE WAVE

Boardriders are dreamers.
    They dream of things that never were...
  and sometimes they make them happen.

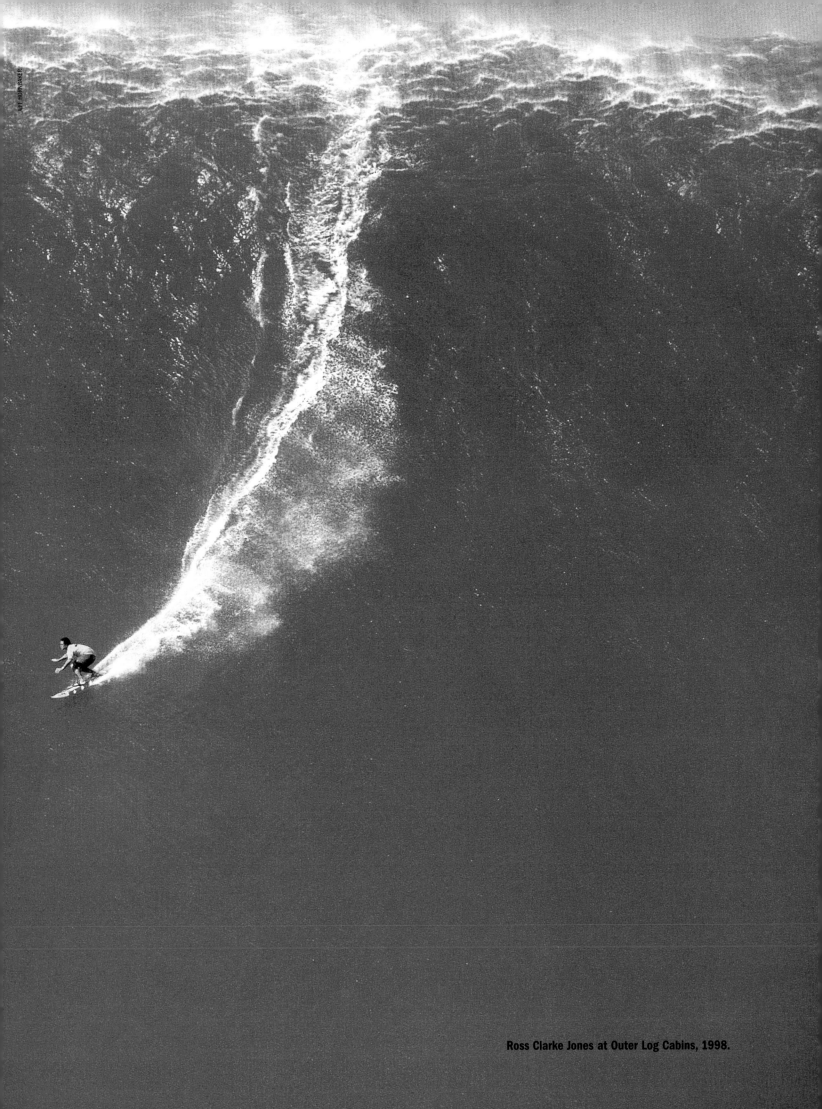

Ross Clarke Jones at Outer Log Cabins, 1998.

They dream of perfect places in the sun,
and glassy little peaks.

Kassia Meador, Indonesia, 2004.

Or deep cavernous pits..

Strider Wasilewski, Teahupoo.

Eric Jackson, New Zealand, 2003.

Or defying the bounds of the possible in the world's most exotic places.

Danny Way, Great Wall of China, 2005.

**Of sending salt spray
rumbling through the jungle.**

Kelly Slater, Indonesia.

And this is where our dream began.

Bells Beach, Easter 1975.

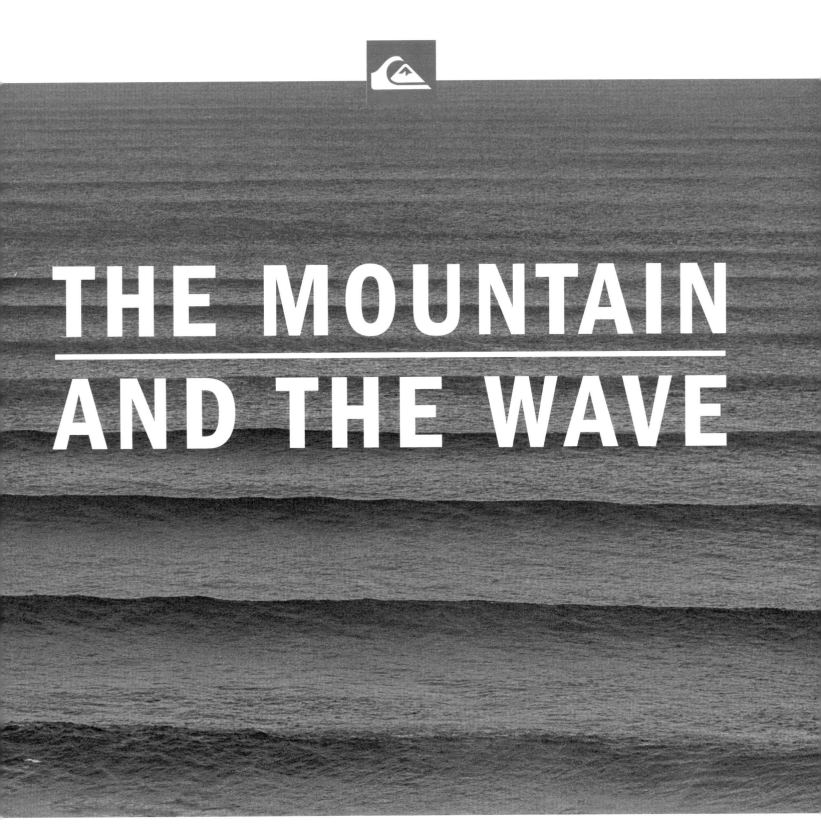

THE MOUNTAIN
AND THE WAVE

The Quiksilver Story

Phil Jarratt

CONTENTS

BERNARD TESTEMALE

Kelly Slater with a long
Hossegor wall ahead.

KELLY SLATER

Caption

Kelly...numbers don't count

Kelly Slater's contribution to Quiksilver can never be quantified in numbers.
Seven world titles...eight? How many covers? How many column inches?
How many kids in the queue for his autograph? It simply doesn't matter.
When Quiksilver signed him in 1990, CEO Bob McKnight wrote: "Don't
ever get confused and think that we only signed you because of your
potential to become a world champion. We signed you because you're a
good kid, a great surfer and a fine image for our company." Nothing has
changed. Yo Kelly! Salut! Good on yer, mate!

7X WORLD CHAMPION!

Does this mean what I think it means? Brazil, 2005.

How We Got Started

When we started designing the first Quiksilver boardshorts, we just wanted to make them better than the others. I suppose you could say that was our first mission statement, except that we didn't know what a mission statement was!

"We" was me and two mates, Carol McDonald from Ocean Grove and Tim Davis from Torquay. It was the start of the last summer of the 1960s; the hippie movement was all over the mainstream news and, in our little world, the summer psyche was all-pervasive. Surfboard design was progressing in leaps and bounds, making them more maneuverable and manageable. Jet travel was almost affordable and you could even run a car, as long as your mates waxed the petrol (or, as in my case, your Nanna gave you wheels for your 21ST!).

Indo was being whispered around, and the best surfers were starting to travel, chasing the seasons. There was a total buzz about surfing, and for me it was quite simple: I wanted to build my life around it. So we made boardshorts.

We sometimes get credited with designing the first "technical" boardshort, but the truth is, we used snaps and Velcro instead of flies because I'd bought a supply of them when I started making Rip Curl wetsuits. (And, although Carol was a bloody good sewer, maybe she didn't know how to do flies!) The yoke waist, which was higher at the back than the front, was the other difference; they hugged your back and still hung low on your hips. They were distinctive, functional, comfortable boardshorts, and two-toned yokes made them different from the rest. Surfers seemed to like them.

Our first customer in the world was the Klemm-Bell surf shop in Gardenvale, Melbourne, and a few months later, their branch in Torquay. Reg Bell was a good mate of mine, and after rejecting my offer of a partnership in the wetsuit company that became Rip Curl, he felt like he owed me one. Anyway, they sold like stink, and soon I was driving up and down the coast, supplying every surf shop I could find in between surf sessions. It wasn't a bad life. You made the shorts, you went out and sold them, then you started again. It was a lot easier than it is now!

As the years went by, people came and went. Brewster Everett joined me pretty early in the piece, and he was a vital creative cog in the business. Then John Law joined me in '76, and we moved into our first proper factory, Jeff Hakman came to town, won the Bells contest and put some drunken proposition to us about starting up in America. And, well, you know the rest. Or you will when you've read this book.

Quiksilver has given me a great life so far, and I'm looking forward to surfing, skiing and sharing the good times with Quiksilver people around the world for many years to come. The thing about this company is that it's never been about one person, not in the beginning, not now. None of us ever believed that the brand should be guided by individual, stand-alone intelligence. Quiksilver has evolved through interaction of a group of five or six people who think globally and act locally and rule the brand through rough consensus. And I mean "rough," because if you agree with everything that's going on everywhere, then you're not contributing much.

Quiksilver is in good hands; I'm sure of that. I'm proud of what we, the founders, achieved, and I know I'll be equally proud of the road that lies ahead for our brand.

—Alan Green, *Torquay, February 2006*

Alan Green in his office at 29 Pride St, Torquay, February 1976.

30 Years of Mountains and Waves

In the beginning...

I grew up in and around the beach...started surfing at 12 when a friend pushed me into a wave on a longboard. I loved the rush: riding on a moving medium. I was hooked! We had a pretty committed surf gang in high school and we trekked up and down the coast as much as we could. Then my dad gave me a movie camera and I started filming. I just fell in love with the whole deal—the adventure, the travel, the bonfires on the beach, hanging out with buddies, trying to emulate the good surfers—the fun of it all.

I just knew surfing was what I wanted to do, but I went to USC because I wanted to get a business degree and because I really wanted to get a good job. I was hooked on surf, though, and I started traveling and surfing the most beautiful tropical waves. Then I met Jeff Hakman in Bali and we started talking about these trunks called "Quiksilver."

I was always in awe of the way great surfers ripped waves apart and how cool they were. So hanging out with Jeff was a way to keep surfing, live near the beach, sell some boardshorts and stall graduate school and getting a real job.

There was no premeditated business plan. We just learned about manufacturing and fabrics and doing business as we went along. That was our first step. Our second was taking our shorts, like precious little gold bars, up and down the coast, trying to sell them, meeting the surf shop retailers and getting to know them. We gave them something new to sell. Back then surf shops sold boards and wax and maybe a tee shirt or two. We introduced them to apparel.

Our third step was learning how marketing worked, making ads for the magazines, getting great pictures of our guys and using them to make our statement. We were the first surf company to use action shots instead of just product. We were making it up as we went along, and in some ways, we still are. We had no one to follow, no business model. No core company had grown beyond $10 million without selling out to the mass market. We did.

Passion...

I'm passionate about surfing and the board sports lifestyle, and so are most people in this company. If I hadn't been I would have gone into some other business. To build a brand you need to have a product you believe in, that you're passionate about. In our world you have to be passionate about marketing, building the right team. The riders have to be the best fit for the brand, and we have to create the right events, kick-ass hangtags, windows, website and retail stores. Most of all, we have to be passionate about protecting the core of our sports. That's what drives our support of our core board sports shops, no matter how big we get. That's why the core marketing, team and events are so important. And that's why we're passionate about our commitment to our Quiksilver Foundation, which focuses on supporting agencies that support kids, ocean, science, education and the environment. Educating our kids about caring for their planet, and in particular their incredible natural playgrounds in the mountains and the waves, is one of our major goals.

I'm passionate about having good, hard-working people in the company who are as passionate about the board sports lifestyle as I am. Not just the marketing guys but everywhere—I want finance guys, sourcing people, designers, salesmen and computer experts who go surfing at lunchtime, who take their families to the snow, who get what we are about and understand that this company will only be successful as long as we remember that and participate. I want people who understand water.

What we aspire to be...

There were no board sports business models when we started, but we wanted to build a great brand. How do you do that? We looked at role models, at other great lifestyle brands. Nike, Starbucks, Mercedes, Coca Cola—they share a lot in common. They all have an unwavering commitment to and passion for good, innovative product. Marketing is key, and a positive consumer experience and "word of mouth" from users is paramount. A lot of time is spent building the brand which gives it history and in turn earns it authenticity. In this way each of our role models has forged a global following. These brick-by-brick foundations have given these great brands "consumer permission" to get big and extend into new products.

We have tried to emulate these brand truths in everything we do at Quiksilver, growing but still staying true to our core values. Each of our brands has to operate in its own universe, have its own values and stay true to them. The company itself provides a shared infrastructure and support to all of them. We want to be proud of each one. And we want to keep growing, because if you don't you go backwards. Every person in our company wants to grow in his or her life, so our job is to facilitate that while keeping it cool.

Bob at the office.

What I've seen along the way...

On my watch I've seen a lot of companies come and go, and a few good people within them fall by the wayside. On the other hand, I've seen our company grow big but keep it real. I've seen the pride in people's faces when they do something within our company and/or our industry that they can be proud of, whether it's the development of a new product, the creation of a killer DVD, winning a sports title or hitting a really big number in sales. I love to see that pride of ownership at every level in our company, whether it's picking up paper clips to recycle them or coming up with a new and improved system for doing their jobs.

I hear from people who walk into our buildings around the world for the first time that they feel the energy and passion of the people who work for us. I've had so many great shared experiences with our staff—on business trips, at trade shows, on surf or snow trips, or hanging out talking about projects, products and the future. I get such a buzz that I can still relate to kids and how they feel.

What I'm most proud of...

We're a $2.5 billion company and we still operate like a nimble little family company. I'm proud of the fact that we've been able to bring so many of our team riders into the company and so many lifestyle people like myself who still feel that they belong in our family. I'm proud of the generations working within the company and how kids grow up and become so important to our company.

And I'm proud of the fact that we support the true legends of our sports and give them a vital role to play Wayne Lynch, Jeff Hakman, Mark Richards, Simon Anderson—the list is as long as the names on it are awesome. And that's what this company is really about.

I'm proud that we have kept the balance between salt and EBT. We need people with salt and snow in their veins at Quiksilver, just as much as we need the MBAs. Everyone said that wasn't the way to create a management team, but in fact we're leading the way. Now we're the business model that schools study, the one that wasn't around when we started. It's all about being inclusive, not exclusive. It's about growing the pond. It's about protecting the core. As SIMA Waterman of the Year for 2006, I'm proud that our industry looks to us to show the way.

The boardriding culture and industry that Quiksilver helped create now influences all facets of life: fashion, sport, music, cinema, television, food, language, art, design and style.

I'm not just proud of Quiksilver, I'm proud of the whole industry we've helped create.

—Bob McKnight, *Huntington Beach, April 2006*

90
KELLY SLATER SIGNS WITH QUIKSILVER

BIG WAVE EVENT, THE "QUIKSILVER IN MEMORY OF EDDIE AIKAU" WON BY KEONE DOWNING

WORLD CHAMPION HALFPIPE SNOWBOARDER SHAUN PALMER SIGNS WITH QUIKSILVER

STEVE O'BRANDOVICH STARS IN "SIDE-OUT" VOLLEYBALL MOVIE

QUIKSILVER DENIM (QSD) HITS THE MARKET

QUIKSILVER STARTS TO MANUFACTURE WETSUITS

TRANSITION FROM SKI FOCUS TO SNOWBOARD EMPHASIS

QUIKSILVER INTRODUCES "ROXY" BRAND TO SURF MARKET

"KELLY SLATER IN BLACK AND WHITE" PRODUCED, THE TOP SELLING SURFING VIDEO OF ALL TIME

ANDY IRONS RIDES FOR QUIK

91
QS "BOYS" BEGINS. "SILVER EDITIO DIVISION BEGINS WITH "QUE"

QUIKSILVER INC. ACQUIRES QUIKSILV EUROPE, MOVES TOWARDS CREATING O GLOBAL COMPANY

QUIKSILVER SPONSORS VOLLEYBALL CHAMPION KARCH KIRALY

QUIKSILVER LICENSES IN TURKEY, QUIKSILVER LICENSES INDONESIA

TOM CARROLL WINS THE PIPE MASTERS

89
20 YEAR ANNIVERSARY OF QUIKSILVER BRAND

"MONDO EXTREME XPERIMENT" 1ST SURF, SKATE, AND SNOWBOARDING VIDEO PRODUCED

QUIKSILVER CREATES "GEN X" PRODUCT GROUP

88
QUIKSILVER LICENSES IN SOUTH AFRICA

QUIKSILVER AND TOM CARROLL CREATE SURFING HISTORY WHEN THE TWICE WORLD CHAMPION SIGNS AN EXCLUSIVE CONTRACT FOR $1 MILLION, THE MOST LUCRATIVE DEAL IN THE SPORT

87
QUIKSILVER SPONSORS HALFPIPE WORLD CHAMPION SNOWBOARDER CRAIG KELLY

JACK JOHNSON SIGNS WITH QUIKSILVER

MEL GIBSON WEARS QUIKSILVER IN "LETHAL WEAPON"

QUIKSILVER LICENSES IN BRAZIL

86
QUIKSILVER INC. IN THE UNITED STATES GOES PUBLIC

QUIKSILVER LICENSES IN NEW ZEALAND

CLYDE AIKAU WINS EDDIE CONTEST AT WAIMEA

83
"WARPAINT" THEME BY SIMON BUTTONSHAW INTRODUCED ON BOARD SHORTS

ROBBY NAISH SIGNS WITH QUIKSILVER

84
1ST "QUIKSILVER IN MEMORY OF EDDIE AIKAU" BIG WAVE CONTEST HELD AT SUNSET BEACH, HI, WON BY DENTON MIYAMURA

"PERFORMERS" PRODUCED BY HARRY HODGE & BRUCE RAYMOND FIRST BRANDED VIDEO RELEASED

QUIKSILVER LICENSES NA PALI TO MANUFACTURE AND DISTRIBUTE THROUGHOUT EUROPE. FOUNDERS ARE HARRY HODGE, JEFF HAKMAN, BRIGITTE DARRIGRAND AND JOHN WINSHIP

QUIKSILVER LICENSES IN CANADA

A HISTORY OF FIRSTS

QUIKSILVER

69 AT THE RIP CURL FACTORY IN TORQUAY AUSTRALIA, ALAN GREEN STARTS WORKING ON PROTOTYPES FOR A NEW KIND OF BOARD SHORT, USING ASPECTS OF WETSUIT TECHNOLOGY, SUCH AS SNAPS AND VELCRO FLIES

70 QUIKSILVER BOARD SHORTS WITH A SWAN LOGO MAKE THEIR FIRST APPEARANCE IN AUSTRALIAN SURF SHOPS. SOON REPLACED BY THE FIRST "MOUNTAIN AND WAVE" LOGO

72 KELLY SLATER BORN 2-11-72

74 UG MANUFACTURING (QUIKSILVER) FIRST EXPORTS BOARDSHORTS TO THE LIGHTNING BOLT SHOP IN HAWAII

76 JEFF HAKMAN WINS THE BELLS BEACH CONTEST

JEFF HAKMAN IS GRANTED THE QUIKSILVER LICENSE. JEFF HAKMAN AND BOB MCKNIGHT TEAM UP TO START QUIKSILVER USA IN NEWPORT BEACH. START SELLING BOARDSHORTS OUT OF BACK OF GREEN VW BUS

JOHN LAW BECOMES PARTNER IN QUIKSILVER

77 QUIKSILVER EXPORTED TO JAPAN

QUIKSILVER SPONSORS "BAND ON THE RUN"

78 "QUIKSILVER COUNTRY" PRINT THEME INTRODUCED

QUIKSILVER EXPORTED TO FRANCE

QUIKSILVER SPONSORS ITS FIRST TEAM RIDERS, RABBIT BARTHOLOMEW AND BRUCE RAYMOND. RABBIT GOES ON TO WIN THE WORLD TITLE

79 QUIKSILVER GARMENTS FOUNDED IN AUSTRALIA TO LEAD AND SERVICE QUIKSILVER LICENSES WORLD WIDE

80 QUIKSILVER INTRODUCES "ECHO BEACH" BOARDSHORTS FEATURING RADICAL PRINT DESIGN WITH POLKA DOTS HARLEQUINS, STARS AND CHECKS

81 "ST COMP" STRETCH BOARDSHORT INTRODUCED WITH NEW LOGO AND GRAPHICS

QUIKSILVER LICENSES IN JAPAN

THRASHER MAGAZINE SKATEBOARDING AD CAMPAIGN FEATURING TODAYS SKATE LEGENDS: CHRISITAN HOSOI, STEVE CABALLERO, PIERRE ANDRE, LANCE MOUNTAIN, ROB ROSKOFF, KEVIN STRAAB, SPIDEY DEMONTROND

QUIKSILVER COMMISSONS LOS ANGELES DESIGNER RAY SMITH TO UPDATE THE MOUNTAIN AND WAVE LOGO

82 QUIKSILVER LICENSES SURF N' SPORT MANUFACTURE AND DISTRIBUTE, IN FRANCE

History

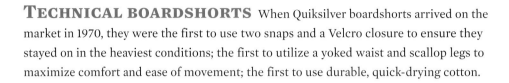

TECHNICAL BOARDSHORTS When Quiksilver boardshorts arrived on the market in 1970, they were the first to use two snaps and a Velcro closure to ensure they stayed on in the heaviest conditions; the first to utilize a yoked waist and scallop legs to maximize comfort and ease of movement; the first to use durable, quick-drying cotton.

THEMED PRODUCT LINES Quiksilver's first themed offering, Quiksilver Country in 1978, offered retailers and customers a complete package for the first time. The soulful prints and panels of the garments were reflected in the advertising and in-store displays. All told a story about a place of perfect waves, a place where surfers wanted to be. Echo Beach and Warpaint carried the themed approach through the 1980s and into the '90s, identifying Quiksilver as a lifestyle, not just a brand.

GEOMETRICS The arrival of Echo Beach in late 1980 caused a sensation. With its geometric designs, bold colors and bad attitude, the new line was the first to capture the mood of the new generation of beachgoers, and it is still being reinvented today.

STRETCH Quiksilver was the first to introduce stretch fabric boardshorts with ST Comp in the early 1980s. The hi-tech functional trunks reflected the new professionalism of surfing's nascent pro tour. Athletes wanted to look like athletes.

BRANDED VIDEO Almost a quarter century ago, Quiksilver saw the birth of video and the coming of home entertainment, and moved quickly to change the way that surfers watched their heroes. Quiksilver's *The Performers* was the first surf film to be released as a home video, and within a year the whole surf film industry had shifted from cinema to lounge rooms. Quiksilver continued to lead the way through the '90s with groundbreaking work like *Kelly Slater in Black and White*.

GO PUBLIC In 1986, Quiksilver's initial public offering and subsequent listing on the NASDAQ exchange provided funds for growth more than a decade before the other companies had even thought about it. In 1998 Quiksilver's move up to the New York Stock Exchange underlined its ambitious approach to business in the new century.

100% SPONSORSHIP The first to establish 100% sponsorship of athletes, with Tom Carroll's 1988 "top to toe" contract for $1 million.

BIG WAVE CONTESTS First to recognize the big-wave revival and establish the Quiksilver in Memory of Eddie Aikau and the Mavericks Men Who Ride Mountains events.

of Firsts

SNOWWEAR The first surf company to adapt the style and feel of the beach to technical outerwear for alpine sports, first skiing and then snowboarding.

WOMEN Quiksilver recognized the increasing influence of women in surfing early in the '80s, but when Roxy, the first dedicated female surf brand, was created in 1990, the bar was raised to a level that the other companies have yet to reach.

DENIM Quiksilver was the first to recognize that boardriders wanted jeans that jeaners didn't make, so it hired denim guru Mel Matsui and created the industry's first genuine denim division.

OWN BRAND RETAIL STORES With the establishment of the first Quiksilver Boardriders Club in Waikiki in 1992, Quiksilver led the way into branded concept stores, a new way of retailing that has impacted the entire industry. With 500 stores worldwide in 2006, Quiksilver still leads the way.

ENTERTAINMENT With the establishment of Quiksilver Entertainment in 2000, Quiksilver became the first surf brand to create a genuine multi-media entertainment portal, facilitating the production of board sports related films, TV series, books and magazines.

BILLION DOLLAR CLUB First boardriding company to break through a billion in sales, with revenue of $1.3 billion in 2004.

MAJOR ACQUISITIONS Having globalized the company through acquisition of its licensees, Quiksilver became the first boardriding company to focus on acquiring major, likeminded brands, such as DC Shoes in 2003 and Rossignol in 2005, with a view to building a family of brands covering the outdoor sector.

GLOBAL MANAGEMENT First boardriding company to fully globalize its management structure with autonomous regional structures.

CHARITY With the establishment of the Quiksilver Foundation, Quiksilver became the first to formalize its social responsibility and expand its altruistic work for a range of educational and social causes, such as Asian tsunami relief and reconstruction.

QUIKSILVER MASTERS WORLD CHAMPIONSHIPS
MAKAHA, HI
1-20 TO 2-01

00

TODD RICHARDS RIDES FOR QUIKSILVER

"ALEX GOES" IS LAUNCHED

QUIKSILVER, INC. ESTABLISHED THE QUIKSILVER TRADEMARKS WORLD WIDE WITH THE ACQUISITION OF ALL OF THE SHARES IN QUIKSILVER INTERNATIONAL

FORM ALLIANCE WITH TONY HAWK TO CREATE SIGNATURE APPAREL LINE, "HAWK" IS LAUNCHED

FIRST ROXY STORE OPENS. FIRST ROXY SURF CAMP ESTABLISHED

QUIKSILVER EUROPE [NA PALI] ACQUIRES OTCHA EUROPE

01

KELLY SLATER WINS 10TH "SURFER POLL AWARDS"

KELLY SLATER GOES BACK ON THE TOUR, UN-RETIRES

02

QUIKSILVER DESIGNS A REVOLUTIONARY NEW WETSUIT. "THE CELL" IS FOR ALL DEGREES OF SURFING. REVOLUTIONARY DESIGN, INCREASED FLEXIBILITY, LIGHTER IN WEIGHT, TOTAL FREEDOM!

QUIKSILVER INC. AND QUIKSILVER ASIA PACIFIC MERGE TO FORM GLOBAL OPERATING ENTITY

DANNY KASS WINS SILVER AT 2002 WINTER OLYMPIC GAMES FOR SNOWBOARDING

"THE CROSSING" GOES THRU EUROPE

KELLY WINS THE EDDIE

UNION FOUNDED

03

BOARDRIDERS CLUB STORE OPENS IN TIME SQUARE NEW YORK

QUIKSILVER CONTINUES INVOLVEMENT WITH ENVIRONMENT, EDUCATION AND SCIENCE WITH PROJECTS "QUIKSCIENCE CHALLENGE" AND "ADOPT-A-VILLAGE"

ROXY TEAMS UP WITH MTV TO LAUNCH "SURF GIRLS" TV SHOW

Q.S. ENTERTAINMENT TEAMS UP WITH FOX TV TO LAUNCH 54321 TV SHOW

"FIDRA" SPONSORS GOLF LEGEND, ERNIE ELS

QUIKSILVER ANNOUNCES JOINT VENTURE FOR RETAIL EXPANSION INTO MAINLAND CHINA WITH PARTNERS GLORIOUS SUN

QUIKSILVER LAUNCHES GLOBAL MEN'S SHOE PRODUCT

QUIKSILVER BECOMES PRESENTING SPONSOR FOR THE BOOST MOBILE WCT TRESTLES SURF CONTEST

QUIKSILVER ENTERTAINMENT INTRODUCES ROXY "LUNA BAY" BOOK SERIES

KELLY SLATER AUTHORS AUTOBIOGRAPHY, "PIPE DREAMS"

QUIKSILVER RINGS OPENING BELL NEW YORK STOCK EXCHANGE, JUNE 4, 2003

QUAMAV (QUIKSILVER UNDERGROUND ARMY MOBILE ASSAULT VEHICLE) HITS THE ROAD

04

QUIKSILVER, INC. DOES $1 BILLION IN SALES

QUIKSILVER ACQUIRES DC SHOE COMPANY

EDDIE WENT/ BRUCE IRONS WINS

QUIKSILVER OPENS BOARDRIDERS CLUB IN LAS VEGAS

"THE QUIKSILVER CROSSING" COMES TO AMERICA

KELLY SLATER HOSTS HIS FIRST EVENT "THE KELLY SLATER INVITATIONAL" IN FIJI

QUIKSILVER GLOBALIZES TECH DIVISION FOR SUNGLASSES, WATCHES, WETSUITS AND ACCESSORIES

QUIKSILVER OPENS A STORE IN SHANGHAI CHINA

TSUNAMI HITS INDIAN OCEAN. NIAS FOUNDATION FORMED

"RIDING GIANTS"

QSE PARTNERS W/ AIRSTREAM

SOFIA MULANOVICH WINS THE WOMENS WORLD TITLE

05

QUIKSILVER SIGNS LEGEND CHRISTIAN HOSOI

BOOST MOBILE AND ROXY TEAM UP

TONY HAWK GUEST STARS ON CSI:MIAMI

QUIKSILVER FOUNDATION IS ESTABLISHED

QUIKSILVER ACQUIRES ROSSIGNOL (DYNASTAR, LANGE, CLEVELAND)

DANNY WAY JUMPED THE GREAT WALL

WALL STREET JOURNAL FEATURES QUIKSILVER

DANNY WAY VOTED "SKATER OF THE YEAR" BY THRASHER MAGAZINE

CHELSEA GEORGESON WINS THE WOMENS WORLD TITLE

KELLY SLATER WINS RECORD BREAKING 7TH WORLD TITLE

99
LIB TECH BUILDS SKATE DECKS AND REDEFINES SNOWBOARDS WITH "AIR CORE"

THE "QUIKSILVER CROSSING" IS LAUNCHED. THE GREATEST SURF ADVENTURE EVER WITH A STRONG ENVIRONMENT FOCUS

QUIKSILVER BOARDRIDERS CLUBS OPEN IN LONDON (COVENT GARDEN) AND IN PARIS (CHAMPS ELYSEES)

QUIK JEAN AND ROXY JEAN DEBUT

THE FIRST "QUIKSILVER MAVERICKS MEN WHO RIDE MOUNTAINS" CONTEST HAPPENS, WON BY FLEA VIROSKO

ROXY LAUNCHES "HULA SCENT"

JOHN ASHWORTH REDEFINES GOLFWEAR AT QUIKSILVER WITH "FIDRA"

"QUIKSILVER TRAVEL" IS BORN

"EXTREME" HITS GLOBAL IMAX THEATERS

QUIKSILVER INC. MOVES TO HUNTINGTON BEACH

QUIKSILVER MOVES WCT CONTEST FROM G-LAND TO TAVARUA, FIJI

QUIKSILVER EUROPE MOVES INTO NEW BUILDING

QUIKSILVER SPONSORS THE SILVER EDITION MASTERS IN LAFITENIA, FRANCE

92
KELLY SLATER WINS HIS FIRST PIPE MASTERS

KELLY SLATER WINS THE ASP WORLD TITLE

QUIKSILVER BIARRITZ SURF MASTERS

KELLY GOES "BAYWATCH"

"KEEP YOUR BALANCE" CAMPAIGN

QUIKSILVER OPENS FIRST "BOARDRIDERS CLUB" IN HAWAII

93
ROXY LAUNCHES "DOUBLE HEART" LOGO

QUIKSILVER ACQUIRES "RAISINS" SWIMWEAR

94
LISA ANDERSEN SIGNS WITH ROXY AND BECOMES WOMEN'S ASP WORLD CHAMPION

KELLY SLATER WINS HIS SECOND ASP WORLD TITLE

QUIKSILVER LICENSES IN ARGENTINA AND CHILE

QUIKSILVER INVENTS "QUIKSVILLE" IN STORE CONCEPTS

ROXY INTRODUCES FIRST GIRLS BOARDSHORT

95
KELLY SLATER, LISA ANDERSEN AND RUSTY KEULANA ARE AGAIN ALL QUIKSILVER WORLD CHAMPIONS

QUIKSILVER SETS THE ULTIMATE IN STANDARD IN PROFESSIONAL SURFING EVENTS BY STAGING THE INAUGURAL "QUIKSILVER PRO" AT G-LAND IN INDONESIA

QUIKSILVER SNOW TEAM TRAVELS TO REMOTE GREENLAND

QUIKSILVER LICENSES IN CHILE

98
KELLY SLATER WINS HIS SIXTH ASP WORLD TITLE AND QUIKSILVER GOES ONE, TWO, THREE IN THE WORLD WITH KELLY, MICK CAMBELL, AND DANNY WILLS

QUIKSILVER INC. LISTS ON THE NEW YORK STOCK EXCHANGE. BELL RINGS FOR ZQK

QUIKSILVER LICENSES IN MAURITIUS

CONDITION BLACK JAN 1, 1998 HUGE SURF, EDDIE WOULDN'T GO. OUTSIDE LOG CABINS TOW SESSION WITH ROSS CLARK JONES CHARGING, LARGEST SURF EVER RIDDEN

QUIKSILVER OPENS FIRST NEW YORK STORE IN SOHO

ASR MAGAZINE VOTES QUIKSILVER "MANUFACTURER OF THE YEAR" AWARD

KELLY SLATER RETIRES

96
QUIKSILVER PRO AT G-LAND AGAIN HAILED AS "THE ULTIMATE SURFING EVENT"

KELLY SLATER WINS FOURTH PIPE MASTERS AND FOURTH WORLD TITLE

FIRST ROXY STORE OPENS IN HONOLULU, HI

QUIKSILVER CREATES "WINTER SPORTS DIVISION" WITH BOARDS, BOOTS, BINDINGS, ACCESSORIES AND OUTERWEAR IN CONJUNCTION WITH MERVIN

QUIKSILVER ACQUIRES MERVIN SNOWBOARD MANUFACTURING COMPANY

97
QUIKSILVER.COM

QUIKSILVER FIRST ADVERTISES IN "ROLLING STONE", "GQ", "SEVENTEEN", AND "SPIN" MAGAZINE

KELLY SLATER HIGHEST MONEY EARNER IN ASP HISTORY

ROBBY NAISH CONTINUES TO DOMINATE WORLD WINDSURFING

QUIKSILVER LAUNCHES INTERNET WEB SITE

"MR. SUNSET" RELEASED. THE COMPLETE STORY OF JEFF HAKMAN TOLD

QUIKSILVER "CLICKER BAR" LOGO INTRODUCED

In Their Own Words

Kelly Slater *champion*

When I got back to California, my manager called me and said, "You're going to ride for Quiksilver. They made a great offer at the last minute, and you're with them." I was speechless...I was with a company every surfer wanted to ride for.

Martin Potter *champion*

As a grommet I always wanted to be sponsored by Quiksilver, that was the ultimate dream. It was one of the only companies that was run by surfers, which made it really grass roots. It's more of a surf company than anything out there. There are so many dynamic people who work at Quiksilver worldwide that I have huge respect for. My job allows me to work with my mates, travel the world and remain in touch with every level of the sport.

Mark Richards *champion*

I had two absolute favorite pairs of Quik boardshorts. I remember being stoked when Greeny and John Law allowed me to custom order. They were beautifully made and the first shorts I owned that were actually comfortable to surf in. In those days every good surfer in the world wore Quiksilvers, even if they had to pay for them. They were the iPods of the '70s; you just had to have 'em.

Titus Kinimaka *legend*

Quiksilver has meant the fulfillment of my surfing career, every dream come true. Since I was a kid I just wanted to be a professional surfer and travel around the world, and now I've been from the top of the world to the bottom, from Scotland all the way down to Australia. My most memorable moments have been on The Crossing, visiting islands so beautiful you can't believe they're real.

Peter Townend *champion*

Quiksilver was the new thing coming from

Australia, and Australia was the hot thing then. The magazines were full of us. In 1977 I had two covers of *Surfer* in three issues, and I was wearing Quiks in both of them. Do you think that helped them get up and running?

Simon Anderson *guru*

I had a brief involvement with Quiksilver back in its very early days, when I was a junior. At that time out of all the companies Quiksilver was the company that you wanted to be sponsored by. I appeared in one ad only; I still have it today. Nice little cutback as I recall. Thirty years later I'm back involved with the Quiksilver board program, so I'm stoked.

Steve Pezman *publisher*

Quiksilver was the first surf company to get into the $100m plus range and keep its cool. I'm not sure how you do that. Probably having surfers driving the company helps because they refused to do stuff that garmentos would do.

Doug Warbrick *Rip Curl co-founder*

We've always co-existed well. In fact, more than that. We've helped each other. In the early pro era, lots of surfers existed on complementary Rip Curl and Quiksilver sponsorship. As pro surfing developed and you had to have real contracts with the

surfers, there was competition for endorsements. With that happening, we had to have a non-competition agreement, so that we didn't get in each other's way. When that ran its course, we ripped up the agreement and became competitors.

Michael Tomson *Gotcha founder*

The first time I saw Quiksilver boardshorts was when I was staying with Jeff Hakman at his place at Pupukea. He had a pair and I wanted them! They were gems, man. Then Greeny started sending them to me and I was on the team! I wore them all the time. For the first time, you really felt you were wearing shorts that were made to surf in.

Wayne Lynch *guru*

If it wasn't for Quiksilver I wouldn't still be in the

surf industry. I think Quiksilver has always put more back into the sport than the others. They've done it via sponsorships and creating innovative projects that have given many of us work and a chance to stay involved.

Robby Naish *champion*

Quiksilver has been a really big part of my life. In fact my growth in life and my success has been a kind of parallel to Quiksilver. When I started with Quiksilver more than 20 years ago, all they made was boardshorts and tee shirts, and windsurfing was just starting. Now everything I'm wearing is Quiksilver...my underwear, my shoes, my socks, my glasses, my watch...everything. I don't own

anything that isn't Quiksilver—I'm proud of that.

Mark Cunningham *bodysurfer*

Quiksilver means quality top to bottom, from what they make to what they stand for to who they are.

You have the best surfers in the world riding the best waves in the world with the best photographers and writers in the world documenting it. It's a company founded by surfers and it's all about surfing, and I hope they never lose that.

How the Surf Industry Began

[ABOVE] Greg Noll Surf Shop, Hermosa Beach, 1963. [OPPOSITE] 1940s ribbed wool trunks by Gantner and Mattern.

The Baby Boomers built the surf industry, but its roots go much deeper than the extraordinary half century of change we have just witnessed in the sport, lifestyle and industry of surfing.

The first surfers carved their boards from trees—either koa or wiliwili—and fashioned them according to their caste. The *a'ali,* or Hawaiian royalty, rode *olo* boards of perhaps 17 feet in length, while the commoners rode the *alaia,* about half that length. For perhaps a thousand years they rode their surfboards naked, standing cross-armed and majestic as the surf carried them across the coral-cased bays of their beautiful island chain, preferably against a backdrop of the setting sun.

Captain James Cook's discovery of the islands, which he named Sandwich in 1778, signaled the beginning of the end for Hawaiian surf culture in its original form. Over the next century, Calvinist missionaries stamped out surfing and other pagan rituals. The writer Mark Twain alerted the world to the fact that the sport of surfing was in danger of extinction in 1866, but it was not until the beginning of the twentieth century that the renaissance of the sport began in earnest, this time reported by another famous writer, Jack London. And this time around, the surfers wore clothes.

The first "surf trunks" worn by the Hawaiian watermen were little more than loincloths, but by the time a "Hawaiiana" craze swept the United States between 1912 and 1914, the cool look was the woolen "tank suit." Posters for the 1912 Olympic gold medalist swimmer and Hawaii's best surfer, Duke Kahanamoku, feature an artist's impression of a young man wearing nothing but woolens that stretched from high on the thigh to just under the navel.

Surfing first received serious attention on the American mainland in 1908, when an Irish-Hawaiian named George Freeth gave a series of exhibitions in Southern California, first in front of tobacco millionaire Abbot Kinney's Italianate Venice canal development on Santa Monica Bay, and culminating the following year in a summer of demonstrations in front of railroad baron Henry Huntington's "Redondo Plunge" indoor pool. Freeth went on to teach surfing up and down the coast, as well as passing on the skills of carving solid wooden boards.

But the sport was difficult to learn and slow to catch on. By the time the United States entered World War II, in December 1941, there were still only two or three hundred active surfers

in California, most of whom rode solid redwood planks of their own design, there being only two companies producing surf and paddle boards. The hero of the nascent surf scene was Tom Blake, a Wisconsin-born eccentric who had refined the Hawaiian surfboard design, produced the first hollow plywood boards and introduced California's first surfing competition at Corona Del Mar in 1928. Blake cruised the coast, followed by a small group of disciples.

This small cell of rebels was bohemian in outlook, but the spirit had not yet permeated their dress sense. The snapshots of pioneer surfer and photographer, the late Dr Don James, shot during his youthful summers between 1936 and 1942, reveal a motley crew of handsome, tanned misfits, dressed in all kinds of ill-fitting garb from high camp sailor gear to army greatcoats...nothing to label them a tribe. It wasn't until after the war, when the decades of prosperity began, that the style of the surfer started to emerge.

Just before the war, American *Vogue* featured an action surfing photo on its cover. Seen gliding down the face at Wakiki, a girl on the front of his board, the un-named surfer was wearing a pair of high-waisted, short-legged surf trunks, although the magazine didn't label them as such. They were a cross between gym trunks and the belted swimsuits popularized in the 1930s, and were almost certainly the product of boutique swimwear brand Lyn's of Waikiki. By 1950 Lyn's had cornered the Hawaiian tourist market with snug trunks with the trademark stripe down the leg. Duke Kahanamoku was frequently photographed in a pair with an Outrigger Canoe Club logo patched on the front of the leg, and in 1961 Elvis Presley wore an extra tight pair for his simulated surfing scenes.

As popular as they were with some surfers, Lyn's trunks were still considered to be all-purpose swimwear, like the styles being pumped out by mainland companies such as McGregor, Catalina and Jantzen. Looking for a more authentic (not to mention cheaper) look, pioneer Hawaiian surfers Woody Brown and John Kelly began wearing modified high school gym shorts in the surf. Manufactured in a sewing room at the back of the H. Miura General Store in Haleiwa, on Oahu, these shorts

Tom Blake and Duke Kahanamoku, Waikiki, late 1920s.

Chubby Mitchell wearing komebaige trunks, Malibu, 1962.

combined good fit with sturdy fabric, and featured stripes in various school colors down the side.

But if H. Miura was the true pioneer of custom surf trunks, it was another small operator in Hawaii who cashed in. M. Nii was the name above a tiny tailor's shop at Waianae, on the road to Makaha on Oahu's dusty Westside, and after the introduction of the Makaha International Surfing Championships in 1954, more and more surfers began to drop in to order custom trunks. Walter Hoffman, later to become one of the big wheels in the surf industry as a supplier of fabrics, recalls visiting M. Nii to order trunks in the early 1950s: "You'd walk into this tiny little room where there's just two sewing machines, and this little Japanese guy with one leg is behind one and his wife is behind the other. Mrs. Nii would take your measurements while Mr. Nii shouted instructions. Then you'd wait forever for your order, but it was worth it. They were good quality and, at the time, they were what you had to have."

Meanwhile, in California, some of the more outrageous surfers were making their own bold fashion statement. Led by former merchant marine Dale Velzy, a group from Los Angele's South Bay beaches began buying white sailors' pants at thrift shops and cutting the legs off just below the knee to create the prototype "baggies." The contest was to wear them all summer long without removing them, and Velzy, an emerging hero of the surf scene, was the clearcut winner.

Velzy is also credited with opening the world's first surf shop, although this claim is subject to a fairly arbitrary definition of "shop." Velzy had started shaping surfboards under the municipal pier at Manhattan Beach, and when the city finally chased him off and cleaned up his piles of wood shavings in 1950, he hung his Velzy Surfboards shingle above a tiny and dilapidated shopfront space a few blocks away on Pacific Coast Highway. Here he shaped and sold surfboards and nothing else.

In 1952 Northern Californian surfer Jack O'Neill opened "The Surf Shop" in a beachfront garage on the Great Highway in San Francisco. It too sold only surfboards initially, but O'Neill had such faith in his big idea that he trademarked the name. The following year Hobie Alter, a young shaper from Laguna Beach, opened Hobie Surfboards at Dana Point, the first purpose-built surf shop, with more floor space than its two predecessors combined. Other retail outlets followed and faced the same

vogue

INCORPORATING VANITY FAIR

HOLIDAY TRAVEL
RESORT FASHIONS
DECEMBER 15, 1938
PRICE 35 CENTS

V   O © THE CONDÉ NAST PUBLICATIONS, INC

This 1938 travel issue of *Vogue* featured surfing on it's cover.

With the publication of his novel *Gidget* in 1957, Kohner became the first outsider to grasp the magical appeal of the surf culture and then exploit it.

WATCH OUT BRIGITTE... HERE COMES GIDGET!

COLUMBIA PICTURES presents

GIDGET

co-starring SANDRA DEE · CLIFF ROBERTSON · JAMES DARREN with ARTHUR O'CONNELL · MARY LaROCHE and THE FOUR PREPS

Screenplay by GABRIELLE UPTON · Based on the novel by FREDERICK KOHNER

CINEMASCOPE   Produced by LEWIS J. RACHMIL · Directed by PAUL WENDKOS   EASTMAN COLOR

The joyous movie based on *that* book!

SONY PICTURES

Cliff Robertson and James Darren hold Sandra Dee aloft in the first *Gidget* movie poster.

challenge. The market wasn't big enough to support single-product stores.

Commercial surfboard production grew quickly in the 1950s as lighter construction and new design made the sport easier to learn. Lightweight balsa overtook solid planks and hollow boards, and a fin facilitated direction changes. But for six months of the year in California, the greatest impediment to surfing's advancement was not any surfboard design element, it was the climate.

O'Neill was among several Californians who had toyed with ideas for easing the chill of winter surfing. He knew that during World War II, US Navy frogmen diving in cold water had worn rubber pants and vests over their long underwear. Depending on the quality and fit of these outfits, they were either "wet suits" or "dry suits." When the water seeped through, it was quickly warmed by body temperature, so that the divers remained wet but warm enough to function.

This was O'Neill's starting point, but he realized that a surfing wetsuit would have to be more durable, and preferably in one piece. He found a rubber source and a pattern maker and began producing a limited number of wetsuit vests out of The Surf Shop. Meanwhile, at the University of California at Berkeley, a physicist named Hugh Bradner was experimenting with neoprene—a material used in other applications, such as refrigerator insulation—as a lightweight, flexible insulation for Navy divers. The military declassified his findings in 1952, and O'Neill was one of the first to read his report.

As O'Neill rushed to get his neoprene wetsuits into production, Los Angeles County lifeguard and well-known surfer Bev Morgan was looking for partners to share the burden of his South Bay water sports store Dive 'n' Surf, since his original partner Hap Jacobs had gone off to make surfboards with Velzy. He found them in identical twins Bob and Bill Meistrell, surfers and divers like him who had also just read the Bradner report. More inventors than marketers, the Meistrells called their suits "Thermocline," and Thermocline they remained for years, until finally they hired a young marketing consultant named Duke Boyd to come up with a sexier name. When Boyd asked them about the selling features of their suits, Bill Meistrell replied: "Well, they fit like a glove." Bingo! Body Glove. Boyd got an artist to knock up a logo of a gloved hand, picked up his pay

check and moved on, realizing that the fledgling surf industry was rich with possibilities.

The California surf boom of the early 1960s was predicated on the appearance at Malibu, in the summer of 1956, of a five-foot-nothing fifteen-year-old named Kathy Kohner...but not for long. By mid-summer the Malibu "Pit Crew" had renamed her "Gidget" (as in girl midget), taught her to surf and let her into their raunchy male-dominated inner sanctum. Far from being horrified, her father, Czech screenwriter Frederick Kohner, delighted in her contagious enthusiasm for her beach adventures, and soon saw in them a commercial opportunity.

With the publication of his novel *Gidget* in 1957, Kohner became the first outsider to grasp the magical appeal of the surf culture and then exploit it. Not that the Malibu Pit Crew cared much at the time. When *Gidget* charged up the best seller lists, *Life* magazine dispatched a team to Malibu to capture the essence of this new beach cool. They were told by a Pit Crewer: "If I had a couple of bucks to buy a book, I wouldn't. I'd buy some beer." Yet when the inevitable feature film followed in 1959, most of the crew happily accepted jobs as stunt doubles, including the diminutive Mickey Munoz, who surfed in a blond wig and bikini as a double for Sandra Dee. While Kathy Kohner gave up surfing and went to college, good old dad turned Gidget into a thriving franchise of novels, movies and television series throughout the 1960s and beyond.

Although the big screen *Gidget* was Hollywood's first surf-themed movie, the surf documentary genre had been around since the earliest days of moving pictures, when the Edison Company's Robert Bonine pointed his camera at the Waikiki surfriders to make the 1906 "actuality," *Surf Board Riders, Waikiki, Honolulu, Hawaiian Islands*. After World War II, when movie cameras became more affordable, surfers such as Bud Browne began shooting their adventures for posterity, then later for profit. Browne spliced his footage together in a 45-minute reel and premiered *Hawaiian Surfing Movies* for a full house at a high school auditorium in Santa Monica in 1953. The success was enough for Browne to give up his day job (teaching), and he became the world's first full-time surf moviemaker. By the end of the decade others—notably Greg Noll, Bruce Brown and John Severson—had joined him.

In 1960, Severson hit on a bright idea to promote his latest surf flick, *Surf Fever*. He utilized an emerging technology to download "still frame" photos from his movie and published them in a 36-page magazine he named *The Surfer*. The 5,000-copy print run was snapped up and the surf magazine was born. By year's end there were three titles in California, but only *Surfer*, as it was known by then, survived and thrived.

Surfing's media-ization was continued with music in 1961. A surfer/musician named Dick Dale began rocking the dance crowd at the Rendezvous Ballroom in Newport Beach with

LEROY GRANNIS

"We have the new shapes." Grannis ad shoot for Jacobs Surfboards, 1963.

wailing guitar reverb instrumentals. The "king of the surf guitar" soon shared the Billboard charts with "surf" instrumental bands such as the Surfaris and the Chantays. Soon vocal groups like the Beach Boys and Jan and Dean had created a softer-edged, more commercial variant with words you could sing along to, and by 1963 all of teenage America was "Surfin' USA."

By 1963 there were more than 40 dedicated surf shops in Southern California alone, with another 20 or so sprinkled along the East and Pacific Northwest coasts. Their stock in trade was still surfboards, but they also sold wetsuits, tee shirts (usually advertising their brand of surfboards), surf wax, surfboard repair

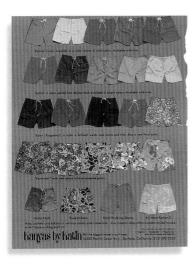

Early '60s trunks ads.

Walter and Nancy Katin, early 1960s.

San Onofre crew.

materials, imported Hawaiian shirts and, increasingly, brand-name surf trunks.

The first genuine Californian brand-name surf trunks were Kanvas by Katin. Walter and Nancy Katin made and sold canvas boat covers from a small premises in Surfside near Long Beach when in the late 1950s they were asked by a young neighbor, 12-year-old Charles "Corky" Carroll, to style him a pair of tough canvas trunks. Future champion Corky Carroll's red Katins lasted long enough to create a market for as many pairs as the couple could produce, and soon they had competition in the form of Birdwell Beach Britches, made out of heavy duty sail cloth. The

two brands vied for shelf space in the minuscule area within surf shops allocated to non-surfboard products. In 1960 a third brand, marketing wiz Duke Boyd's Hang Ten, which specialized in nylon trunks, crowded in.

But as the surf craze peaked in the mid-1960s, the brand trunks that made the most impact had nothing to do with durability or fit. They were long-legged, baggy pareo print shorts in dazzling colors, held up with a draw-string, and they were called Jams. The creation of former Santa Monica lifeguard Dave Rochlen, by then living in Hawaii, they took the tiny surf market by storm and soon became all-purpose beachwear. Rochlen's Honolulu-based company Surf Line Hawaii soon cracked the lucrative department store market, and while mass merchandising would later kill many brands, Jams somehow managed to retain credibility with the surfers.

Although Makaha had hosted an international surf meet since 1954, it was not until 1964 that an official "world championships" of surfing was held, at Manly in Australia. But while this was big news in Australia, it made very little impact in the American main-stream media. However the following year saw the inauguration of an event in Hawaii that would capture the imagination of the American public and kick-start the career of one of surfing's best-loved champions.

Now in his 75th year, Duke Kahanamoku was becoming increasingly frail, and his agent and sometime business partner, an entrepreneur named Kimo Wilder McVay, wanted to honor the legend's lifetime contribution to surfing. Although Duke's name had already been pinned to various McVay enterprises, including a Waikiki restaurant and bar, the announcement of the Duke Kahanamoku Invitational Surfing Championships was received well by both the public and the media, with the CBS television network securing the broadcast rights.

Held at Sunset Beach on the North Shore in the week before Christmas, 1965, the Duke was won by the smallest and youngest competitor, 17-year-old schoolboy Jeff Hakman. The baby-faced Hakman touched a special chord with Americans as they watched him negotiate waves four times his height. Overnight, he became surfing's biggest star and, already known by his teachers at Honolulu's prestigious Punahou School as a thinker, he began to ponder the means by which he might parlay his momentary surfing fame into a lifetime career.

1965 saw the inauguration of an event in Hawaii that would capture the imagination of the American public, and kick-start the career of one of surfing's best-loved champions.

LEROY GRANNIS

Jeff Hakman at Sunset, 1965.

Australia:
The Early Days

Alan Green's Ford Customline on the beach at Double Island Point, 1967.

[TOP] **On surfari, summer '68. Alan Green and friends take a roadside break.**
[ABOVE] **Greeny in trim at Noosa.**

Bells Beach had the best big waves in Australia, and everyone knew it, especially after the Bells Beach Easter surf contest was instigated in 1962. But ironically, in the years that followed the introduction of the Malibu chip balsa surfboard to Australia in 1956, surf culture grew faster around the place that had the worst waves in the southern state of Victoria.

Port Phillip Bay, around which the city of Melbourne is built, churns with southerly squalls that create waist-high wind waves. Along most of the bay, the chop falls formless on open beach, but Brighton Beach, just a few miles from the city, had a stretch of beach bounded by a concrete seawall and a pier, between which the wind slop would smooth out then break in a peaky left. It was garbage, but whenever it happened Brighton's surf-starved gremmies would "hit the stormies."

One of the keenest of the Brighton storm riders was Doug "Claw" Warbrick, whose family lived in a rambling house on the esplanade. He was usually the instigator of weekend surf trips to Bells in the older Pat Morgan's Holden panel van. The mattress in back was reserved for another Brighton surfer, Rod Brooks, and occasionally a tiny 11-year-old prodigy named John Law. They often shared a beach campfire with surfers from Torquay and Geelong, including a student teacher named Brian Singer.

While Singer was at university and Brooks and Morgan studied the building trades, Claw worked at a variety of jobs, but his dream was to open a surf shop in Brighton. The grandly titled Bayside Surf Centre was a low-rent hole in the wall on Railway Walk, but it didn't look so bad after Claw filled it with second-hand boards and his own special blended surf wax. It was successful enough to bankroll his second shop, this time next to Torquay's only beatnik coffee house.

By 1964 Claw had closed down the Bayside and relocated permanently to Torquay, and that summer he and Singer opened a seasonal surf shop under the Cumberland Hotel at Lorne, another beach town about an hour down the coast. Lorne had a more established summer tourist scene, and while the partners didn't make a lot of money, they met a lot of girls. In 1966 they opened the Bells Beach Surf Shop at Torquay. By this time Claw had secured the agency for America's White Stag Wetsuits, a company that had followed the leads of O'Neill and Body Glove. But just as sales took off, Australia's best surfer, Nat Young,

won the world surfing title in San Diego and returned home with a contract to represent White Stag throughout Australia. Bitterly disappointed, Warbrick and Singer vowed to stay away from wetsuits in the future.

When the Warbrick/Singer partnership dissolved under financial pressures, at least temporarily, Claw lit out for the warmth of Queensland and its long-peeling right-hand point breaks. North of Brisbane, at a place called Noosa Heads, perfect small waves rolled into four bays when the right conditions prevailed, and here Claw stumbled into a laboratory of surfboard experimentation led by a diminutive surfer and shaper from Sydney named Bob McTavish. Fueled by the music, energy and drugs of the "summer of love," McTavish and his acolytes were developing the surfboard designs that would ultimately lead to Australia's shortboard revolution.

After that inspirational winter, Claw started the long drive back to Torquay, breaking his journey in Sydney, where he discovered that the leading board manufacturers were already turning Noosa dreams into commercial realities, complete with psychedelic graphics. Claw quickly secured Victorian rights to McTavish's "Plastic Machine" model, then prevailed upon the shaper to allow him to cut into the line and get custom Plastic Machines for himself and the new teenage surfing sensation, Wayne Lynch. McTavish's own board at the time featured a big psychedelic logo with a mushroom cloud over

Bob McTavish pushing the limits at Honolua Bay on a V-bottom "Plastic Machine," December 1967. [FACING PAGE] **Summer of love at Noosa, 1967.**

it encapsulating the words "Hot Kid Rip Board." As he drove south from Sydney, Claw had a mind to go one better, just as soon as his new board came.

Lynch's Plastic Machine arrived first, and by the time Claw's arrived, everyone from Lorne to Torquay was talking about

the young goofy-footer's incredible moves. Before trying his own board, Claw commissioned local artist and surfer Simon Buttonshaw to produce a freaky flower power logo. The two then tried to come up with their own slogan. The brainstorming resulted in the phrase "Rip Curl Hot Dog," and McTavish Plastic Machines bearing this legend sold like hotcakes in the revitalized Bells Beach Surf Shop. Later Warbrick and Singer cut a longer-term

deal for unbranded boards from new Sydney manufacturer Shane Stedman, who didn't like the look of the four-word artwork. Within days Buttonshaw had mailed a new psychedelic logo, accompanied by a simpler "Rip Curl."

The following summer, the Rip Curl partners rented an old bakery and went into production for themselves, taking out their first advertisement, a full page in *Surfing World* heralding "the dawning of Rip Curl Surfboards" with the promise: "We know what we're doing and we'll be around for a long time."

A couple months before the Rip Curl ad appeared, a Bells regular named Alan Green pulled up outside the bakery in a 1953 Ford Customline, a recent 21st birthday present from his grandmother. He grabbed a bulging bag of patterns and samples off the back seat and marched in to do business.

Born in 1947 at Pascoe Vale in the working class suburbs of Melbourne, Green had learned to use his fists. When a teacher slugged him from behind for some alleged insolence, "Greeny,"

Reno Abellira streaks across a Bells Beach wall at the world titles.

as he was known to all, turned around and "king hit" the man. Expelled from school over the pleas of his parents, Greeny got a job in the mail room at Ansett Airlines, and soon became the personal "gofer" of Sir Reginald Ansett, the airline's founder and one of Australia's most dynamic and ruthless businessmen. Ansett liked the boy's spirit, but he advised him to finish school. A friend was about to enroll at Footscray Technical College to study accounting, so Greeny tagged along, lied about his high school diploma and was admitted to the course.

While still at school, Greeny had hitch-hiked on summer weekends down to the coast at Ocean Grove, where he learned to surf on the old boards stored in the surf club. As soon as he was old enough to drive, he started borrowing his mother's Mini Minor and taking his Pascoe Vale friends along. One of them, Robert Ashton, recalls: "He was a bit of a bad-ass. He'd go into a shop and order a toasted cheese sandwich, and while they were out the back making it, he'd help himself to a carton of smokes. He was bold and brave and he always seemed to get away with it."

Rip Curl bakery, Torquay.

The entire Torquay surf industry gathered for Friday afternoon beers, Sovereign Hotel, Torquay, 1975.

The Pascoe Vale punks took a road trip to Cactus, a recently-discovered series of breaks off the remote desert of the Great Australian Bight. Once their Ford Falcon station wagon hit the desert back roads, Greeny perched on the hood and fired his .22 caliber rifle at anything that moved and much that didn't. With 15-year-old Ashton at the wheel, the vehicle crested a hill and collided head-on with another car, as Greeny dived into the brush to save his life. They camped out for three days waiting for replacement parts.

Later, when Grandma bestowed the Customline, Greeny put the old team back together, made sure they had enough money to cover the gas bills and headed for Noosa, a two-day drive north. While the older guys slept, Ashton, still too young for a driving license, drove through the night. But the passengers woke up quickly when he smashed the birthday car into a guardrail. Ashton recalls: "Greeny inspected the damage, abused me a bit and then went back to sleep while some one else drove. But the next morning he walked around the car, made a note of every dent and scratch it had ever taken and told me I'd have to pay to have them all fixed."

With most of his classes at Footscray Tech at night, Greeny took a day job as a trainee accountant at a winery (perhaps laying the foundations for a legendary love affair with wine later in life), and then as bookkeeper at Australian Divers in North Melbourne. With a steady job and a time-consuming passion for surfing, Greeny dropped his accountancy course without a diploma.

Australian Divers was the creation of a "Commander" Batterham, a former career naval officer who had worked with the famed undersea expert Jacques Cousteau during World War II. After the war Cousteau became a major investor in Batterham's enterprise. By the time Green became their bookkeeper, Australian Divers made or imported everything a recreational or professional diver needed, including neoprene wetsuits. When Greeny pressured his boss to diversify into surfing wetsuits Batterham said: "You should leave and do it yourself. I'll even sell you the materials at cost to get you started." Greeny borrowed $1,500AU from his father and set out to give the wheels of industry a spin.

By the time Alan Green walked through their door at Boston Road in the early summer of 1968-69, the Rip Curl partners

Alan Green pulls on his Rip Curl for a session at Jan Juc, 1975.

[ABOVE] **Sparra Pyburne in the wetsuit cutting room.**
[BELOW] **First print advertisement, Breakaway, 1974.**

were starting to realize that the slim profit margin on surfboards would take them only so far. Even as they penned their "We know what we're doing and we'll be around for a long time" slogan, Brian Singer and Doug Warbrick wondered how true this would be if they didn't diversify. Greeny convinced the partners that he knew how to make wetsuits and Singer and Claw saw the potential market, so the three young men shook hands, cleared a space at the back of the bakery and tacked up a "Rip Curl Wetsuits" shingle.

"The first ones were a complete disaster," Greeny recalls. "John 'Sparra' Pyburne was a hot, young local surfer on the way up, so I decided to make the prototype for him. He'd stand there while I cut and glued the panels around him, but it was such a mess that he got the shits and took over as cutter. He's still cutting rubber at Rip Curl today."

Some time during the southern summer of 1969-70, Greeny's mind wandered to another challenge. In his view the surf trunk, or boardshort, screamed for innovation. The dominant Australian brands, Platt's and Adler's, both of which had evolved from the sewing machines of the mothers of well known surfers, were a bulky fit, and the heavyweight fabric often caused rashes and chafing on the upper legs. The few imports, usually canvas or nylon, were not much better. A couple of Torquay surfers had begun tinkering with new designs—part of a general process that Claw called the "creative soup" of the surf-mad town at that time. Greeny decided to see if he could do any better.

The Australian Divers wetsuits incorporated a shoulder entry secured by a Velcro strip and a metal snap at each end, and Greeny had brought this design feature (and a huge supply of snaps and strips) with him to Rip Curl. Now, as he fitted the

snaps into the neoprene and tested the closure, it occurred to him that the same system could replace buttons and flies on boardshorts. That night in the Torquay flat he shared with his schoolteacher girlfriend, Barbara, he sketched some designs on a pad, focusing on fit. Making use of wetsuit parts, Greeny developed the first technical boardshort. He drew a yoked waistband, higher at the back than the front, with scallops on the legs to ensure ample movement. The next morning he delivered two bolts of cotton in contrasting colors and his sketches to one of his wetsuit sewers. He said: "Do us a little favor, would you love?"

In 1970, with no room left at the Boston Road bakery, Greeny's Rip Curl boardshorts division operated out of a series of rented flats and shop fronts around Torquay. At the sewing machine, Carol McDonald turned out 20 to 30 pairs a day while Greeny added the snaps. The Rip Curl partners had already decided on a separate brand for the board-shorts, but it was left to Greeny's girlfriend to come up with a name. Barbara Green recalled many years later that she had just read a definition of the word "quicksilver" that seemed to match ele-

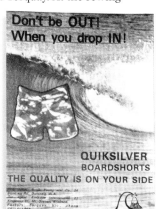

ments of her boyfriend's personality—"elusive, mercurial." It helped, too, that a favorite album on the couple's turntable was by the San Francisco psychedelic band Quicksilver Messenger Service. So Quicksilver it was.

At Cash's, a Melbourne labeling company, Greeny flipped through volumes of logo designs and selected a swan, or a "duck"

Alan Green being interviewed for Tracks in Quiksilver offices, Pride Street, Torquay.

Brewster Everett (left) and Alan Green outside the Pride St office, 1976

as he preferred to think of it. But then he began to have second thoughts about the rights to the name. Without the money to do a trademark search, he decided to play it safe, changing the name to Kwiksilver and even designing the lettering, until McDonald pointed out that a "k" next to a "w" was an embroiderer's nightmare. Finally he settled on Quiksilver, thus ensuring that the fledgling brand would forever be misspelled.

Quiksilver's first customer was the Klemm-Bell Surf Shop in the outer Melbourne suburb of Gardenvale. Greeny had offered Terry Klemm and Reg Bell a partnership in the wetsuits

before he took the idea to Rip Curl, and since they had turned him down they felt obliged to stock his boardshorts. But the designs sold well and Klemm-Bell ordered more. Other clients included Speaky's Surf Shop in Torquay and Tony Olsen's Melbourne Surf Shop, by far the biggest surf retailer in the city. By Christmas "duck" Quiksilvers had sold out, but Greeny was too busy with next season's wetsuits to oversee another production run, so the project was put on hold until the following spring.

Quiksilver soon moved into a shop next to the post office on Pearl Street, Torquay, and Greeny hung up a shingle. With plans for a wider range, he needed fabric at a good wholesale price and, through a friend of his father's, he met a German immigrant rag trader. Joe Ronic had contacts behind the Iron Curtain in East Germany, where excess stock piled up in the wake of another unrealistic Soviet five-year-plan. Though he specialized in dress fabric, Ronic also had access to a double-twisted poplin used mainly for raincoats. Greeny asked Ronic how they might structure a deal. The older garmento must have liked the kid, because he said: "You tell me how much you want and what colors, I dye it for you and you pay me when you sell your range." This generous arrangement, which remained in place for several seasons, put Quiksilver on a footing for future profit. It was a kick-start that Alan Green never forgot.

If Quiksilver boardshorts were going to take on the world, the duck had to go. Greeny again pulled out his sketch pad and began playing with the shape of a wave. He drew the outline of a breaking wave with a few droplets of foam hovering around the lip. Then, for good measure, and for balance, he added a tiny snowcapped mountain underneath it. While surf and snow were not the kindred spirits they are today, Greeny felt that they both represented nature's A-list. He took his sketches back to Cash's where designers refined them into a square patch with QUIKSILVER in capital letters across the bottom. It was a difficult and expensive logo, but by the time it went into production, Greeny was convinced that the little mountain and wave on the bottom of the left leg made a profound statement about the new brand's commitment to its cultural roots.

The second season sold well. Flush with success, Greeny found Quiksilver a bigger home at 29 Pride Street, Torquay. The boss designated the master bedroom as his office and the living room as the production line. The large garage served as the stock room. Greeny also took on a new partner, Brewster Everett, a laidback local with an artistic streak who took over much of the design and production work, freeing Greeny to concentrate on expanding the sales base.

To stay alive, Quiksilver had to either expand its geographic reach to warmer winter climates or develop a winter product...maybe both. During the summer of 1971 Greeny drove north along the Australian east coast, taking orders from tiny surf shops. The farther north he went, the longer the summer and the bigger the sell-in. And one thing was clear—the top surfers recognized the superior cut and quality of the new shorts, and happily served as walking billboards in return for free pairs.

On one of his trips north, Greeny noticed that sheep-skin "ug" boots were becoming quite popular with surfers. Sydney surfboard manufacturer Shane Stedman had registered the name "Ugg" as a trademark and gone into production, selling through surf shops, but in fact the boots and the name had been around in rural communities since the early part of the century. Greeny knew that Victorian surfers would adopt the boots for chilly mornings, so he skirted the trademark issue by registering his business as Ug Manufacturing.

Ug boot production kept the company busy through the winter of 1972, but Green knew that he had to focus on the growing

ART BREWER

"It was creative soup back in '68. Everyone in Torquay was trying to come up with something to sell. Mostly they were creative surfer types who just wanted to have some fun, but Brian Singer and Greeny and I wanted to go on with it. We had a vision the others didn't have."

—DOUG WARBRICK

Michael Peterson on his way to winning the 1973 Rip Curl Pro at Bells Beach.

reputation of Quiksilver boardshorts. Many of the Australian team members competing in the world titles in San Diego that October wore Quiksilvers that Greeny had given them, but it wasn't until the following year, when the Bells Beach contest went professional, that Torquay surf products made a major impact on the style setters and opinion leaders of the surfing world.

Pioneer Australian pro surfer Mark Warren recalls: "We called ourselves professional but no one got real money. It was all about stuff, and boy, did we get a lot of stuff that year at Bells!"

The Rip Curl Bells Beach Pro was the brainchild of Claw Warbrick, and Australia's first pro event was certainly a marketing success for its sponsors, but a stand-alone contest so far away from home was not going to attract all of the best surfers from the northern hemisphere. So Claw was ecstatic when the Australian distributors of Coca Cola and a Sydney radio station announced joint sponsorship of a big-money event in Sydney right after the Bells meet the following year.

The 1974 Down Under pro season attracted all the big names, got widespread television coverage and established a new generation of Australian surfing. Both the Rip Curl Pro and the inaugural Coke Surfabout served as unofficial trade shows, with the captains of industry exchanging board designs and clothing concepts in the beach parking lots. Quiksilver even scored its first offshore client, when contest judge Jack Shipley smuggled 20 pairs of boardshorts inside his surfboard bag to sell at his Lightning Bolt Surf Shop in Honolulu.

The day after the Surfabout finished some visiting pros scored the best surf of their visit when a solid ground swell hit and was caressed by an unseasonally warm offshore breeze. The world's leading pro surfer, Jeff Hakman, arrived at Whale Beach near the tip of Sydney's northern peninsula with only a wetsuit. Fellow pro Mark Warren loaned him a pair of Quiksilvers. "Wow! These feel real good," said Hakman.

He surfed for three hours, drove to the airport and took a flight to Bali. Warren never saw his shorts again.

Celebrating a new partnership in Torquay, 1976. Left to right: Geraldine and John Law, Barbara and Alan Green.

John Law Becomes a Partner

By early 1976 Alan Green's original partners, including production boss Brewster Everett, had moved on, and with Rip Curl's Claw Warbrick and Brian Singer also looking to separate their financial interests, Greeny was looking for an active partner. He didn't need to look beyond Torquay.

One of the finest young surfers in Victoria in the early '70s, John Law had finished third in the Bells Beach Pro in 1974, but he had already seen a career in the surf industry, rather than taking his chances on the new pro tour. After working briefly for a Melbourne stockbroker, "Lawo" had worked for Fred Pyke in Torquay, cutting rubber for the Body Glove wetsuits Pyke made under license, then designing boardshorts and working in sales. Lawo was respected as much for his business acumen as his surfing ability, and Greeny stayed in touch with him when Law and his new bride, Geraldine, left for extended travels in Asia and Europe in 1975.

John Law races a Winki Pop wall, 1974.

Lawo was enjoying the early summer surf and good life of Hossegor in France when Greeny caught up with him to offer a partnership. It didn't take him long to accept, and he returned home to buy the Rip Curl shares and take up his new role at Quiksilver.

ESSAY BY
PETER
TOWNEND

THE BIRTH OF PRO SURFING: WE HAD A DREAM

I sit here on the VIP deck at the 2005 Quiksilver Pro Gold Coast and know, nearly 30 years on, that our dream for pro surfing has been realized.

Back in the '70s, a bunch of us shared this dream, that surfers could be legitimate sportsmen and women. It was about the same time that Greeny starting making and selling trunks to fuel his passion to stay in the water, and we were trying to figure out the same thing, only our version happened to coincide with the "money contests" that began to pop up all around the world.

The birth of pro surfing was coming, and a few of us saw it, particularly the Australians and South Africans who annually made the pilgrimage to Hawaii's North Shore. We were reading books about pro tennis, pro golf, and Formula One motor racing, and we used to say to ourselves, 'We can be like those guys.'

The push for pro surfing had come from Hawaii, due largely to Fred Hemmings, who, since winning the 1968 world amateur title in Puerto Rico, believed with a passion that surfers could become professional athletes and make a decent living from their sport. He began to establish money contests on the North Shore, notably the Smirnoff Pro/Am and Pipe Masters. Fred's contests, along with the Duke and Hang Ten American Pro, were on American television, and if you were in them, you felt like it was big time, especially when ABC's Jim McKay came down the beach to interview you for "Wide World of Sports." At the same time, the Rip Curl Bell's contest went money in '73; there was the Gunston 500 in Durban, South Africa, and the Coke contest, launched in Sydney in '74, offered the biggest money so far, and a lot of mainstream media attention.

In this period, a lot of surfers were on a mission of adventure and discovery, looking for their own "Endless Summers," chasing waves in new locations. It made sense to schedule the search around the events so that sometimes you could win a few extra bucks. We started calling it "The Gypsy Tour."

The real deal, though, began to jell in 1975, when a handful of the Aussies formed the Australian Professional Surfers Association (APSA) and established ratings based on those used for Formula One car racing. These were first published by a young surf journalist named Harry Hodge, in Australia's *Breakway* magazine in September 1976. I remember Terry Fitzgerald commenting, "Wow! You mean I'm doing that good!" as he read of his fourth-place ranking in the international standings.

Finally there was a measurement that wasn't based on how many photos you had in the mags or whether you'd starred in the latest surf movie, but on actual competition results over a season, and with the formation of International Professional Surfers (IPS) by veteran competitor and administrator Fred Hemmings and his sidekick Randy Rarick, surfing began to get its act together.

Through this whole period, there was a surf industry evolving that also helped professionalism along. In Australia, Quiksilver, Rip Curl, and Billabong—and in America, Hang Ten, Op, and Lightning Bolt—were all giving out free trunks to surfers, putting them in their ads in the surf mags and occasionally even putting some money into the contests.

All of these things came together—the money contests, the surf brands becoming established, the APSA and IPS—and in 1976 Randy Rarick was able to convince Fred Hemmings that a ratings system, like the one published in *Breakway*, was the way to go.

Us old pros still debate exactly how it all finally came together, but just prior to the Hawaii contests that year, Fred announced that IPS would crown a world champion based on the money contests of '76—starting with the New Zealand Pro that Michael Peterson had snuck over and won at the beginning of the year without us even noticing!

Fortunately, I hit the Gypsy Tour hard that year, and coming into Hawaii I was poised to win. With a solid North Shore season, making three of the four finals and missing the Pipe Masters final by just one slot, I had enough points on the board to be declared the first IPS World Champion.

Greeny sent me my first pair of pink and black scallop-legs in '74, and I wore the same-design Quiks all the way to that title, and that probably helped land me on the foldout cover of *Surfer* magazine's Holiday Issue of 1976, along with Rabbit's controversial "Bustin' Down the Door" article. They even made the *Surfer* logo pink to match my shorts! Of course I wasn't the only one to land on a surf magazine cover wearing Quiks. In fact, if you look back at the covers from that era, just about everyone was wearing them!

To think now that you could launch a brand that could become a billion-dollar company by giving away free trunks to the best surfers in the world is quite laughable, but that's exactly what happened!

So here I sit, 30 years later, watching Mick Fanning beat Chris Ward in front of thousands of cheering fans at Coolangatta's Superbank, while hundreds of thousands more all over the world are watching the webcast, listening to Shmoo and Pottz on quiksilver.com. Pro surfing has sure come a long way into its fourth decade.

Fanning walks away with the Quik Pro title and a 30-grand check, more than my total earnings as the World Champ in '76. The dream is realized! Well, getting there, anyway.

Pro surfing's first world champion, Peter Townend has enjoyed a long and successful career in the surf industry and media. A longtime advertising director and publisher of Surfing *magazine, he also served as Rusty's marketing director and coached the U.S. national team for the National Scholastic Surfing Association.*

JEFF DIVINE'S TOP 10

Surf photographers are a special breed, not much given to nostalgia or romanticism...at least not in so many words. They really do believe that a picture is worth a thousand words, which is why it's a lot easier to get 10 photos out of them than a few hundred words to accompany them.

Nevertheless, we prevailed upon some of the genre's leading exponents over the past three decades to share with us some of their favorite Quiksilver-related images, and to tell the story behind them. The brief was pretty simple. Just pick 10 shots that summarize the brand for you...its surfers, events, adventures, whatever. Did we mention that surf photographers aren't real good at math either? Ten shots became 12 or 15, or maybe even 9.

Jeff Divine is one who can count...and he was there from the beginning.

As a surf photographer I preferred TC's carving power turns and straight line speed barrels.

—JEFF DIVINE

I guess if you asked most surfers, they'd say that Tom Carroll's snap at Pipe was his most famous move. As a surf photographer I preferred his carving power turns and straight line speed barrels. This one hit the inside sandbar with Tom disappearing and then getting spat out.

Over time there have been surfers who are photogenic simply because of the big moves they pull. No wiggle waggle through the difficult section, just a solid power turn into the snap and on down the line. Willy Morris always displayed both qualities.

On small days at Off The Wall, Mark Richards schooled everyone on his twin, first a collaboration with Ben Aipa and later his own designs. November of '78, two photographers in the water, three on the beach and not a bodyboarder in sight.

Mark Richards with twin fin at Off-the-Wall aka Leongs, Kodak Reef December, 1978. This was the era where a surfboard was shared and Quiksilver boardshorts were worn by all the best surfers in the world purely for their functionality with no monthly check involved.

Marvin Foster grew up
in Haleiwa and was the
cutting-edge surfer at
Pipeline in the 1980s.
He was radical yet poised
in the eye of the storm.
One of the best free
surfers Quiksilver ever had.

Marvin was radical yet poised
in the eye of the storm.

—JEFF DIVINE

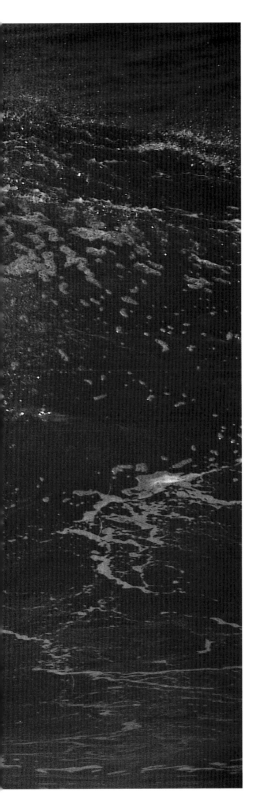

You have to literally claw your way up the cliff for this angle on Sunset. Dozens of mosquitoes probed my legs and I only lasted about a half hour at the sharp-edged volcanic perch. Long enough to catch Ross Clarke Jones snagging one of the best set waves, and then I was back on the beach.

The mid section at Sunset is where the surfers gain speed to set up for the inside bowl. Ross is always a master at judging exactly what he needs to do to put it all together.

Quiksilver has always seemed to have
the knack of recognizing Hawaiian talent
early. Fred Pattachia started out surfing
the white water at Haleiwa. By the time
I took this photo of him being spat out at
Pipeline, he was a Quik team veteran.

My photographer friends were ragging on me for still having my gear set up as the clouds moved in and the rain threatened. I was just about to tell them that Slater was still out there and that the day's work was not yet done when he pulled this move. They groaned as my camera whirred. I turned back to them with a sneer and a Bart Simpson laugh. A month later it was on the cover of *Surfer.*

Imagine that this wave is lined up for another 30 yards in front and you've already surfed for 50. That's exactly what Jimmy Rotherham is experiencing here at his backyard break, a place that has helped him develop into one of the best surfers in Latin America.

TEAM RIDERS
1970s

In late 1977, Wayne "Rabbit" Bartholomew, the number two surfer on that year's IPS world pro tour rankings, became the first official Quiksilver-sponsored athlete when he signed a contract for AU $5,000, rising to AU $8,000 the following year, should he win the world title—which he did.

Rabbit was soon joined on the athlete payroll by Bruce Raymond, a rising young Australian pro. But the fact was that neither of these surfers was new to Quiksilver. They had been wearing the brand for years, since their very first recognition in the sport, at which time Quiksilver founder Alan Green had quickly "flowed" them pairs of boardshorts. In fact, by the mid-1970s, Greeny was flowing shorts to just about every prominent surfer in the world, and in return, the surfers were happy to be associated with the brand in editorial and advertising.

The first team rider ad in the world appeared in the short-lived Australian magazine *Backdoor* in 1975, featuring Gerry Lopez, then the highest-profile surfer in the world, whose own company, Lightning Bolt, had not yet branched into apparel. It was followed a couple of months later by a color ad in Australia's *Surfing World*, featuring the young Sydney surfers Bruce Raymond and Steve Jones. Meanwhile, in the editorial pages of the magazines, while Quiksilver made no official "team" claims, among the surfers seen wearing Quiks were: Terry Fitzgerald, Nat Young, Rory Russell, Michael Ho, Paul Neilsen, Mark Richards, Dane Kealoha, Wayne Deane, Michael Tomson, Peter Townend, Mark Warren, Simon Anderson and Rabbit Bartholomew.

It was a great look for the young brand, but as the pro era dawned, it couldn't possibly last. When Bob McKnight and Jeff Hakman brought Quiksilver to the U.S. in 1976, they built their marketing around the existing flow program, adding local surfers like J. Riddle (Malibu), Mike Armstrong (Laguna and North Shore) and Ed Farwell (Newport), but relied on the PTs and the MRs to bring in the covers and centerspreads. When PT won the 1976 world title, he began to complain to Alan Green that he was being exploited on both sides of the Pacific for the price of a few pairs of shorts. Mark Richards took it a step further, refusing to wear Quiks any longer unless there was a payday. So the era of the great free-for-all ended, but not before it had positioned Quiksilver as the choice of champions.

⬆ Mark Warren

One of Australia's best young surfers in the early 1970s, Mark Warren became one of Quiksilver's first sales reps in order to subsidize a tilt at the pro tour. In that role in 1974 he introduced Jeff Hakman to the brand, opening the door for the emergence of Quiksilver, Inc. After peaking as world number four in '76, Warren joined the Bronzed Aussies promotional team and later left pro surfing to pursue a television career. In recent years he has returned to the fold and now manages Quiksilver's event webcasts.

⬇ Terry Fitzgerald

This flamboyant surfer/shaper from Sydney's speed jive North Shore performances in the early 1970s made him one of the highest-profile surfers on the planet. Although his Hot Buttered Surfboards brand eventually turned to apparel, "Fitz" was a Quiksilver rider through most of the '70s, which didn't stop him from pulling on a pair of Hang Tens for a paid gig!

➡ Michael Ho

The pint-sized Hawaiian powerhouse was third in the world in '78 when he joined Quiksilver's Hawaiian team. Michael spent 13 years on the pro tour but always reserved his best form for the home season on the North Shore, where he continued to dominate into middle age, finishing second in the Pipe Masters at the age of 40.

⬇ Mike Armstrong

This Laguna Beach surfer made a name for himself at Pipeline as a charger in the mid-1970s. When Quiksilver started in the U.S. in 1976, ad salesman Army sold them their first ads in *Surfing* magazine. Jeff Hakman realizing that the salesman could also be the star, quickly put Army on the team and featured him in future ads.

DAN MERKEL

AITIONN

⚲ Michael Tomson

Along with his cousin Shaun and Australia's Rabbit Bartholomew, Michael Tomson led the backside charge at Pipeline in the mid '70s, securing his place in surfing history. But the eloquent South African had more on his mind than winning surf contests. After his stint as a Quiksilver team rider, he considered taking the brand to South Africa, but instead started his own, Gotcha. Within a decade his sales had overtaken Quik's, before returning to earth with a thud in the 1990s.

⚲ Wayne Lynch

Mysterioso goofy-foot from Lorne, Victoria, Wayne grabbed the spotlight with the release of Paul Witzig's *Evolution* in 1969 and has been attempting to avoid it ever since. Although he showed flashes of brilliance in his on-and-off pro career, Lynch has always been the ultimate soul surfer, saving his best performances for solo sessions at remote reef breaks. A Quiksilver rider since the beginning, he is still part of the team.

DAN MERKEL

⚲ Rory Russell

Although he spent much of his career in the shadow of his Pipeline mentor Gerry Lopez, Rory was one of the most colorful of the 1970s Quiksilver team members until following Gerry to Lightning Bolt. Always a standout on the North Shore, Rory also did well in most places he competed during his few years on the pro tour.

AITIONN

◄ Dane Kealoha

North Shore power surfer in the mould of Barry Kanaiapuni (also a Quik rider for a time), Dane burst onto the pro tour in the late '70s and finished runner-up to Mark Richards in 1980. An amazing tube rider, Dane was a favorite of the photographers' gallery at Off The Wall, putting the mountain and wave logo in tight focus on magazine covers around the world. Dane went on to become the proprietor of a Quiksilver Boardriders Club store.

◄ Simon Anderson

Before he invented the thruster, the gentle giant from Sydney's Dee Why carved some pretty heavy lines on a single-fin. It was during this period that he was a Quiksilver team member, seen wearing Quiks during his clean sweep of the Australian pro tour in 1977. Still one of the most popular figures in surfing, Simon is back with Quiksilver's surfboard program.

◄ Chris Byrne

Determined little pro from Australia who emerged at the same time as that other tiny dynamo, Tom Carroll. "Critta" joined the Quik team in the late '70s and was a serious performer around the world through the '80s. Then he worked for Quiksilver marketing in Europe.

THE TEAM

Mark Richards

Rabbit Bartholomew

Bruce Raymond

Peter Townend

Simon Anderson

Wayne Lynch

Nat Young

Paul Neilsen

Maurice Cole

Mark Warren

Terry Fitzgerald

Wayne Deane

Dane Kealoha

Danny Kwock

Michael Tomson

Jeff Hakman

Michael Ho

J. Riddle

Buzzy Kerbox

Chris Byrne

Cheyne Horan

Steve Jones

Rory Russell

Gerry Lopez

Jackie Dunn

Mike Armstrong

Jeff Crawford

Barry Kanaiapuni

DAN MERKEL'S TOP 10

The lean, muscular form of Dan Merkel was a common sight throughout the '70s and '80s as the world's leading surfers dropped into tight barrels at Off The Wall, Backdoor or Burleigh. Before taking an extended sabbatical for much of the '90s, then re-emerging reinvigorated in the new century, Merkel was the credit behind some of surf's most electric images. Here are just a few.

MR had total control when he flew off the lip, a very fluent surfer. Every day at Off The Wall back then was a duel between Shaun and MR.

The bottom turn with the arms down by his sides was really MR's defining statement and this is the classic photo of it. Total control, so relaxed. This was at Off The Wall in the '76 season. It was a poster in *Surfing*.

Rabbit's aggressive style got him into trouble when the Aussies first came to Hawaii. He really did bust down some doors! But in the water, oh man. He was really radical and those guys would do just about anything to get the best shots.

Rabbit at Sunset was another story. Powerful and radical. These guys that came out of the Gold Coast had only ridden small waves. They were known to be radical when it was small and playful, but when they came to Hawaii, they just brought the same attack with them and used it in big waves.

Wes Laine was a gentleman of the surf. A good, solid surfer without being too radical. This was one of the more radical images of him I ever took.

Buttons always cracked me up. He was an excellent surfer and such fun to be around. This was at Ehukai Beach Park after a Pipe session, givin' me the shaka from the shower, bra! Surfing used to be fun, man. It's gone too corporate.

I shot water footage for Big Wednesday alongside George Greenough, but I also shot some stills whenever I could. Here you have actor Billy Katt and his girlfriend of the time, PT and his wife of the time, and George. All the others were in period surfwear from the '60s because they were in front of the cameras. George was behind the camera, so he got to wear what everyone wore in the '70s—Quiksilvers. The photo was taken on location in El Salvador.

In August 2005 I traveled up the West Australian coast with Nathan Fletcher, Danny Fuller and Reef McIntosh. When we got up north we hooked up with Ry Craike, although he wasn't with us the day we got Red Bluff really firing. The locals reckoned the tide was too low, but our guys just paddled out and shredded it. Reef is a very accomplished big wave surfer, a guy I've seen just power all over the world. Danny Fuller rips too, but I don't like his driving music selection so much. I don't think I ever traveled with young guys like that before. It was cool, but I couldn't believe they'd run into the motel room, grab all the beds and leave the old guy on the floor.

I shot the panoramic of the Quiksilver Pro Gold Coast contest site from across the bay at Kirra, just as it was getting dark. It looked like this weird city on the beachfront and it reminded me of how far surfing contests have come.

...ogo

...uiksilver boardshorts of 1970
...al but rather plain solid-color
...turing a square leg cut, narrow
...ro fly and single snap closure.
...ed logo patch was not the
...t is now instantly recognized
...ld, but a rendition of a silver
... background—essentially
...offered by the company's first
...ksilver's Mountain and Wave
...—a compelling allusion to surf
...s—made its first appearance
...remained the company's
...ce.

Michael Ho in early Quiksilver Country panels.

Mid-'70's solids

By the mid-'70s, Quiksilver had defined the style that set its boardshorts apart from all others. Design and fabrication were unique, particularly the wide "yoke" waistband that rode low on the hips. Double snap and Velcro closure made for an easy and secure fastening and ensured the boardshorts would stay on even in the most turbulent surf. Solid-color bodies were accented by a contrasting colored waistband, sometimes with a third color piping trim. The boardshorts came in three silhouettes —square leg, scallop leg and arch leg—all designed for comfort and freedom of move-ment.

Echo Beach 2

The Echo Beach name was inspired by the 1980 song from Canadian New Wave band, Martha and the Muffins, but the line of surf trunks continued to be a hit long after the record dropped off the charts. The Echo Beach line was carried over for several seasons in many re-interpretations from Quiksilver's creative designers and helped make the Surf Look an undeniable and permanent icon of American sportswear design. The look was reprised yet again in the new century with a retro range for summer ' 06 that brought back not only the patterns but a modified shorter leg.

Heat Wave

This watercolor-style abstract print could be considered an extension of the Echo Beach line. Its name was also borrowed from a New Wave pop hit of the early '80s and its color story was resonant of high summer. By this time original artwork prints had become a hallmark of Quiksilver's boardshorts line and designers were inventing new ones both in Australia and California. It was not long before a third tier would be at work in southwest France too, as a license had just been granted for Quiksilver in Europe.

Early '90s Warpaint

Wild artwork, often with "primitive" motifs were becoming a mainstay of surfwear, as evidenced by this boardshort from Quiksilver's early '90s Warpaint line, a reinterpretation of a successful mid-'80s design. Surfers traveling to exotic locations as far afield as Africa, Indonesia and South America had long been inspired by the different cultures they found along the way. Now, in the aftermath of surf culture being co-opted by mainstream fashion, core surf labels like Quiksilver countered with tribal insignia that set surfers apart from the non-surfing populace, drawing from eclectic sources for a distinctive look.

Tom Carroll in cup-hugging Neo Geos.

...ar

...rfwear, just as in the broader
...s, a distinctive style goes
... cycles of rediscovery and
...ere was nothing new about
...rs on a solid-color background
...r placed this boardshort in
...he early years of the new
...78 World Champion Wayne
...omew had favored a red pair
...ite stars at the start of the
...But in modern microfiber
...ed with silver appliqué—as
...ater—this retro revival had a

2000s Roxy

In the new century Roxy's boardshorts styles have evolved to cater for the broader market, from hardcore surfer to fashionista. The Lisa Andersen-designed originals still live on and are favored by girls who care as much about function as fashion, but there are also styles of varying length that are more for partying on the beach than tearing it apart in the surf. Cool prints have taken over from solid colors as the most popular style.

The History of Quiksilver Boardshorts

Since its rather crude beginnings in 1970, Quiksilver has combined function, fit, art and fashion in developing the boardshort into the core item of surfwear, imitated around the world. From basic beginnings with one color, one fabric—cotton—Quiksilver boardshorts have evolved into an ever-changing array of solid colors, prints and bold new art concepts from the most tuned in artists and designers on the planet. Styles have come and gone, and come back again, but there has always been one constant: quality.

Duck [...]

The very first [...]
were a functio[...]
cotton trunk fe[...]
waistband, Ve[...]
The embroide[...]
familiar icon t[...]
around the wo[...]
swan on a blac[...]
generic clip a[...]
contractor. Qu[...]
trademark log[...]
and snow spo[...]
in 1971 and ha[...]
marque ever s[...]

Kong in Echo Beach.

Echo Beach 1

Surf style and New Wave pop music coincided in 1980 with Quiksilver's Echo Beach line of boardshorts. Featuring both all-over prints of checkerboards, harlequin diamonds and brightly colored polka dots in addition to solid-color bodies with side panels of the same graphic look, the hugely successful Echo Beach range of trunks was a "runner"—a springboard to the company's broader success as a full-line surfwear label offering not just boardshorts but walkshorts, tops, jeans, jackets and more.

Ghetto Dog

The cultural phenomenon of graffiti art and the influence of innovators like Keith Haring and Jean-Michel Basquiat spilled over into the surf scene in the late-'80s with boardshorts like this from Quiksilver's Ghetto Dog range. The highly-stylized, gritty motifs—some of them evocative of Aboriginal archetypes—were the brainstorm of Australian designer Peter Webb who fully intended Ghetto Dog to rebut the steady stream of artwork prints being produced by upstart surf label Mambo that had built a reputation and a market with its quirky, irreverent and sometimes scatological graphics.

Gen X

As the surf look was co-opted and knocked-off by mainstream apparel makers, genuine surf labels sought innovative directions to take back the beach and to acknowledge the changing tastes and attitudes of the contemporary youth demographic. This early 1990s example from the "Generation X" line features edgier graphics and less glaringly bright colors—a hint that neon was about to be "x'd" from the surfwear color palette. Boardshorts with a longer length leg also became popular once more at this time, a style that Quiksilver dubbed its "Leggo" silhouette.

Foil S[...]

In functional s[...]
fashion busine[...]
through endl[...]
reinvention. [...]
five-pointed st[...]
when Quiksil[...]
its line durin[...]
millennium. 1[...]
Rabbit Barth[...]
printed with [...]
Echo Beach [...]
fabric foil-su[...]
worn by Kel[...]
whole new l[...]

QUIKSILVER®

Origins of the

One-piece woolen knit "tank" suit, circa 1920s.

High-waisted, belted all-purpose trunk, circa 1930s.

1950s surf trunk by Take of Honolulu.

In the tropical waters of Hawaii, the only equipment that's really needed for surfing is a board and a pair of boardshorts or a swimsuit. But when Captain James Cook arrived in 1778 and became the first Westerner to see people riding waves on surfboards, the locals didn't bother with any more gear than the absolute essential—they surfed naked.

The missionaries who followed in Cook's wake by the 1820s soon put a stop to that, insisting on a modesty inspired by the social norms of Europe. Victorian age "sea bathing" meant wading into the shallows dressed in what today could pass for street clothing, absent the shoes. While Hawaiian men of the 19th century could still get away with surfing in as little as a loincloth, the constraints of missionary-style modesty appear to have ended a centuries-long tradition of women surfing in Hawaii, the voluminous neck-to-ankle bathing garb being totally impractical in turbulent waves. In fact, the missionary view of surfing—that it encouraged licentiousness and gambling, among other alarming habits— almost put an end to the sport entirely.

When surfing's revival began in Hawaii during the early years of the 20th century, modesty laws in Hawaii, as on the mainland, dictated that not even men could go topless at the beach or in the water. Surfing attire was a one-piece woolen knit "tank" suit with mid-thigh-length legs. When wet, such suits could weigh as much as nine pounds. As surfing spread from the shores of Waikiki to the U.S. mainland and across the Pacific to Australia in the second decade of the century, the one-piece, or by now sometimes two-piece wool suit—trunks with a tank top—remained the legally enforced dress code for men. Women had to wear a similar suit with a skirt or risk being arrested. During the Roaring Twenties, as more liberal attitudes took hold, such social constraints and modesty laws began to disappear, leading to less coverage and more freedom of movement in swimsuits. But there were still no suits specifically designed for surfing.

Specialty surf trunks first made their appearance among surfers and beach boys of Waikiki in the 1930s. The few women who surfed still wore one-piece maillot-type swimsuits, but men were now at liberty to go topless in the surf. Although commercially produced swim trunks were readily available—typically high-waisted and high-cut in the leg—more and more surfers wore custom-made, close-fitting, high-waisted shorts with a mid-thigh leg that helped prevent chafing while straddling a surfboard. Increasingly, a lace-up tie at the waist replaced the less comfortable belt with a cinch or buckle to secure the trunks in the event of a wipeout. Form was beginning to follow function in surf trunk design. A thriving garment industry was developing in Honolulu, as the Aloha shirt and the muumuu became sought-after styles among locals and tourists alike, and it was a simple matter to find a seamstress to sew up a pair of surf trunks from cotton twill or sailcloth. By the end of the decade, there was even a commercially made surf trunk being manufactured by Kahala, the Aloha shirtmaker, sold under the Lyn's label from its retail store located at the Outrigger Canoe Club. Lyn's became the surf trunk of choice for most surfers and beach boys over the next 10 years. The cotton twill short, with its lace-tie waistband and flat-buttoned fly, often featured a stripe down the outside of each leg, and eventually also bore the Outrigger Canoe Club logo. The distinctive style—a specialty surf look—was the precursor of a worldwide surfwear industry.

Trunks, & Baggies

Boardshort

BY PAUL HOLMES

By the mid to late 1950s, several shops on the island of Oahu in Hawaii were known for their ability to make functional custom-made surf trunks including the H. Miura General Store in Haleiwa on the North Shore, Take's of Honolulu on the south side, and M. Nii of leeward Waianae. All by now were selling to local surfers and to the increasing numbers of surfers visiting from the mainland, where specialty surf trunks were still a novelty and most surfers got by with commercially made swim trunks or a pair of cut-off ex-Navy pants. The latter usually featured exaggeratedly long legs, left to fray at the bottom, another indicator of the unique "fashion" element of surf style that would shortly emerge.

Kanvas by Katin, circa 1962.

Los Angeles–based Catalina Swimwear had been making women's bathing suits for years. When *Gidget* hit the silver screen in 1959 and surfing began to explode in popularity, Catalina jumped into the men's market with trunks aimed at surfers. They were soon joined by other West Coast swimwear companies including Sandcomber, Balboa, Jantzen, Campus, and McGregor.

But a highly specialized custom trunk–making cottage industry took root in California during the late '50s, just as it had already done in Hawaii. Surfside-based Kanvas by Katin began making surf trunks after a neighborhood gremmie—future U.S. champion Corky Carroll—asked the canvas awning maker to sew up a pair of shorts for him from the same rugged material. Kanvas by Katin—along with San Diego company Birdwell Beach Britches, founded in 1961—became one of several custom-order trunk makers in California's emerging surf scene and marketplace. As a network of surf shops sprang up on both the West and East Coasts of the U.S. during the 1960s, custom trunk making gave way to a larger-scale manufacturing and wholesale distribution system serving core-market specialty stores.

Hang Ten, circa 1960s.

In 1960, surfer Duke Boyd started making Hang Ten trunks with an embroidered logo of two golden feet—a graphic depiction of one of surfing's most compelling motifs, alluding to a noseride or footprints on an empty beach. Early pairs of Hang Tens were made of canvas or cotton twill, but by 1962 fast-drying nylon was used exclusively. Most grassroots surf trunk makers still favored a lace-tie for the waistband, although more convenient snaps soon became widely used and Velcro became a standard closure for the fly.

When designer Boyd licensed Hang Ten's manufacturing to Ontario-based Don Rancho in 1964, Hang Ten became one of the first major surfwear labels, expanding its line from "baggies," as the looser-fitting surf trunks were commonly called at the time, to sophisticated engineered striped knitted T-shirts, nylon windbreakers, and other items—all embroidered with the distinctive Hang Ten logo. That same year in Hawaii, at the Surfline board shop, Dave Rochlen started making a long-legged surf trunk that featured stylized tropical prints. Rochlen named the clam-digger shorts "jams," because his wife, who'd sewn them up, thought they looked like pajama bottoms. When Mike Doyle wore a pair during the nationally televised Makaha International surf contest that winter, Rochlen was called by a buyer at the Lord & Taylor department store in New York wanting to place a $10,000 order for spring and summer sales back east, where the surfing look was exploding thanks to the *Gidget* movies and the Beach Boys' music.

Jams by Surfline Hawaii, circa 1965.

Boardshorts, at first just a functional style for surfing, had become an iconic youth-culture statement.

Bruce Raymond and Steve Jones model Quiksilver Country designs in the first ever ad shoot, 1975.

Australian Print Interpretation

Thousands of miles from Hawaii in Torquay, Australia, Quiksilver artist and designer Simon Buttonshaw was rendering his own interpretation of traditional tropical prints found on colorful pareos throughout Polynesia. Elements such as hibiscus, bird of paradise flowers, fern leaves and other tropical foliage were motifs manipulated to give a fresh twist to the pareo print story. Silky sateen fabric gave the boardshorts an equally exotic texture, in keeping with the sensual tropical experience of surfing in the Polynesian islands. Selected designs like this one were also printed on utilitarian twill.

panel printing
shorts portend
"neon" color
feature of the

Neon Butt logo

The beach lifestyle became the driving force in sportswear both in the United States and across the globe during the late '80s, with designs from Quiksilver and other Southern California's surfwear companies imitated by everyone from casual clothing makers to couture labels. This "neon" boardshort with its prominent "butt logo" on the back drew both from surf roots and the pro beach volleyball scene for its inspiration and features a return to the narrower waistband and single snap closure.

Pareo Prints Redux

Traditional pareo prints made a comeback in the late 1990s, 20 years after Quiksilver had first incorporated the look into its boardshorts line, but this time around the cut of the boardshort was quite different, with a longer legged silhouette still in vogue among surfers. By now, team rider Kelly Slater had already racked up an incredible record-breaking six world championship titles and when he adopted the look, wearing the tropical print boardshort in both competition and freesurfing appearances, its success in surf shops around the globe was almost guaranteed.

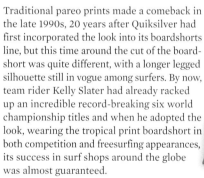

Troy Brooks at work.

Art Series

The Webmaster Art Series, to give it its full title, was created by veteran Quiksilver artist Peter Webb and brought to fruition by "Webby," Natas Kaupas in California and Josh Gurry, an Australian artist working out of New York—a classic example of the worldwide network that now contributes to design and art for Quiksilver. A homage to the Impressionists and other more recent art schools, the Art Series was nonetheless imbued with a distinctly surf look.

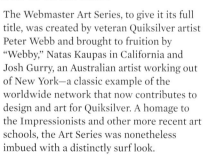

Kelly Slater, North Shore winter '05.

7 Stars

When Kelly Slater won his seventh world title in the fall of 2005, Quiksilver's design team was already at work reinventing the Echo Beach look, stars included. To celebrate Kelly's phenomenal achievement, it seemed only logical to reprise his favorite look of the '90s, the Foil Star. The limited edition 7-Star short was a classic, combining the original designs of the '80s with the microfiber technology of the new century.

Mid-'70's panels

Color-blocking side panels were added to the Quiksilver range of boardshorts shortly before the U.S. license was granted to Bob McKnight and Jeff Hakman in 1976. The first Quiksilvers seen in the US market were imported from Australia, but Quiksilver USA soon began making its own range locally with U.S. product adapted from the Australian patterns so that the boardshorts were consistent in design and appearance on both sides of the Pacific. As the decade progressed, however, in the US alternative fabrics were introduced including faster-drying cotton/poly blends.

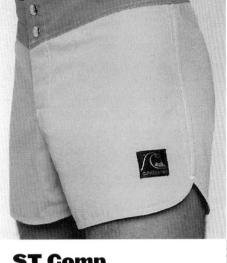

Hoffman prints/ Quiksilver Country

Starting in the mid- to late '70s, Quiksilver's boardshorts became available in various prints specially produced by Hoffman California Fabrics of Mission Viejo. The artistic flair of Hawaiian tropical prints seen in the "Aloha" shirts of the 1940s and '50s had long been identified with surfers and surfing. In the 1970s airbrush artists had taken tropical surf and beach scenes to new heights of fantasy as decoration on surfboards and for printed tee-shirt graphics. Quiksilver adapted the look into a variety of fabric prints for boardshorts as part of the theme it called "Quiksilver Country."

ST Comp

By the mid-'80s professional surfing's world tour had been in existence for a decade and was continuing to grow. The ST Comp boardshort represented both technical innovation and style inspired by the pro surfing scene. Fabricated from a cotton-Lycra blend, they offered two-way stretch, guaranteeing maximum freedom of movement for high-performance surfing. In keeping with the futuristic approach, a new "engineered" logo—a stylized more modern interpretation of the Mountain and Wave—was introduced during this period. The logo stood the test of time and is still being used to this day.

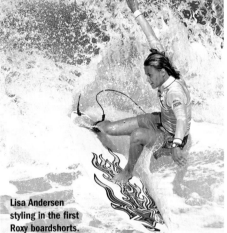

Lisa Andersen styling in the first Roxy boardshorts.

ST Comp 2

The bright accents in the side of this style of ST Comp board the arrival of the "Day-Glo" or story that would be a dominan Surf Look in the late 1980s.

Neo Geo

Quiksilver's success with boardshorts, the essential element of any authentic surfwear label, was by no means driven solely by innovative graphics. This mid-'90s Neo Geo boardshort constructed from two-way stretch Lycra coincided with the company's entry into wetsuit manufacturing and the snug-fitting, ultra-flexible style echoed the huge technological advances made in wetsuit technology since suits were first introduced in the mid-'50s. Two-time World Champion and 1990 Pipeline Master Tom Carroll took a liking to the Neo Geo and his endorsement helped launch the fast-drying, technical athletic-wear style.

90s Roxy

By the mid-'90s, women and girls had begun taking to the waves in unprecedented numbers, partly inspired by the Girl Power movement. Quiksilver proved to be in tune with the changing times, launching its Roxy line of surfwear, sportswear and accessories virtually simultaneously with the start of the phenomenon. Roxy's women's boardshort—a first for the surfwear business—was both feminine and functional, stylish and sexy, especially when worn by a Girl Power icon like four-time World Champion Lisa Andersen.

Cell

Art and science, function and form, and just plain fun—what surfing's all about—come together in the contemporary interpretation of the boardshort. In Quiksilver's 2005 range, the technology of fast-drying microfibers, two-way horizontal stretch fabrics and stitchless welded seams are still merely a canvas for creativity. A print that melds op-art, new wave and gothic elements comes alive with the pair of 3-D glasses included. Oversized tropical floral prints sprout from a bed of dynasuede. A fin key, bottle opener and wax comb—a tool that every surfer can use—comes with the Lycra hem and neoprene fly. Want solid

Bunny Cooker

This limited edition 2005 style features original artwork with a bombardment of embellishments including screen prints, embroidery and appliqué. Each boardshort is topped off with graffiti-style, hand airbrushing, essentially customizing each individual pair—a truly futuristic innovation that is sure to find favor in the increasingly cookie-cutter world of the 21st century. A neoprene-fly utilizes Quiksilver's wetsuit technology, adding to the comfort factor by eliminating Velcro and making it easier to get into and out of. Reinforced Lycra constructed hems prevent knees from catching while surfing in the longer leg boardshort.

ESSAY BY
DREW
KAMPION

INVASION FROM OZ:
THE BACKSIDE ATTACK

The initial and defining drama of the so-called Australian Invasion of world surfing came in huge surf at the Banzai Pipeline during the winter of '75-'76. Referred to as the "backside attack," this unparalleled assault on the elements and the status quo wasn't only about regulars and goofy-foots, Australians and South Africans. It was also about showmanship, balls, and ultimately— once the smoke had cleared and the battleground was again serene —salvation and humility, too. That groundbreaking winter brought a charmed coincidence of attitude and opportunity, as regular-footed Wayne "Rabbit" Bartholomew of Queensland, Australia, and cousins Michael and Shaun Tomson of Durban, South Africa, led the charge to fill a kind of charisma void in the surfing world and establish themselves as the new force in power surfing.

Gerry Lopez, who had succeeded and outshone predecessors Butch Van Artsdalen and Jock Sutherland to become the definitive "Mr. Pipeline" in the early '70s, cast his sights elsewhere with the discovery of the longer, less crowded barrels of the Indian Ocean archipelagos, first at Ulu Watu and then at Grajagan. Thus, Lopez was not so much deposed or eclipsed; rather, he abdicated to a cohort of Pipe aficionados that included Rory Russell, Jackie Dunn, Mike Armstrong and Jeff Crawford. These guys had surfed with Gerry and very much followed the Lopez formula at Pipeline: Be patient, get the right wave, take off deep, fade if you can, find the cleanest line on the wall of the barrel, don't let the lip hit you in the head and surf elegantly. Like Lopez, these guys were all goofy-footers, but the new kids from the Southern Hemisphere weren't.

That winter was the time for these kids... and they *were* kids; Shaun and Rabbit were just 20, and Mike was 21. But they came to the North Shore with this *attitude* that anything was possible, maybe even fated.

Whenever and wherever they surfed, they *went* for it, full-bore. And when the west-northwest swells started concentrating energy on second-reef Pipe, they went for it there, too. It was as if they were living with a sense of déjà vu—as if they knew what was coming and that this was their time—and these three backsiders blew the roof off Pipeline. They hurled themselves over precipitous ledges into impossible vertical drops—way too late, way too deep, way too committed—and they reaped a shitload of punishment. But, much more often than they probably expected, they made it! And every time they survived, the field of the possible was stretched further.

"I always thought there were only three people involved in the backside attack," Shaun Tomson recently commented, "and out of everyone, Mike Tomson was the gutsiest." Nonetheless, it was Shaun who won the 1975 Pipe Masters, and the Australians, by sheer strength of numbers, who got the column inches and full-page shots.

That winter, every day seemed like a realized opportunity, as if these three guys and the other young men from Down Under (Peter Townend, Ian Cairns, Mark Richards, Mark Warren, Bruce Raymond, Paul Neilsen, Terry Fitzgerald, and so on) saw a crack in the door to another dimension and were determined to push through. Every session was a contest, each wave a new benchmark. All action and no talk, Richards won the Smirnoff and five thousand bucks at Waimea Bay, followed by Cairns and Rabbit. The Australian Invasion was on! They charged Sunset, surfed Waimea more than respectfully, and rode deeper than anyone at Rocky Point, V-Land and a new spot called Off the Wall.

To make matters even more interesting, these new young guys got sudden and extraordinary media coverage. Their surfing had an abandon that caught the imagination of the media. Photographers were caught up in a feeding frenzy that kept the magazines happy over the next nine months. In large measure, this was the work of a handful of skilled and physically fit lensmen, who increasingly did their work in close proximity to the impact zone. Dan Merkel was especially notable, along with Art Brewer, Steve Wilkings, Jeff Divine and a handful of others. The up-close-and-personal nature of their images effectively captured the charisma of the new surfers: They were bold, colorful, and they surfed with a wild passion that made the previous coterie of top guns appear a bit staid. And, of course, they became the stars of Bill Delaney's influential '77 flick, *Free Ride*.

The real moment of truth for the Australian Invasion came at the onset of the following season, with the arrival of Rabbit on Oahu in October of 1976, embarrassingly coincident with the publication of Rabbit's *Surfer* magazine cover-story proclamation that he and his mates were prepared to descend on Hawaii and really "bust down the doors" this time around.

Unfortunately, the slim Caucasian and future president of the Association of Surfing Professionals appeared in the magazine wearing the garb (including the boxing gloves) of Mohammad Ali. This may have sent the wrong message to committed local surfers, because shortly after Bugs arrived, he was caught in a slap-down with the North Shore *hui*—a locals-only society—and subsequently fitted with a new set of front teeth.

That winter ('76-'77) was a dark time on the North Shore— the Aussies received death threats and were holed up at the Kuilima Resort for weeks. It took the intercession of big-wave rider Eddie Aikau and his family to get things sorted out. Still, the die was cast.

Just before Rabbit's arrival on the North Shore that year, the International Professional Surfers (IPS) was created, and retroactively selected events qualifying for the year's pro rankings. Thus, Queensland surfer Peter Townend emerged as pro surfing's first world champion. The kids from Down Under had maneuvered a quick coup d'état, and Hawaiians and Californians alike felt outflanked.

No matter. It was a *fait accompli,* and the men from Down Under would continue to dominate the new world of professional surfing for a decade, until the ascendancy of California's Tom Curren in 1985.

One-time editor of both Surfer *and* Surfing, *Drew Kampion brought the reckless style of New Journalism to surfing in the late 1960s and 1970s. His opinionated coverage of pro surfing's formative years influenced a generation of surf writers.*

Quiksilver in the US: The Early Days

Jeff Hakman ponders a broken board and an imminent business career, North Shore, 1976.

[TOP] **Bob trains the state-of-the-art Sony at the surf, c. 1970.** [ABOVE] **Bali crew 1974. Bob is third from left.**

In the summer of 1974, USC business major Robert Buchner McKnight Jr, 20, led a group of friends on a surf trip that would change his life forever.

While sailing through Southeast Asia on board the World Campus Afloat student cruise ship the previous summer, McKnight had discovered the romance, adventure and, above all, the incredible surf of the island of Bali. He had been scheming to get back there ever since, and now, having recruited 10 fellow adventurers, he had a free Pan Am ticket, a backpack full of surf trunks and wax, two surfboards in a sailcloth bag and, of course, his beloved Sony Super-8 movie camera.

Born (1953) and raised in the affluent L.A. 'burbs of Pasadena and San Marino, Bob McKnight had been a surfer since his early teens, a surf moviemaker almost as long. After a downturn in his father's business career, he had helped pay for his college studies by showing his home-made surf movies up and down the coast. Now McKnight intended to combine his passion for making movies with his business education and forge a career in the film industry. But that was later. For now all he cared about was surfing those magical, pristine waves of Bali.

A couple of months into the trip all his friends had gone broke and gone home. Having the time of his life, McKnight hung on, eking out a cheap existence in a *losmen* (or guesthouse) on the edge of the jungle and surfing every day with a new friend, Australian surfer Phil Byrne. One day while he and Byrne were resting after a day's surfing, another young filmmaker rode past on his motorcycle and yelled: "Hey, McKnight, hope you got plenty of film left. Hakman just arrived."

Although he had never met him, McKnight knew all about Jeff Hakman. Everybody did! Since winning the first Duke Kahanamoku contest at Sunset Beach in 1965, the frail little boy who had looked so vulnerable riding those giant waves had grown into a powerful man who was widely recognized as the best pro surfer in the world. There were no ratings and no official world tour, but Hakman's performances in the Duke and the recently established Pipeline Masters events had given him the edge over other surf heroes like Gerry Lopez and the Australian powerhouse, Michael Peterson. Hakman may not have been god, but he was damn close!

McKnight found that Hakman, far from having a surf star attitude, was friendly and engaging with a wicked sense of humor. They soon became friends and stayed in touch after they each went back to their separate worlds. McKnight was delighted when his surf-star buddy started inviting him to spend winters at his simple A-frame cottage on Hawaii's famous North Shore, and upon his graduation from 'SC at the beginning of 1976, he gladly accepted Hakman's offer to house-sit in Hawaii while the champion competed in Australia.

McKnight found his friend somewhat distracted on the eve of his Australian tour. "He kept going on about swimsuits," he recalls. "Jeff always seemed to be passionate about something, and now it was these Australian surf trunks called Quiksilvers. To be honest, I didn't pay much attention."

Despite some drug adventures that had got him into trouble with the law in the late 1960s, Hakman had served an apprenticeship in the nascent surfwear business under the California-based entrepreneur Duke Boyd, first at Hang Ten and then at Boyd's new brand, Golden Breed. Now Boyd had again recruited Hakman as he sought to turn the successful surfboard brand Lightning Bolt into an even more successful apparel brand, but Hakman had become obsessive about the Australian trunks that fellow pro surfer Mark Warren had introduced him to, and he planted the obsession in his friend McKnight.

Jeff Hakman on his way to winning the 1976 Bells trophy.

Winners are grinners at Bells. (Left to right) Shirley Rogers, Jeff's girlfriend Joey, Jeff, Rory Russell.

While Bob McKnight looked after the Pupukea house, Hakman enjoyed his best-ever Australian season, winning the prestigious Rip Curl Bells Pro. What happened on the night of his victory has become one of surfing's great legends. Fueled with excitement, adrenaline, red wine and God knows what else, Hakman approached Alan Green's table in a Torquay restaurant and brought up a familiar topic—his obsession with obtaining a license to make and sell Quiksilver in the U.S.

"Greeny, what do I have to do to make you understand how much I want this license?" Hakman pleaded. Green, considerably the worse for drink himself, pointed to a decorative cloth doily in the center of the table. "Eat the doily," he said. Hakman did not hesitate, grabbing the doily and eating it, washing each mouthful down with a swig of wine from Green's bottle. Rolling on the floor with laughter, Alan Green gave up. "Okay Hakman," he wept, "You've got a license!"

The phone call woke McKnight in the middle of the night. "Buzz...we got the license!" At first McKnight ("Buzz" to Hakman, after a famous Hawaiian big-wave rider) had no idea what his friend was babbling about. Then the penny dropped. Hakman had the Quiksilver license and the two friends were in the surfwear business. Oh my God, thought McKnight, what do we do now?

As it turned out on Hakman's return to Hawaii, he didn't really know either. They had a verbal license agreement from a guy who had never licensed before and whose Australian business was doing less than $400,000 in sales. Green had given Hakman two pairs of shorts and a cheery "good luck"—that was it! Fortunately, by the time McKnight had established the business at his rented apartment on Seashore Drive in Newport Beach and Hakman had relocated from Hawaii, a small package arrived from Alan Green. In it the partners found a pattern on thin paper, a small square of cotton poplin, a patch logo, a metal snap, a length of

Jeff and Bob, c.1974.

Velcro and a note from Greeny spelling out the royalty agreement (one percent, for a trial period). At the end of the note, Greeny had written: "If you need any advice, see Walter Hoffman."

Somehow the partners found enough materials to get started and a team of seamstresses at bikini house Summer Girl by Sandi, in Encinitas. Despite the fact that Quiksilver USA only managed to dribble out a small number of pairs in the late fall of 1976, the arrival of the "boardshorts" from Down Under created quite a stir in the surfing community. Hobie's Surf Center in Dana Point put up a sign on the sidewalk in front: "Quiksilvers are coming!" When McKnight and Hakman made their first delivery in Bob's battered VW bus, the sign was changed to: "They're here!" They sold out in a matter of hours.

While their meager working capital dwindled and they searched for a third partner to help them finance production, McKnight and Hakman took Greeny's advice and went to see Hoffman, boss of Hoffman California Fabrics, supplier of fabric to brands like Hang Ten, Hobie and the new Ocean Pacific brand. The fabric guru's first words echoed those of Bob's father: "You guys are out of your freakin' minds!" But later Hoffman provided them with industry contacts, while McKnight Sr. put them in touch with some investment brokers who agreed to bankroll Quiksilver USA's production runs for a 30% stake in the company.

Now they were getting serious. McKnight, who had somehow imagined that the business would be like a summer fling before getting back to a real career, realized just how serious when he found himself freezing in snowy New York City just before Christmas, learning about warp and weft from a helpful salesman named Chris Glynn at fabric giant Milliken's headquarters. Fortunately for the surfers turned garmentos, in Milliken they found an ally, just as Alan Green had found one in Joe Ronic.

Limited by the fabric they could afford to purchase from Milliken, some of the early Quiksilver boardshorts featured unfortunate color combinations, but the main problem the partners encountered was that their shorts were 65% polyester while Greeny's were pure cotton that shrank to a tight, hip-hugging fit, while the blended fabric tended to hang loosely. But McKnight and Hakman were on a learning curve, and their product improved with each run, particularly after they moved production to the home factory of a Thai woman named Sunanta Vailles. Sunanta and her workers were fastidious and they devoted themselves exclusively to Quiksilver. And when Hakman and McKnight moved into their first factory, on 17TH Street in Costa Mesa, Sunanta was just around the corner.

In the spring of 1977, Quiksilver began its first advertising campaign, a series of full-page, full-color ads in *Surfing* magazine. Since they still could not meet demand, the ads were an indulgence, but Hakman was determined to reinforce their market positioning as "real boardshorts" by identifying the brand with the leading surfers who wore them. The first ad featured an action shot of

Bob (centre) and the newly-sponsored San Marino gang, 1976.

Sales rep Tom Holbrook (left) writes some sales at an early trade show, 1978.

reigning world champion Peter Townend and the lines, "A Sense of Style! The Quiksilver look: often copied but never matched."

As Quiksilver USA geared up for summer '77 production, the partners ran out of money again. Asked to fund the business again, the investors demanded another 30%. McKnight knew that it would be fatal to surrender control, so he looked for another solution and found it in Pete Wilson, a San Marino surfer and 'SC fraternity brother who had organized the rental deal for

their Quonset hut factory in Costa Mesa. An architecture graduate, Wilson had made some money renovating and selling houses, and this he used to buy a stake. Although he hadn't studied it, Wilson had a natural flair for business, and with the help of his father he organized a bank line of credit to fund production and moved into the role of general manager of the young company.

By the end of the summer, Quiksilver USA had overtaken the sales of its Australian parent company. Realizing that the trial period seemed to be over, Greeny had a proper licensing contract drawn up, giving the American partners five years with an option for another five. Meanwhile, John Law, a Torquay surfer and former stockbroker who had become Green's partner in 1976, began to investigate the possibilities of duplicating the American license in other markets, like Japan and Europe.

One afternoon in the spring of 1978 McKnight, Hakman and Wilson sat in their makeshift office at the front of a Quonset hut feeling pretty pleased with themselves. They could see that their fledgling company had survived the first hurdles. Summer orders were good; the brand was gathering momentum.

Suddenly car doors slammed at the rear entrance and tires screeched as a car took off at speed. The three men ran to the far end of the hut and found a sliding door open and their entire stock of size 36 boardshorts gone. One hundred pairs, a tenth of their inventory. "Unbelievable," said McKnight. "Kids,"

The hottest hundred yards: Danny Kwock at 56th Street, Newport, 1980.

said Wilson. "Maybe," chuckled Hakman, "but they'd have to be really chubby little buggers."

A few days later a scrawny kid turned up at the factory. "I know who ripped you off," he told McKnight. "It was Danny Kwock and Preston Murray."

The Kwock monster. McKnight and Hakman knew who he was, a pint-size surf terrorist who operated between 52ND Street and 56TH Street in Newport Beach, blatantly stealing every wave he could paddle into without fear of reprisal, because no one would hit such a shrimp. Perhaps his luck had run out, thought McKnight. He made a few calls, then dialed the number he had been seeking.

Of Hawaiian, Chinese, Dutch and Japanese ancestry, Daniel Christopher Kwock II was born in Honolulu in 1961 and spent his early years living behind his aunt's store, Helena's Hawaiian Foods. His father, who ran Hawaiian entertainment at fairs and travel shows around the world, had accumulated 11 children from two marriages. Danny learned to surf on the South Shore beaches of Oahu, but just as he was starting to make progress his mother moved the family to California, first to the hot, smoggy, land-locked San Fernando Valley, then to a "thrasher pad" opposite the infamous Newport Wedge on Newport's Balboa Peninsula.

The Wedge, where ocean swells refracted around the Newport Harbor entrance and broke with ferocity in a doubled-up shorebreak, was a staple of the early surf magazines and movies for the visual spectacle of body-surfers hitting its backwash and

[CENTER] **Kwock clowning around 54th St.** [ABOVE] **Steve Obradovich jumps high in Quik court shorts, 1979**

Tom Holbrook, Pete Wilson with Bob and Jeff in Bali, 1977.

elevator-dropping headfirst into the sand. Danny Kwock started surfing the place standing up on a borrowed bodyboard, then, as he grew in confidence, on a proper surfboard. His reputation growing along the strip between Balboa and the River Jetties, Danny soon graduated to the beach between 52ND and 56TH Streets, home to the hottest young surfers in Orange County, and within months he was king of the kids, leading the way in mutating the latest fashions depicted in the surf magazines and movies.

Kwock and Preston Murray, his school pal at Newport Harbor High, pestered a local surf shop proprietor to "flow" them pairs of Quiksilver trunks, the hottest new thing to hit the California coast. When he refused, Preston told Danny: "I know where their factory is, man." The plan wasn't really thought out. They just "borrowed" Preston's mom's car and drove up the hill to Costa Mesa. They parked a few blocks from the Quiksilver factory and Preston explained to Danny that he would be the getaway driver. Barely able to drive or to see over the dash, Kwock edged up on the factory, Murray disappeared inside and emerged running, his arms filled with trunks. The passenger door slammed and Danny put the pedal to the metal.

Danny was lucky that it was he, not his mother, who picked up McKnight's call. "Listen to me, you little asshole. We know it was you and your buddy and unless you get your scrawny butts up here right now, you're goin' down!" An hour later the Quiksilver partners faced off against the two trembling kids. Kwock was quickly in tears as McKnight read the riot act. They would pay for all the trunks they couldn't return. They would

become company slaves, spending all their time outside of school hours at the factory, cleaning the washrooms, washing cars, running errands. And whenever the partners appeared in the surf at Newport, the two thieves would quietly paddle to the beach until their elders and betters had finished their session.

Murray made a couple of appearances at the Quonset, borrowed money from his parents to repay the debt and was never seen again. Kwock reported for duty every afternoon, sold his surfboards to pay off part of his debt and reached an agreement to work off the rest. After a while the partners conceded that it was kind of cool having him around. Danny was their conduit to the kids on the beach. He was the guy with his finger on the pulse of the new generation. By the end of the year he was a team rider, being flowed not only Quiksilver boardshorts but also Rip Curl wetsuits and McCoy surfboards.

Between Pete Wilson's arrival in the summer of '77 and the end of the decade, Quiksilver moved into a bigger factory at Production Place in Costa Mesa, signed up sales agents for Hawaii (top surfboard shaper Tom Parrish), the East Coast (Bob Merrigan), Texas (Don Shelton) and the Rockies (John Thompson and Terry Fisher). Closer to home, the partners hired McKnight's former bartending buddy, Tom Holbrook as California sales rep, and at the end of '79, they were joined by former Australian pro surfer Bruce Raymond who would assist Hakman in marketing while Bob was continuing to learn the trade behind the scenes.

A stylish young surfer who had been impressive during his couple of years on the pro tour, Raymond had become Quiksilver's second sponsored surfer (after Rabbit Bartholomew) just two years earlier. When he quit the tour he was hired by Alan Green and, after a short Torquay apprenticeship, he was sent to California with the mission "make them just like us"—effectively Raymond's and Quiksilver's first licensing position.

Raymond went to work designing magazine ads and working up deals with editors and photographers to expand Quiksilver's editorial coverage. A savvy operator with a big reputation as a surfer, Raymond had simply to offer himself and Bartholomew as models, then head for Mexico or Puerto Rico with a suitcase full of Quiksilver's latest range and go surfing while a photographer stood on the shore shooting covers and gatefolds. Says McKnight: "Bruce really invented the branded product shot. He was a genius at that."

And the whole time Raymond made his rounds, he was followed like a faithful hound by Danny Kwock, the former thief who would become marketing manager when Raymond returned to Australia to run Quiksilver's licensing company.

Meanwhile, Pete Wilson's dream run at the helm of the business side of the company had ended. While he was an effective manager, he was also a forceful personality, and Hakman and McKnight often found themselves at loggerheads with him over the direction in which the company was heading. Wilson favored fast-tracking growth by selling to the specialty store giant Nordstrom, for example, while the others believed that the brand needed to stay true to its surf shop roots. In the end the matter was resolved when Alan Green flew in and negotiated an amicable parting of the ways. But Wilson had accumulated 44% of the company, and neither McKnight nor Hakman had the funds to buy him out, so again they looked for equity partners, and again they found them in the old San Marino crew.

Larry Crowe was the elder brother of Charles Crowe, another surfing and school buddy of McKnight's. He had experience in the financial industry and, more importantly, he had the money to buy out Wilson. But Crowe came with other issues. As the deal evolved, it turned out that he was actually splitting the investment with his brother and another friend, Randy Hunt, and all three would become working directors of Quiksilver. It soon became apparent to McKnight that this was not a match made in heaven, but he decided to bite his lip and try to make it work, particularly when he realized that his original partner and surfing idol was on a downward spiral.

Although he was born in California, Hakman had moved to Hawaii as a child and never felt comfortable living and working in Orange County. The everyday pressures of business, things that McKnight and Wilson took in stride, weighed heavily on him, and to escape he slipped back into daily drug use. By 1982, now responsible for his girlfriend and young son, the former surf star was a hopeless heroin addict. In the toughest decision of his career so far, McKnight told his friend that he would have to leave the company and try to find himself again.

In September 1980, Quiksilver in Australia introduced a radical new range of boardshorts and tee shirts in outlandish colors and patterns featuring bold harlequin stars and polka dots. "Echo Beach," the creation of Alan Green and artist Simon

Bruce Raymond, Bob McKnight, G-Land, 1983.

Buttonshaw, was actually based on the style of clothing worn by jockeys (horse-racing being another passion of Green's), but the theme also carried with it the rock-and-roll feel of a new decade and a new generation. In California, its disciple was, of course, Danny Kwock. Kwock was the king of the peak at what the surf magazines had begun to call "the hottest hundred yards," the stretch of beach between 52ND and 56TH Streets at Newport, and photos of him and his posse wearing the bright new Quiksilvers soon dominated the surf media. The second California surf boom had begun, and Quiksilver USA's sales soon shot through the $3 million mark, more than trebling Australia's.

In 1985 Quiksilver's sales skyrocketed by 80%, placing it, at $12.8 million, in the top five companies in the rapidly expanding industry. Faced with the enormous job of funding another year of similar growth, the partners came to McKnight with a proposition.

"We think we should float the company," they said.

"What?"

"Go public. Lead the industry into the future, not to mention securing our own, Bob."

McKnight was initially horrified. The only public companies in surfing were the licensing corporations that had specialized in taking authentic brands and putting them on toilet seat covers for quick profits and certain extinction. But as time went on, he saw that some hard-earned cash could come out and shares could be awarded to loyal managers. It would be a bold, audacious move, but wasn't that the Quiksilver way?

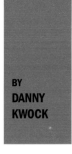

BY
DANNY
KWOCK

ECHO BEACH:
"THE HOTTEST 100 YARDS"

I was born and raised in Hawaii where I learnt three things: 1) you can go to school barefoot, 2) there is nothing wrong with playing the ukulele, and 3) the ocean is the best playground you can have.

I learnt how to surf with my friend Andrew Coutts (an ex-Quiksilver team rider) and wiggled my first turns on one of my mentors' boards (a surfer/shaper named Martial Crum who became a Quiksilver designer and artist).

Surfing was the ultimate choice of play for any kid growing up in Hawaii, an amazing creative outlet. When our family moved to Newport Beach, CA, I burst onto the scene as the crazy kid who rode a stand-up board at the Wedge—unheard of at the time. I surfed giant south swells in front of thousands of spectators lined up to see blood. To me this was the ultimate—fun, thrills and sharing it with others, even if it was nuts! That's where I began to understand how entertaining surfing could be.

Fast-forward to the late '70s, and I've become a Quiksilver-sponsored surfer, trying to make it as a pro while dealing with growing up at the same time. Very stressful time. All I could think of was this stuffed clown I had as a toddler, and I guess I tried to copy that style, wearing crazy shorts and painting polka dots on my boards. I remember one of the partners at Quiksilver opening up *Surfing Magazine* to find my first big spread and just going ballistic.

He wanted to know why they gave Kwock free shorts when he shows up in a magazine wearing girls' running shorts! The problem was that boardshorts had become boring and predictable, and while the partner might not have liked my response to that, the other people in the company suddenly wanted to see my designs and ideas.

Bob McKnight had seamstress Shirley "Bird" Ashbury run up a pair of size 28" pink arch legs with black and white hand-sewn, quilted checker panels to my design and I wore them in the first US ad for Echo Beach. The name came from a song by Martha and the Muffins but it had been picked up as a nickname for Bondi Beach in Australia and was perfect for a new urban surf look. Before I'd started experimenting with a new look, Alan Green and designer Simon Buttonshaw in Torquay had come up with some ideas taken from the clothes that jockeys wore. Greeny was a real horse-racing freak and he thought the harlequins and polka dots might translate to surfing. So that's how Echo Beach was born.

We launched the theme with the Echo Beach Pro-Am Surf Challenge at 54TH Street in Newport Beach, and photographer Jack McCoy shot an ad campaign that featured Tom Carroll, Preston Murray, Craig Brazda and myself lying on silver tanning blankets sporting wrap shades! Craig was the only professional model and he asked to be paid for the shoot. My boss Bruce Raymond told me: "Tell Brazda he gets clothes for life." Craig wanted a couple of hundred bucks cash at the time. At last count his annual shopping spree at the Quiksilver warehouse had topped $25,000!

Echo Beach became firmly rooted on a stretch of sand in Newport between the 52ND and 56TH Street jetties—a place that became known in the surfing magazines as the "hottest 100 yards." We had other names for it, like Kodak Sandbar and Studio 54. Whenever there was a clear, sunny day accompanied by a south west swell, the place was taken over by the freaks and the fotogs. We were the freaks, surfers trying to get famous with a radical maneuver. The fotogs were the surfing photographers, trying to hit pay dirt with a cover shot for *Surfer* or *Surfing*, back in the days when there was no autofocus.

All of this went down at a break once guarded by single fin soul surfers in black wetsuits. Why did it get so much attention? Was there a change in the way waves were being ridden? No, not really, although we liked to think so at the time. Was there a revolution in surfboard design? No, not at our beach. What was so remarkable about the whole Echo Beach thing was that it grew out of a bunch of young people having fun and being creative about their personal style...setting trends in surf fashion for the first time. It was the spark that helped light up the surf industry and set it on its way to becoming the multi-billion action sports industry of today.

The Echo beach crew was similar in many ways to the skateboarders of today who got the Jackass thing going in youth entertainment. The idea was the same—putting the fun back in. I remember giving a pair of polka dot shorts to a kid in Cocoa Beach, Florida 25 years ago. He thought they were pretty cool. His name was Kelly Slater. Then a dozen or more years later a young lady asked me if it was cool to paint polka dots on her board like I had. Her name was Lisa Andersen. I laughed to myself as I walked away. Echo Beach was still colorful and fun, still making people happy. Now that's what surfing is all about.

[ABOVE] **Kwock in his kingdom.** [OPPOSITE] **Echo Beach crew: Craig Brazda, Preston Murray, Tom Carroll and Danny Kwock at 54th Street.**

MIKE MOIR

JACK McKOY

ART BREWER'S TOP 10

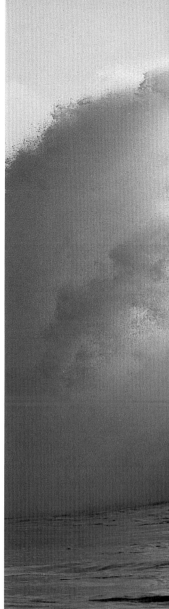

[ABOVE] **This was the first time I ever saw Padang Padang break. It was 1981. Lopez had left two days earlier but Peter McCabe was there. It was me and Grub and Rory and Walter Hoffman; we pretty much had it to ourselves. I never swam as much in my whole photographic career as I did that day. Grub McCabe was the star that day.**

[LEFT] **I stayed with Wayne down in Victoria for a couple of weeks back in 1978 and got to know him pretty well. I spotted the Evolution board when we were looking for something else behind his house. He pulled it out and I shot it.**

[RIGHT] **Nathan Fletcher in the Mentawais, 1998. This was his first *Surfer* cover. Nathan had bailed on surfing to do motocross for a while and that had really strengthened his torso. His strong airs and deep barrels were exceptional.**

I really like the Paterson brothers. They're tough, gritty guys, always kind of under-estimated, always in the background. There's this roughness and crudeness about them and not many people know what they're about. This was my attempt at keeping them in disguise, keeping them down and dirty and unknowable. The pure grit of Australian surfing.

Hakman's clean lines and power turns were always beautiful to photograph. Conversely, on the beach he was always goofing around, like here at Trestles.

Lisa was the first girl they said surfed as good as a guy. Remember that *Surfer* cover line? But she never surfed like a guy. She was always fast, fluid and graceful.

Kelly was pushing for his third world title this year and basically unstoppable. My little visual joke was that you'd have to tie him up to lose. My initial idea was to hang him by his feet out of a tree in front of Jeff Johnson's house (at Pipe), but he wasn't going along with that. In fact he wasn't real happy about being tied up either. He couldn't see where I was going with it, but he was happy when he saw the result.

The shot at Lance's Rights was from the Tomorrowland or September Sessions trip, depending on where you stand on that. I was there with Ted Grambeau and I was lucky enough to get a shot that he didn't. Later I did a shoot for Pepsi with (soccer star) David Beckham and I imposed him on the Kelly shot. People looked at it and went, "No one does rail grabs like that except Slater." I said, "David Beckham does."

How many shots of Tom in his helmet at Pipe can you bear? One more please. I like this for the stark power of the wave and the strong yet casual lean into the turn. Classic TC.

I shot this portrait of Tom in his backyard at Rocky Point. This was in between color takes. You can't keep him serious for too long. Here he was coming on like a brown dog.

Rabbit North Shore power cuttie. He's been pulling direction changes like that for 30 years.

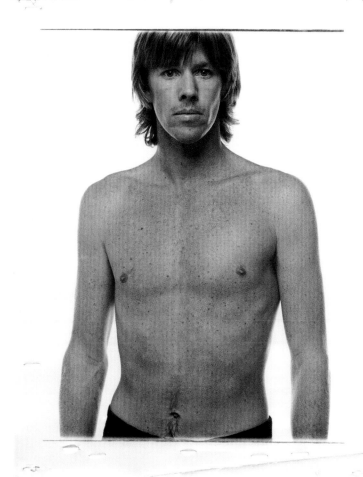

Rabbit came by the magazine [*Surfer*] one day and I pulled him into the little studio and shot five or six rolls of his Mick Jagger persona. This was after the "Bustin' Down the Door" session; he was pretty relaxed with me. It was 1977 so he wasn't really welcome in Hawaii, but he had other ways of making a statement.

BY
ALAN
GREEN

EASTER '81:
A SURFER'S TALE

To many who were there the Rip Curl Bells Pro 1981 is still the greatest surfing contest of all time, etched in the memory by virtue of the fact that it was won by Simon Anderson, riding huge and perfect waves on a new three-finned board he called the "thruster." For some, however, like Quiksilver founder Alan Green, what lingers in the memory occurred not at Bells, but just around the corner at a break called Winki Pop.

When Paul "Smelly" Neilsen and I went down to Winki Pop around midday it was very big, regular and perfectly offshore. We made ready to go out and I told Smelly that we needed to make for the "button" area, to get trajectory with the rip, so we rock-hopped along under the cliff at high tide.

From out of nowhere a big set hit the point and sent a five-foot wall of whitewater sideways along the base of the cliff. I dived behind a boulder and braced myself. When the impact had passed, I looked for Smelly. Gone, somewhere down the line with three or four waves still to deal with. I held on until the end of the set, then had no alternative but to jump on the outflow and paddle out.

The rip drags you down the reef and you need a surge to get you past the break, but the waves were constant and I ended up down in the little bay where I found Smelly, still chirpy but looking like a piece of flotsam. We started to paddle again but 10 to 12 foot waves kept breaking in front of us. Then finally a lull, and the surge took us quickly into the lineup out the back of Boobs.

The monster set had taken care of the other surfers, but as we stroked to get over another 15-foot set, we saw someone way out in the take-off zone. As we drew closer we realized it was Nat Young, sitting out in the middle of the bay alone. We paddled out to him and compared notes. Our main concern was getting in at high tide without being crushed against the cliffs, but we put that out of our minds temporarily as we marveled at the huge corduroy perfection of the sets.

We caught a couple of waves each and things began to settle down a bit. Then suddenly another huge set loomed outside and we paddled frantically for the horizon. I'm halfway up the face of the biggest wave I've ever paddled over and Nat turns and yells, "Greeny, this one's yours!" Smelly started laughing and I think I did too, but only when I knew I was going to make it to the other side.

When the set subsided we sat there and took in the markers, trying to establish where we were. It was ridiculous, we were out in the shipping lanes! This was really huge, the swell probably peaking right then. As we sat waiting, the talk turned again to the problem of getting in. I'd had enough and I think Smelly had too. And Nat, too, or perhaps he just didn't want to be out there alone again.

Smelly was terrified of coming ashore at Winki and favored paddling around and catching one in at Bells, through the middle of the contest. We'd been in the water more than two hours and I was certain that the tide would have backed off the cliffs enough for it to be safe. My plan was to pick up a wave way up the point, bail out in front of the target landing zone and get pushed in by the rolling whitewater.

My wave came and I took off and felt my way through a slow bottom turn and into trim. Jumping off a big wave was tricky for me—total lack of experience, for one thing—but I kept an eye on the cliff-line and as it seemed to be dead ahead, I turned up into the top of the wave, dropped back down as far into the pit as I could, and stepped off the back of the board. I got tumbled along, but I was behind the primal action and covering distance. I caught a breath and the next two waves were easier, just rolling whitewater, and there I was at the landing, safe and sound.

As I reached the top of the cliff, I heard a PA announcement from the contest, and looked out across the bay to see Smelly and Nat paddling way outside of Rincon and the "heat currently in the water," as I heard an alarmed announcer describe it. A set appeared and Nat took the first huge wave and rode it from Rincon to the sand. Smelly took the next, an even bigger wave. He pulled high into it and drove across the saddle at high speed until the huge face started to barrel in front of him. Smelly set his trim and pulled into the barrel, never to emerge! Meanwhile, the contestants in the water just watched and wondered.

Smelly's was one of the most exciting waves I've ever seen ridden at Bells on the most exciting day I've ever seen there. Big call, maybe, but the whole package—the waves, the weather, the vibe of the contest, the bar afterwards—it just doesn't get any better.

[ABOVE] **Alan Green and Paul Neilsen stroke for the horizon as a widow-maker hits Winki.** [OPPOSITE] **Alan Green pushing hard off the bottom with a long wall ahead.**

Europe:
The Early Days

Guethary, on the Basque Coast of southwest France, Quiksilver's home in Europe.

In the mid 1970s, **Maritxu Darrigrand**, a young female surfer and skier of some repute in France, married another well known surfer and adventurer, Yves Bessas, and together they formed a company called Uhaina to distribute snow and surf films in Europe. They compiled a program of surf and ski footage from around the world that they called *La Nuit de la Glisse*, and, after a low-key start at the Pax Cinema in Biarritz, *La Nuit* played to packed houses all over Europe.

Quiksilver Australia partner John Law had met Bessas in Europe and, hearing of their success with surf film distribution, asked the French couple to distribute Quiksilver products in France. So Uhaina handled surf products too, with Rip Curl wetsuits, Lightning Bolt surfboards and California Tee Shirts soon joining the group.

Maritxu Darrigrand recalls: "We were living at my family farmhouse outside Biarritz, and big packages would arrive from Australia every few weeks. We had no idea what would arrive, but whatever came, we would try to sell the stuff to the few surf shops we had in France."

The two businesses proved complementary. The movies promoted the lifestyle and created a market for the clothes. And as both businesses grew, Uhaina needed partners. Bessas knew Alan Tiegen, a young American surfer who had worked in the surf film business before marrying a local girl and returning to California to finish college. Yves and Maritxu visited the Tiegens in Santa Barbara and offered them a partnership. Having just finished his business degree, Alan accepted. Ferme Landeretche, the Darrigrand farmhouse, now became home to two couples and two businesses.

Both distribution businesses thrived, but the personal chemistry did not. Finally it was resolved that Bessas would take Uhaina and do his films, the Tiegens would run the surfwear business through a company called Surf 'n' Sport, and Darrigrand would leave them to it, flying to her sister in Australia.

Alan and Francoise Tiegen broadened Quiksilver's distribution throughout France while Law tracked down distributors elsewhere in Europe. In 1979, just as windsurfing took off all over Europe, Lawo had trekked through Holland, Belgium, Germany and Switzerland, finding distributors in each. These small markets for Quiksilver's limited and summer-based range collectively represented a significant market, and once

SYLVAIN CAZENAVE

JOHN WITZIG

Maritxu Darrigrand and Yves Bessas, 1978.

Bruce Raymond took over the licensing business, he formulated a plan to create a united sales base in Europe.

Surf 'n' Sport was granted a manufacturing and distribution license for France, Spain and the UK in 1982, and the Tiegens rented a small factory in Biarritz and went into production. Alan Tiegen knew that to make inroads in Europe, the product had to be "Europeanized," so the first garments off the Surf 'n' Sport production line were boardshorts with slips or linings inside, placing them somewhere between surf culture and the promenade poseurs of Nice and Cannes.

Alan Green was outraged, but Law and Raymond convinced him to bite his tongue until they could see if Europeanization boosted sales. It did. In 1983 Surf 'n' Sport, now with a production team of 12, sold 20,000 pairs of boardshorts for gross sales of around a quarter million dollars. It was still very much a one-product, one-short-season business, but the Tiegens had samples of the new Echo Beach jackets and pants and were looking to steadily grow their sales base.

The problem, as the Australians saw it, was that the Tiegens weren't moving fast enough. Francoise Tiegen felt strongly that the business should grow at the sedate pace of French provincial life and remain in the hands of the family, rather than taking in equity partners to fund faster growth. Sitting somewhat uncomfortably on the fence between two cultures, Alan Tiegen recalls: "Quiksilver had their business plan and we had ours. There was a growing sense of frustration with our different objectives."

Band on the Run crew: Brian Cregan, Paul Neilsen, Bruce Raymond and Rabbit Bartholomew.

In 1976 a young Australian photojournalist named Harry Hodge started working on the project of his dreams—an adventure surf film that picked up where *The Endless Summer* had left off.

Jeff Hakman and Harry Hodge on the sales trail, 1985.

For his stars he chose a former Australian champion named Paul Neilsen, unknown Brian Cregan and two of Quiksilver's earliest unpaid "team riders," Rabbit Bartholomew and Bruce Raymond. For cast, crew and investors, it became the adventure that never seemed to end. It was 1981 before Hodge's *Band On The Run* finally opened in cinemas to lukewarm reviews and low box office.

Bruised if not broken, Hodge retreated to the village of Angourie on Australia's east coast with his French girlfriend, Brigitte Darrigrand, to work on his golf swing and a new plan. When Bruce Raymond passed through on a surf trip, Hodge confided in him that he needed a job. Raymond, now managing Quiksilver's licensing company, promised to put in a good word with Green and Law. Hodge and Darrigrand moved south to Torquay a month later, he to work in marketing, she in design.

Despite his own film's disastrous financial performance, Hodge had undoubted talent as a cinematographer and producer, and Quiksilver soon put them to use. During his time at Quiksilver USA, Raymond had put together a deal with filmmaker Scott Dittrich in which Quiksilver anted up two surfers (Raymond and Rabbit Bartholomew) for a shoot in Puerto Rico in return for a five-minute cut of action and product footage. Raymond gave a dupe of the short (*Quiksilver Country*) to every roadshow man in

After work party at the Darrigrand farmhouse, Jeff Hakman on right, 1984.

the business. The free commercial played worldwide for more than a year.

Another short, *Black Betty*, followed, and by 1983 Green, Raymond and Law had begun to talk about getting Quiksilver-branded entertainment into the surfing market. Raymond recalls: "Video was the big new thing, but the price was ridiculous. I felt that if we could keep the retail price down, a branded surf movie for video would work." In fact, the project, called *The Performers*, revolutionized the financing and marketing of the genre and side-lined the surf roadshow men—at least until a revival decades later.

Hodge and surf cameraman Jack McCoy shot the Hawaiian North Shore winter season of 1982-3, focusing on Quiksilver team riders Gary Elkerton, Bartholomew, Chappy Jennings, Bryce Ellis, Wes Laine, Willy Morris, Mickey Neilsen and Marvin Foster. Editor Nick Glover set the footage to rock tracks and the movie sold well, once surfers warmed to the idea of buying a movie at a surf shop, rather than watching it on the big screen.

With *The Performers* in the can, Hodge and Darrigrand decided to spend the northern summer vacationing in her native France, checking out the Teigens' Surf 'n' Sport operation while they were there. By the end of the summer they had made up their minds. France would be their new home.

When he returned to Torquay in fall 1983, Hodge began to invent a freelance marketing role for himself in France. He outlined a position in which he would do all the marketing

Brigitte Darrigrand and John Winship cut samples, 1984.

Quiksilver Pro France, Hossegor.

dog-work for the Tiegens while building the brand all over Europe through creating editorial packages using team riders, as Raymond had done in America. Green was skeptical.

At the traditional Australian Friday "beer o'clock" drinks session at Quiksilver, Greeny got off the phone after a long session with Alan Tiegen. He and Law were fuming over Surf 'n' Sport's inability to see the bigger picture. Hodge offered some poorly timed advice and Greeny snarled, "Well, if you're so frickin' smart, Harry, why don't you go over there and run the business?"

It was an idea conceived in a heated moment, but the more Greeny considered it, the more sense it made. He recalled years later: "Harry had proven himself to be a pretty good field marshal, so I started to think that maybe it was worth a shot. And, of course, he had a good local support base through Brigitte's family. I knew it was a risk, but we've always been risk takers."

Hodge and Darrigrand decided to take up the challenge. While Law and Raymond terminated the Surf 'n' Sport license, Hodge drew up a business plan, searched for finance and pondered his team. As Greeny had noted, Hodge was a leader, and he knew marketing. Darrigrand had built a bikini business in Australia and excelled in design and production.

But a vital ingredient was missing. In surfing terminology it was known as the stoke. Hodge knew someone who had it to spare.

When Jeff Hakman, his girlfriend, Cherie, and baby son, Ryan, arrived on the Gold Coast of Queensland in May 1983, their lives had nowhere to go but up. Their departure from California had been a blur of drugs and humiliation. Only seven years after he had moved to California to start Quiksilver with Bob McKnight, Hakman had left it a tragic figure.

The Hakmans rented a small apartment at Burleigh Heads and Jeff tried to regain his health by surfing every day. Cherie applied for a single mother's pension. They had no car. They walked to the store to buy what groceries they could afford. Jeff heard that the Brothers Neilsen store in Surfers Paradise was advertising for a sales assistant. He walked to the corner phone booth and called his old friend, Paul Neilsen.

Few people in the surf industry had spoken out against drugs as loudly as Paul Neilsen. Hakman's heroin addiction horrified him, and he felt that the last thing he needed in his life was a disintegrating junkie behind the counter at his premier store. But he was also a loyal friend, vulnerable to Hakman's cry for help. Jeff had a job—at $200 a week—the next day.

Hakman stayed clean and sober all winter and, as the Australian summer began, he launched a surf school, giving lessons to tourists outside store hours. The business developed quickly, and Hakman was considering focusing exclusively on it when Hodge phoned.

Hodge recalls: "We were both losers on the comeback trail. We both had something to prove, both to ourselves and to our friends. And I wanted Jeff in because he'd done all this before, and he had that X-factor. He could win people over with his enthusiasm."

Hakman had reservations, mainly about weathering the pressures of a startup again, but when he flew to Torquay to compete in the longboard event at the 1984 Bells Beach Easter Classic, he told Hodge he was in.

By mid-year the group had a fourth partner in John Winship, a South African designer who had worked for Quiksilver in California and moved to the Gold Coast with Hakman. They also had a base at Ferme Landeretche and a new company they named Na Pali SA, after the rugged Kauai coast. Na Pali had start-up capital of just two million French francs (approximately $230,000), a lot more than Hakman and McKnight had had just eight years earlier, but not nearly enough. The money had come from a grab-bag of investors that included the working partners themselves (who put up about half) and Quiksilver family and friends from around the world. A non-investor, Raymond was appointed to represent the Australian investments while he oversaw the establishment of the licensee.

Years later, after Quiksilver Europe had become a success, Hodge told an interviewer: "When you think about it, how unlikely was it that three foreigners who spoke no French, and a French woman returning after so many years away, could make something of an Australian brand in this far corner of France? When we arrived we had no office, no cars, no work papers and absolutely no experience of running a business in France. Perhaps that's why we made it through the tough times. If we'd known what was ahead of us, we never would have started."

By the end of the summer, Na Pali SA had moved out of the farm and into a thousand meters of factory floor in a new industrial estate north of Saint Jean de Luz, thanks to Brigitte's family putting up property security for bank loans. Fortunately the partners found a friendly bank manager in Monsieur Henri Pomares.

Brigitte set up a cutting room and basic production facility, and, by also "piggy-backing" on Ug Manufacturing's production, Na Pali achieved five million francs turnover in its first full year of operation. The distributors elsewhere in Europe, most much wealthier than Na Pali, paid for their stock with letters of credit that provided cash flow, and the company, against all odds, flourished.

For the first year or two, Hodge and Hakman spent much of their time on the road, riding trains or driving from one end of Western Europe to the other, selling the brand. Their manufacturing presence in France significantly boosted domestic sales, but in the rest of Europe the brand was represented by distributors who had several brands in their portfolios. Getting them to focus on Quiksilver, and believe in its long-term viability, was a strategic imperitive as rival brands such as O'Neill, Chiemsee and Oxbow vied for market share.

In 1985 the Na Pali partners opened a Quiksilver retail store in downtown Biarritz and hired a New Zealand-born professional rugby player named Jeff Bradburn to run it. The store, the brand's first stand-alone retail operation in the world, succeeded immediately, and Bradburn ascended to the position of export sales manager. In this role he would develop the distributor contacts that Hakman and Hodge had made. In Hodge's words: "His job was to be in their faces, all the time."

By 1988 export sales had surpassed French domestic sales, and, with an increasingly Pan-European focus, Na Pali

The Na Pali partners, 1989. Left to right, Hodge, Darrigrand, Hakman, Winship.

COURTESY NA PALI

(or Quiksilver Europe, as it had been designated) was poised for major growth. It boasted good staff, good product, an aggressive marketing plan and an even more aggressive approach to selling. The ship was sailing smoothly, but Hodge spied two navigational hazards ahead.

The first was that Hakman was doing heroin again. He had begun using occasionally as an escape from business pressures, then daily, then whenever he had to, which was often. By now the partners were paying themselves reasonable salaries, but not enough to support his habit, so Hakman used his company gas card to get cash for drugs. He was stealing from his partners, and the rising tide of resentment and tension was destabilizing the company.

The second was that Hodge's house of cards was shaky. For years he had juggled letters of credit and romanced the banks every few weeks to fund the company's staggering growth. And it was staggering—an average 175 percent over the first few years before leveling off to 40 percent in the late '80s. Quiksilver USA had grown from zero to $3.5 million in sales in its first five years. Quiksilver Europe had grown from zero to $13.2 million over the same period.

The difference was that McKnight's grounding in business made him fiscally conservative, more interested in building a solid foundation. Hodge, ever the flamboyant entrepreneur, erected a skyscraper that could topple. He had done a brilliant job in taking the company this far without new funding, but McKnight and Hakman had needed far more than their startup capital to support much smaller growth, and, despite his own unflagging belief that he would prevail, Hodge couldn't do it either.

The Changing of the Guard

In June 2005 I was invited to attend the grand opening of the Quiksilver/Andaska store in Anglet, France. I went, for the first time, as a guest rather than one of the organizers. This was a little strange for me. In fact I was more than a touch nervous. I had attended so many of these functions that it should be second nature, but this seemed different. Quiksilver Europe had grown so much and was considered a leader in the global company's retail sector, and even though I had been there during huge growth, this was on a different scale.

I saw so many familiar faces as I registered and received my entry wristband. I was pretty pleased that the girls on the desk remembered me! Guy Forget, one of the favorite sons of French tennis, was one of the first people I ran into, along with Bixente Lizarazu, the Basque soccer legend who starred in the French team that beat Brazil in the 1998 World Cup in Paris. I mention these two because for me their involvement with our company illustrates just how Quiksilver's influence has crossed over from the pure board riding sports of surf, skate and snow. Even though they are still our primary focus, our brand has grown beyond that arena and is now recognized as one of the leading sports apparel brands in the world.

Inside I ran into Kelly Slater who had come over especially for the event, and many of our other sponsored athletes, like France's top surfer Miky Picon and snowboarding legend Serge Vitelli. I began to get a sense of how big this event was going to be—the stage area, the number of dignitaries and celebrities. Hell, if Nina Cherry is playing at the after party, then it's big. The opening ceremony was being streamed live on our web site around the world.

Eventually I found Robby Naish. Robby and I have been close friends since the early 1980s when he became involved with Quiksilver and in turn as one of the original investors in Quiksilver Europe. At events like this we sometimes seek solace in each other to "hide" from the crowds and catch up on each other's exploits. Robby's sense of humor is, to say the least, wicked. His commentary on the diverse group was hilarious and we greeted many people whom we both have known for over 20 years in Europe, reflecting on how far we'd come from those early days trudging around Europe attending trade shows in Munich, Amsterdam and Paris, trying to get the Quiksilver brand started.

The formal part of the evening was approaching. The "ribbon cutters," of which I was one, were told to get ready to come up on stage. As Bob McKnight, our CEO, Bernard Mariette, our president, and Pierre Agnes the new president of Quiksilver Europe, delivered their speeches I watched proudly from the side of the stage, looking at all the people gathered for the occasion. The succession plan we had built in Europe had pretty much always revolved around Pierre Agnes becoming the leader. As a founder, I still felt like I was an integral part of Quiksilver Europe, but I was part of its history, and Pierre was part of its future. It was his time.

As Bob finished his speech he called me up on stage. He then asked Jeff Hakman and Brigitte Darrigrand, my co-founders, to join us. Standing there with Jeff, Brigitte, Bob, Bernard and Pierre Agnes, I found myself reflecting on what Quiksilver Europe had achieved. It had been a long journey from 1984, when we started, to this crowning achievement of opening night of one of the finest retails outlets anywhere in Europe.

Standing there with my friends, all of whom had played vital roles in Quiksilver Europe's ascent, my mind panned across all those adventures we had shared. Building something from nothing with Brigitte, Jeff and John Winship, our fourth partner; becoming part of the Quiksilver, Inc. family in 1991 and having to learn those hard lessons about accountability in a public company; watching our sales targets absolutely smashed every season in the early '90s, then, joined by Bernard Mariette in 1994, raising the bar even higher with slicker systems, better products and higher and higher sales. What a roll we were on!

Then I thought about all the fun we had—creating those great events, like the surf/snow cross-over break-through, the Quik Cup, Pierre's annual grom fests at Capbreton, Maritxu Darrigrand's Roxy Jams, honoring the pioneers of pro surfing at the Quiksilver Masters, and of course, our great WCT events in Lacanau, Biarritz and now in Hossegor. And there was the fun we had just for fun's sake—staff days at the beach, where afternoon surf lessons segued into outrageous parties; the many nights at Christian's Ferme Ostalapia or Roland's Rockfood, celebrating this birthday or hitting our numbers yet again. And the great camaraderie of our sales conferences, where hard work and hard partying shook hands.

I snapped back into the here and now as I realized there were now over 60 people up on stage to cut the 100-meter long ribbon. I was standing next to Laurent Boix-Vives, chairman of Rossignol, whose company Quiksilver had just acquired. On the other side were Bob, Bernard and Pierre. I have, in one way or another, been involved with Quiksilver since 1974, spending the last 20 years in Europe, building our base there. As I glanced around the crowd of more than 1,000, I saw the faces of some the people who helped make it all happen. Some of the original sewing girls were waving madly; there was our design team grouped to one side of the stage, waving too. I saw Jeff Bradburn, one of Quiksilver Europe's first employees, whose commitment and work ethic are considered invaluable to where we are today. Our very first employee, Dominique Taylor, who was my personal assistant for so many years, and her husband, Greg Taylor, an Australian who came to look for work at Quiksilver in the '80s

Hodge, late '90s.

and stayed. Then there was Mike McNeill, an American who has lived in France for nearly 30 years and been one of our most loyal employees for nearly 20. Jasper Sanders, Simon Wootton and Belly (Stephen Bell), the core of our marketing team, watched alongside the current group of executive management who are guiding Quiksilver Europe along its journey today, Eugenio Padras, Peter Bloxham, Peter Skelton, Seb Loux and their team.

As the many ribbon cutters were being introduced, again I reflected on the journey of the last 20 years. I felt humbled and proud to have been a part of the journey so far, and realized that even though I would not lead the next phase in Europe, I would always be part of what would have to be described as a truly remarkable success, not only for the brand but for the people who built Quiksilver Europe. At that stage I really wished my wife and kids could have been there. But I realized I was with the Quiksilver family. It had grown, it was different, but it still had the same feeling.

As we were handed our scissors to cut the red, white and blue French national colors, I felt a surge of emotion that I had to struggle to control. Then I remembered that this was just a retail store opening after all. But in fact it was far more than that. It was the beginning of what I believe will be a fantastic voyage for all those involved, not only with Quiksilver Europe, but with Quiksilver as a global brand. My role in the future would be different. When I left Quiksilver Europe in 2003 I was bestowed with the title Chairman Emeritus, something I am extremely proud of.

As the evening's proceedings started to heat up and Nina Cherry came on stage, Robby Naish and I retreated to the back of the store to have a few quiet beers. But emotion got the better of me again, and I decided I needed to deal with the moment in private. I got back to my house in Bidart, opened the best bottle of red I could find, stood outside on the terrace overlooking the Bay Of Biscay and drank a private toast to all those who now are going to take Quiksilver Europe to the next phase. *Salut et votre sante!* Cheers and good health!

Today Harry Hodge is based back in Australia, living on Sydney's northern beaches with his wife, Sandee, and three children, Mathieu, Tommy and Ben. He is an Executive Advisor to Quiksilver and is a board member of the Quiksilver Foundation. He also sits on the international board of SurfAID.

TEAM RIDERS
1980s

Echo Beach drove the brand through the early 1980s and, not surprisingly, new team hires reflected the audacious personality of the theme. In Australia Gary "Kong" Elkerton, James "Chappy" Jennings, Chris "Critta" Byrne and Tom Carroll joined Rabbit Bartholomew in the A Team.

In California charger Danny Kwock (now team manager) was joined by Willy Morris, rising star Tom Curren, 1984 world amateur champ Scott Farnsworth, Doug Silva, Allan Sarlo, Jeff Booth and Jamie Brisick, while back East Wes Laine headed a pack that included Matt Kechele and Sean Slater, and in Hawaii Marvin Foster and Mickey Neilsen were the main men, soon joined by big wave chargers Ken Bradshaw, Ronnie Burns and Derek Ho.

In Europe, the emerging brand hosted a world title in 1986, won by new Quik signing from Australia, Mark Sainsbury, and locally, sponsored surfers like Thierry Domenech of France and Spencer Hargraves of the UK. But Quiksilver Europe also looked beyond surfing to skier/snowboarder Serge Vitelli and to world windsurfing champion Robby Naish, one of the most revered athletes all over Europe.

Profiles by Jason Borte.

◉ Richard Cram

The world tour didn't know a more down to earth bloke in the '80s than the smiling, kinky-haired Australian Richard Cram, but if you ever witnessed one of his shuddering cutbacks you'd finger him a cold-blooded executioner. Waves dissolved under the sheer force, paddlers-by testified they'd been sprayed with machine gun fire, and Richter scales registered phantom readings. The move was both feared and revered. Crammy's 1984 included hijacking Quiksilver's *The Performers*, rising to tenth in the ASP rankings, and being deemed the world's most underrated surfer by Tom Carroll. The next year, unimpressed with competition and travel, the 23-year-old quit the circus cold turkey and moseyed back to Oz to raise a family.

◉ Marvin Foster

The line separating good crazy and bad crazy is no wider than a surfboard stringer, a line over which Hawaiian Marvin Foster has ping-ponged since freefalling onto the scene in 1982. The 18-year-old phenomenon bum-rushed the Pipeline hierarchy and snagged world tour Rookie of the Year honors. In search of new thrills, he upped the standard for backside tube-riding with his "pigdog" lay-forward attack at Backdoor and Sunset and defied death by riding left toward the rocks at massive Waimea. Unfortunately, the daredevil in him also emerged on land, leading to trouble with the law and a career cut short.

Sean Slater

Sean Slater's lot in surfing history is a thankless but crucial one. It was sealed by the age of ten, having already so thoroughly bullied his younger sibling that little bro's life would become one endless series of competitions. The drive that Sean inadvertently instilled in Kelly helped create the greatest surfer the world has ever seen, and it forever cemented Sean's role as the brother of somebody special. That shoe, however, was once on the other foot. That's right, Sean was the kid everybody was talking about, pointing their cameras at, and expecting great things from, while Kelly was the mere tagalong. Things turned around, to say the least, but the fact remains that without Sean there might be no Kelly.

☉ Wes Laine

What the hell was Wes Laine thinking in '82, coming from waveless Virginia Beach, dropping out of college a semester before graduation, heading into the big, bad jungle of pro surfing against a burly bunch of Africans, Aussies, and Hawaiians all weaned on savage surf? He couldn't have imagined he'd reach a Bells final, win tour events in New Jersey slappers and South African mackers, to become the first East Coaster to crack the ASP's Top 10, all within a few short years. What did he have going for him beyond a gentlemanly manner, a U.S. junior kneeboarding title, and two ridiculously long arms hanging from his 6'4" body? Like the procession of East Coasters who have followed his lead, Wes had dedication. And that goes a long way.

☉ Willy Morris

Ogre-sized Willy Morris came into surfing with two strikes —growing up pre-Surfline in the California valley and lumbering into an era (the 1980s) overrun by little men and little waves. Like any worthy slugger, he shrugged off his shortcomings and knocked the next pitch to the moon. Big Willy had a head for the game, walloping all comers in the '81 U.S. Championships and the '85 Katin Team Challenge. The coveted ASP Top 16 lay just beyond his hulking grasp, so he simply filled the camera's frame with own giant frame and became a star. Board and body clad in neon, his mighty, spray-laden gashes on poor, unsuspecting wave faces were undeniably electric. The Powerful One then walked away gracefully, straight to the front office, where he remains today.

⊙ Gary Elkerton

In 1983, the surfing world was introduced to a beefy, aggressive kid reportedly bred in the wild, shark-infested waves outside The Great Barrier Reef. His given name of Gary Elkerton sank to the deep, and he cockily stomped ashore as simply "Kong." In spite of his feral nature, he cleaned up real good and made several world title runs over the next decade. The fact that he fell short was more a sign of the system's failure to grade quality over quantity than any weakness of his own. Kong found worthy domain in Hawaii's North Shore, the only venue to match him power for power. There, he was a force unleashed, the first visitor to singlehandedly dominate. Still an animal, he now roams the world for outer reef beasts.

⊙ Jeff Booth

When other Californians were too cool for school and turning pro, Laguna's Jeff Booth was racking up straight As and NSSA hardware. When they were burning out and dropping off the tour, he was steadily climbing to fourth in the ASP ranks. When they were struggling to find work, he was bringing home bank for getting barreled around the world. When they finally awoke to reality, he'd settled into a secure industry position. Boothy's legacy is the Anti-Spicoli—a composed, thinking-man's surfer who maximized his potential and wasn't above sending a scathing letter to the surf mags or smacking some sense into a lineup loudmouth when the situation called for it.

⊙ Ronnie Burns

The range of adjectives that describe Pipeline goes from gnarly, to violent, to deadly, but when Ronnie Burns surfed it during the '80s, the place looked downright soft. Schooled by quintessential Pipe Masters Gerry Lopez and Rory Russell, he humbly absorbed their counsel and became his peers' choice as The Man. He took off deeper

JEFF DIVINE

☼ Dave Macaulay

During the eight years Western Australian Dave Macaulay spent among the world's Top 16 surfers, he may well have been the most unique of the lot. The only crowd this ordinary chap *would* stand out in is a bunch of pro surfers. He was humble (amid a roomful of egos), religious (way before it was trendy), and self-sufficient (the last elite pro to build his own boards while his pampered competitors barely filled out order forms). The silent assassin worked without notice, except by his adversaries who fell prey to his surgical precision. Aside from tour gods Curren and Slater, Macaulay was the last surfer to "bowl a turkey," winning three consecutive events in 1989.

☼ Ross Clarke-Jones

There are hellmen—fearless chargers who'll push themselves over any ledge, and then there's RCJ. His birthdate (6/6/66) says it all. Ross doesn't loaf around on his laurels waiting for a challenge; he's devoted his life to seeking out deadly situations, sort of the Crocodile Hunter of surfing. The former back 16 pro from Down Under found a new life in the big wave revival, and leads the assault on the world's heaviest waves. Winner of the prestigious Quiksilver in memory of Eddie Aikau in 2001, his peers grant him the ultimate compliment—they regard him as a complete psycho.

ATIONN

than anyone, yet somehow managed to appear saner and calmer doing it. Beyond grace under pressure, his poise was more akin to giving the Grim Reaper a lap dance. After three Pipe finals in five years, he died in a tragic motorcycle accident at the peak of his ability in 1990. Man down, but not forgotten.

THE TEAM

Australia

Rabbit Bartholomew
Chappy Jennings
Tom Carroll
Gary Elkerton
Critta Byrne
Richard Cram
Dave Macaulay
Ross Clark-Jones
Mark Sainsbury
Bryce Ellis

USA

Danny Kwock
Willy Morris
Wes Laine
Sean Slater
Marvin Foster
Michey Neilsen
Jeff Booth
Christian Slater
Preston Murray
Scott Farnsworth
Sunny Garcia
Rob Machado
Ronnie Burns
Richard Woolcott
Derek Ho
Chris O'Rourke
Tom Curren
Tony Moniz
Jamie Brisick
Doug Silva
Matt Kechele
Allan Sarlo
John Shimooka
Ken Bradshaw
Jay Adams
Noah Budroe
Robby Naish
Rainos Hayes
Brad Gerlach
Mike Parsons
Matt Archbold
Shane Beschen
Todd Chesser
Cordell Miller
Chava Greenlee
Fred Couples
John Hanley
Kevin Staab
Steve Obradovich
Steve Cabellero

Europe

Thierry Domenech
Sebastien St Jean
Jean-Louis Poupinel
Spencer Hargraves
Maurice Cole
Didier Piter
Peyo Lizarazu
Serge Vitelli
Robert Teritehau
Nathalie Lelievre

BY
NORM
INNIS

Adventures in Asia Pacific

Bruce Raymond takes the drop at Sunset, late '80s.

Going to work for Greeny and Lawo in 1982 wasn't really such a big decision. I had spent the previous couple of years traveling the world surfing, and as a now-broke surfer living in Torquay, could there be a better option if you had to work for a living?

Quiksilver in 1982 was a completely different animal. The entire management team (outside the USA operation) was in Torquay—Greeny and Lawo, Murray Boyd as general manager of Ug (started in 1979), Dave Moyes (production manager), John Morrison (accountant, started 1981), Harry Hodge (who started in 1982 as marketing manager), and Bruce Raymond (CEO of Quiksilver Garments as it then was, who arrived in Torquay in 1981 after a stint at Quik Inc.) This bunch covered all aspects of design, marketing and sales, but in those days the business was very much dominated by production and planning issues.

Torquay head office in 1982 was very much a factory operation. There were about 60 girls in the factory, another six or eight in the office and the shop (which was attached to the factory), and the only males were the management staff and the guys in the cutting room. Needless to say, the parties were legendary.

The formula was pretty simple. The product line basically consisted of boardshorts and cordshorts. All the shops had to do was order their overall numbers; Greeny told them when they could have them, and the prints/colors they ended up with depended on Greeny's mood of the day when he issued orders to the cutting room. Lawo was responsible for tee shirts which were ordered blank in two drops from the USA each summer (when the Australian dollar was pegged at US$ 1.25!). No such thing as stock service—you pre-ordered, and when they were gone, that was it! The finished goods warehouse was approximately 20 feet by 20 feet, and two people worked there.

The most urgent matter I had to deal with at the beginning of my career was finalizing the June 30 annual accounts for 1982. Total sales turnover was AU $2 million, which included all the export to Europe and Japan. Mind you, the reputation of Quiksilver was much greater than the actual turnover suggested, although at that stage you would be hard pressed to find anyone in mainstream business who had heard of the company.

Things became more serious in 1983. Greeny appointed Jim Fisher (ex Golden Breed rep, Surf' Dive 'n' Ski owner) as sales

Geelong Road factory, '80s.

manager. The product line was beginning to expand, the company was already beginning to source outside its own factory (in Geelong and Melbourne) and sales turnover started to grow rapidly.

Like many small companies experiencing rapid growth, finance was always an urgent consideration. Seasonality was still an issue—winter sales were significantly less than summer sales— and cash, particularly during the inventory build-up to summer, was non-existent. In mid 1983 there was a week we couldn't pay the factory wages, the consequences of which were frightening. Eighty (by this time) angry girls without their pay—I wasn't going to be the one to tell them! Lawo came to the rescue with a loan secured on his block of land in Jan Juc. The bank came to the party and all we needed was Lawo's signature on the documents, but where the hell was he? Out surfing, of course. I found him off Pt. Danger, and after honking the horn of the car, I ended up taking off my shoes and wading out in the freezing water with a pen and the document, which Lawo duly signed after catching a wave close to shore.

Export business was a way around our seasonality problem, and the Johns (Law and Morrison) and Yasuo Tokita put together a deal in Japan that year. The next year (1984) saw Harry Hodge leave Torquay for the Europe operation, but Ug retained export rights for England and Germany, which also helped our off-season business. Turnover reached AU $5 million.

In 1985 we opened new offices in Sydney, further expanded our product line, and with good export markets now, we seemed to have a bright future. But our resources were stretched to the limit. We needed more people, bigger warehouses, more office space, computer systems, etc., so we started to spend the money to acquire what we needed. (When I started there were no computers, no fax machines and only six phone extensions. When Greeny placed the season's bulk order for printed fabric with Japan, it was everyone on hand to man the office doors to ensure no one walked in and stood on the 20-plus feet of telex tape that took an hour to feed into the machine.)

Very soon, profitability began to erode and by June 30, 1986, things were starting to get serious. We massaged the numbers to report a break even—a loss would have meant the bank pulling out its support and we would have been history. Fortunately, at this time Greeny and Lawo were in the process of selling the trademarks for the U.S. to Quik, Inc. so there was cash around from the major owners to prop up the business in the short term. But by the end of the year we had one of those emotional watershed moments when the cleanout of overheads began. Like many such situations, it started at the bottom and not the top, but there were higher-level changes with Lawo moving full time to Quiksilver Garments, and Murray Boyd moving to a contract basis.

In early 1987 I felt the situation hadn't really improved, and I was concerned the business might not survive, so I found another job. I handed Greeny my resignation, which he accepted. A few days later, Greeny came into my office and asked me if I would like to "have a go." It took a few minutes for it to sink in, but only a few seconds to accept his offer to take over the reins.

At 29, I was general manager of Quiksilver in Australia. I didn't really have any idea what I was doing, but I found if I acted confidently enough, people generally didn't question my ideas. We were doing around AU $7million turnover at this point, but still not making a profit. Our expenses had already been cut back significantly, so the only option was growth. Expanded product lines, better throughput, safer inventory control, the usual fundamentals of business that we now take for granted.

At the end of 1987, Greeny appointed me managing director, and he joined Lawo full time at Quiksilver Garments. Greeny and Lawo of course still sat on the board of Ug and we still had long and philosophical discussions about surfing and Quiksilver, Quiksilver and surfing, surfing and surfing, and, occasionally, skiing.

Obviously Quik was still very much about surfing, and authenticity was everything. Hence Greeny's observation at the time that Quiksilver would produce wallets "over his dead body," not to mention shoes, a category that was an issue to the very end. Still, the selective product lines and distribution didn't hold back growth over the next six years and by 1994 turnover had grown to over AU $25 million. In that time the company had become profitable and paid back Greeny and Lawo's loans, although it was still very much run as a family business.

In 1989 we were looking for an accountant. A 35-year-old football fanatic, who didn't surf and barely knew what Quiksilver was, came in one evening for an interview. He was wearing brown slacks, a brown tie, a checked sports coat and sported a mullet hairstyle (very fashionable in Australian football circles.) Despite first appearances, he eventually got the job, and Clive Fitts went on to become the managing director of Ug, and eventually president of Quiksilver Asia Pacific.

In 1993, we needed a new sales manager for Victoria. I bugged Craig Stevenson, a local surfer who was successfully repping for Rusty and Stüssy, to come on board. Greeny actually bet me he wouldn't come over, but I bullshitted Craig, telling him he would one day be national sales manager. He bought it, and who knows where Craig will eventually end up?

Shortly after this, Quiksilver entered another watershed period. Quik, Inc. had gone from strength to strength from 1986 to 1991, and then, along with the rest of the U.S. surf industry, totally hit the wall. I was a regular visitor over those years, and it was not a good feeling to see an industry overcook and crash.

In the wake of this downturn, we had the now-famous Global Directions meeting in France, at which tears were shed and we all did a lot of soul searching. On my return from France, I resolved that what had happened in America would not happen in Australia. Our sales team commenced a review of our total account base and we eliminated all department stores, sports stores and most menswear stores. This was one of the most difficult things I ever attempted, but it set us up for the future.

Retail was changing from strip shopping to shopping centers. Surf retailers couldn't make the margins they needed if they had to compete against retailers who would not only cut prices but would not merchandise the product correctly. We needed the right retailers to carry our product into this arena. Of course, no one would question this strategy now, but it wasn't so self evident at the time.

An even more far-reaching political change emerged at this time, when the Australian government began to wind back the tariff and quota protection on imported clothing. Even though we had outgrown our own factory, all of our production was carried out in Australia—in Geelong, Melbourne, Sydney and other regional centers. Now the writing was on the wall for our domestic suppliers. We began our offshore adventures by going

JOHN MILLS

"You are stealing our spirit"

As Quiksilver's distinctive mountain-and-wave logo became a global commodity, the brand attracted counterfeiters, the knock-off cheats who seemed to infiltrate every clothing market of every Third World country.

By the late 1980s, licensing company boss Bruce Raymond had dealt with the problem around the globe, sometimes actually turning a counterfeiter into a genuine licensee. But the biggest problem for Quiksilver International was emerging closest to home. When counterfeit shirts started appearing in Australia, they were soon traced to the Indonesian island of Bali, Australia's closest neighbor.

When normal business practices seemed to be having no effect, Raymond contacted an Australian martial arts expert, John Wills, who was known in Bali as a champion of *silat*, an art practiced by members of the Pencak Silat Bhakti Negara society. Through Wills, he enlisted the support of a troop of men who would assist in the operation. Raymond had military-style shirts run up in the samples room, then set off for Bali with Wills.

After several days of searching, they located a warehouse full of counterfeit print fabric, and, backed up by the Bhakti Negara, they pounced and seized the goods. At one point during the raid, Raymond jumped up on a cutting table and screamed: "You are stealing our spirit!"

After consultation with the local police, Raymond led a convoy of jeeps out to the low-tide reef at Ulu Watu,

JOHN MILLS

JOHN MILLS

[TOP] **Bruce Raymond lights his counterfeit bonfire.**

where he symbolically burned all the fabric as a warning to other counterfeiters. Photographs of the gesture ended up in media around the world. Within a year Quiksilver had a legitimate licensee in Indonesia.

Craig Stevenson and Burleigh barrel.

to Quik, Inc.'s China sources, but our small production runs, different seasonality and different requirements just didn't prove to be a neat fit. In fact, all our first attempts outside our comfort zones were disasters.

Eventually, during a management retreat, one of the production girls said, "Well, there is no other solution than to get up to Hong Kong and start our own office." She may as well have said, "Let's start an office on the moon." We just had no idea how to go about it.

Around the same time, though, we had started to get involved in sales and marketing in Southeast Asia. I had brought our Singapore retailers to Australia in the early '90s and convinced them to open a "surf shop" in Singapore. We struggled to provide competitive product (at Australian-made prices), but it was up and running and surviving. At the same time, Lawo had licensed Steve Palmer (one of a group of Bali-based counterfeiters) to make Quiksilver legally in Bali from 1991. At first, Ug was not invited to participate in the new company, but by '93 they realized they needed Ug's financial support and expertise to survive. With access to legitimate Asian sourcing from Indonesia, momentum started to shift to allow us to play a role in the region.

In late 1994 Ug did a deal that would bring Australia and Japan closer together via cross shareholdings and develop the Southeast Asian market. It also allowed us to generate the funds to establish our own office in Hong Kong and push on with market development over the whole region.

Although still managing director, I essentially handed the reins for Australia and New Zealand over to Clive and left to co-ordinate our Asian business, returning primarily only for board meetings. Initially it was too big a step to move straight to Hong Kong—I was still pretty adamant about getting a surf now and then—so I based myself in Bali and commuted to Hong Kong once a month. Our strategy wasn't just about sourcing. The plan was to develop the Asian market from a sales perspective. We felt that the Australian market of 20 million people was finite and we wanted access to millions more people, and possibly billions when China matured as a market.

The first couple of years seemed to bear out our most enthusiastic and optimistic forecasts. Our HK office hit the ground running, and our retail development was incredible. I had seen the initial Boardrider's Club in Waikiki just after it was opened in 1991, and it was the answer to my prayer. Previously we had had no way of retailing our product in Asia without going to department stores. No surf stores existed and no one could portray our imagery properly in order to first expose, and then market, our product. Boardrider's Clubs were the answer. With a combination of Australian-made product, Indonesian product, USA product, and with the China product coming on stream, we could suddenly offer retailers a total package.

By mid 1997 we had opened stores in Bali, Jakarta, Thailand, two in Singapore, two in Kuala Lumpur, one in Hong Kong, and one in the Philippines, plus commenced distribution to a wider network of emerging surf stores, and legalised our operation in Bali. In Indonesia alone, we turned over AU $5million in 1996. Quiksilver was on the radar screen in Asia!

At the start of 1997 I bit the bullet and moved to Hong Kong to ensure the sourcing company was fully operational. As I should have expected, not all was well. It's one thing to call in every month for a week or so; it's quite another to work in an organization day in, day out. By September we had a totally new team on board, the senior members of which (Andrew Lau and Rosita Luk) are still there today, and the company employs 100 people with a turnover approaching US $50 million.

I suppose I should have seen it coming. Just as I thought things were looking pretty good, the Asian economies went into meltdown. The first place that went was Thailand; the property

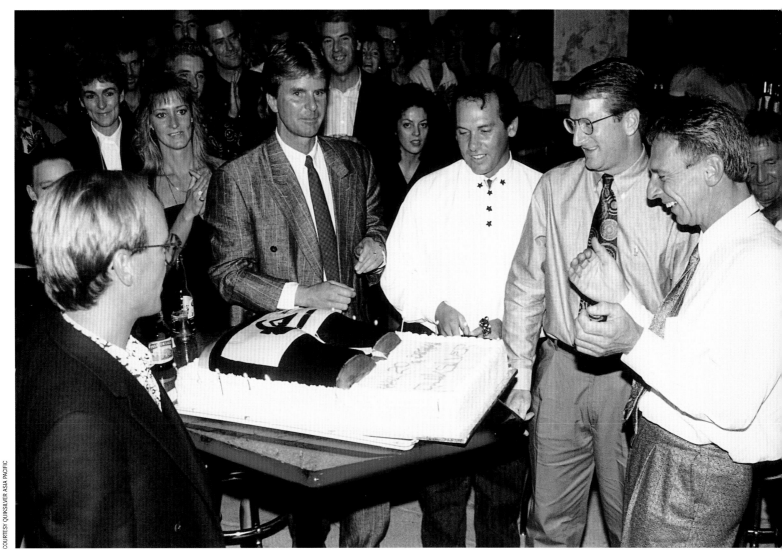

Cutting the 20th birthday cake in Sydney, 1989. Left to right: John Law, Harry Hodge, Bruce Raymond, Bob McKnight, Alan Green.

bubble burst, then the stock market and the currency. One by one, each country followed suit and eventually the disease hit Australia in 1998, dropping the currency from 80c to 50c US. Of course, in our transition from 100 percent Australian-made products to 100 percent imports (purchased in US$), we hadn't factored in the need for exchange cover. We were overstocked, our inventory system was shot and our bankers were not happy.

The Asian development had to go on hold—there was no budget available for capital expansion and no profits to pay me. I returned to Australia at the end of the year.

Of course, putting the Asian market into a holding pattern was one thing, remedying the problems in the parent company was quite another. But a strategy was devised. Craig Stevenson really pushed to get the Roxy trademark for the region and to acquire Omareef. These two initiatives allowed Ug to consolidate the Quiksilver business in Australia and New Zealand and created a platform for future growth. Clive Fitts recruited Greg Healy to the team as CFO, and the "three amigos" (Clive, Craig, Greg) launched an extremely ambitious plan for board approval. Although there was scepticism at first, they hit all their

targets and then reached for the big one—putting the Asian regional plan back on the table.

To really amalgamate the businesses properly, some serious money would be needed. A possible float was one way of achieving the aim; consolidating the business with Quiksilver, Inc. was the way that made the most sense.

After the sale of Quiksilver International to the USA in July 2000, I was fortunate enough to fall on my feet after my return from Asia, coming on board with International as general manager late in 2000. I was kept busy through the period of adjustment to International's new role in the global Quiksilver world and enjoyed working closely with Bruce Raymond, even though we hadn't always seen eye to eye when he represented the licensor and I the licensee! But at the end of 2003 I decided, not without considerable regret, to bring to a close my 22-year association with Quiksilver. It was an adventure from beginning to end, and I would not have missed it for anything.

Norm Innis spent more than 20 years working in the frontlines in Australia and Southeast Asia.

ROAD SONG | AITIONN

"Sometimes the two might just become one...lines on a road map, lines on a weather map. Waves." These words by the great Victorian writer Jack Finlay appeared in *Surfing World* magazine's "Road Song" photo annual back in 1982.

The annual featured a trip down the south coast of New South Wales to Victoria with Quiksilver team groms Gary "Kong" Elkerton and James "Chappy" Jennings, and along the way, we discovered that the road trip was a great device for highlighting character and surfing action against the backdrop of the timeless beauty of the Australian landscape. We were turned on to a vehicle for expressing our vision of the surfing lifestyle, and Quiksilver backed us on it.

As a hardcore surf company, Quik was always up for a bit of roadwork that might produce some magical images, and that is wonderfully illustrated here, in photos from two epic adventures a decade apart.

The year after Road Song's seed had been planted, a full-on West Australian expedition went down, a real survivalist journey to the remotest parts of the continent, with the highlight an awesome groundswell session at the legendary Red Bluff. In an era when surf spots were idealized but never named, our gate passes remained untarnished and the locals friendly, even during pit stops at North Point and Kalbarri, where localism had become an issue. Gary Elkerton in full Kong mode, underground shaper Bruce Fitzgerald, multi-Australian champion Bryce Ellis, WA local standouts Damon Eastaugh and Mitch Thorson, and Victorian Quik guy Paul Hart were the crew. The whole thing was so huge that it resulted in a coffee-table book of its own, *Surfing Wild Australia*.

Ten years later, in 1993, things had moved on. Sponsor trips were common, airs were popped routinely, and surfers were actually making money. But on a project based out of Quik's hometown of Torquay, the MO remained the same: big-country environment, hot and interesting surfers, and no real place names, thank you.

We headed southwest, past breaks originally revealed (with the usual secrecy conditions) by Greeny and Lawo and their mates. Past Johanna to Princetown, along the coast through Port Fairy, Warnambool and Portland, toward South Australia's border. The surfers, under the ... er, management of Quik's "Eddie" Hart and the late Andrew Murphy, were West Australian Jake Paterson, Queenslander Sasha Stocker and Sydney's Dee Why joker Brett Herring. They were joined at various stages by locals Shaun Brooks, Mark Phipps and Nigel Muscroft.

The mix of barrels, nouveau moves, 40-degree (Centigrade) heat and 10-degree water, convict history and an elements-ravaged landscape produced "4000 Ks—A Southern Australia Epic," a 40-page testament to an ideal that we shared with Quiksilver.

Surfing moves on, as it must, and in an era of boats and floatplanes, not to mention surfers with business obligations, the road trip has almost been consigned to the vault. But to this humble punter, it's a vault stuffed full of magical memories.

Hugh McLeod ran Surfing World, *Australia's original surf magazine, with Bruce Channon for more than 25 years. Under his* nom de lens *of Aitionn, his work has appeared around the world.*

Flashes from Surfing Wild Australia.
[LEFT] Blood red Kalbarri sunset, Western Australia, with the
après session figures of Bruce Channon, Damon Eastaugh
and Mitch Thorson winding their way towards the town
with two pubs.
[TOP TO BOTTOM] Kong's quiver of Al Byrne deep channel bottoms,
spread out on the parched slopes of Red Bluff, '82.
Damon Eastaugh driving hard at the Bluff. Twenty plus years
on, Damon's reputation as a charger in West Oz has only
grown. Along with other notables, like the Paterson brothers,
he's now towing into the huge outer reef bommies of WA.
Bryce Ellis, Kalbarri lip bash in silhouette. From the talent
hotbed of Avoca on the NSW Central Coast, Bryce once had
the distinction of holding the state, national and world
junior titles simultaneously. A realist in the early days of
pro surfing, he was also a qualified plumber. But when
Bryce moved into the lineup, his attack was anything but
tradesmanlike.

Solid day at Red Bluff.

[LEFT] Gary "Kong" Elkerton draws a trademark line off the top at the Bluff on a full moon groundswell. Kong's power surfing was always complemented by a certain style factor, drawn from his Queensland Sunshine Coast roots.

[TOP TO BOTTOM] Bluff crew hanging out, refuelling at our desert day camp.

Underground Maroochydore shaper Bruce Fitzgerald about to engage in some undersea exploration at the Bluff. The 1983 caption in SW read: "Fitzy consistently took off on the biggest, hairiest set waves, hauled off the bottom on his tiny 5-9 thruster and, using every drop of experience gleaned from numerous Indonesian campaigns, pulled in and raced, McCabe-like, through dreamtime tunnels."

Red Bluff lineup. The white dots are our two trucks, adding some scale to the scene.

Bryce and a lovely moonrise. Atop our four-wheeler in the pre-dawn, awakened by the rhythmic crunch of the new pulse.

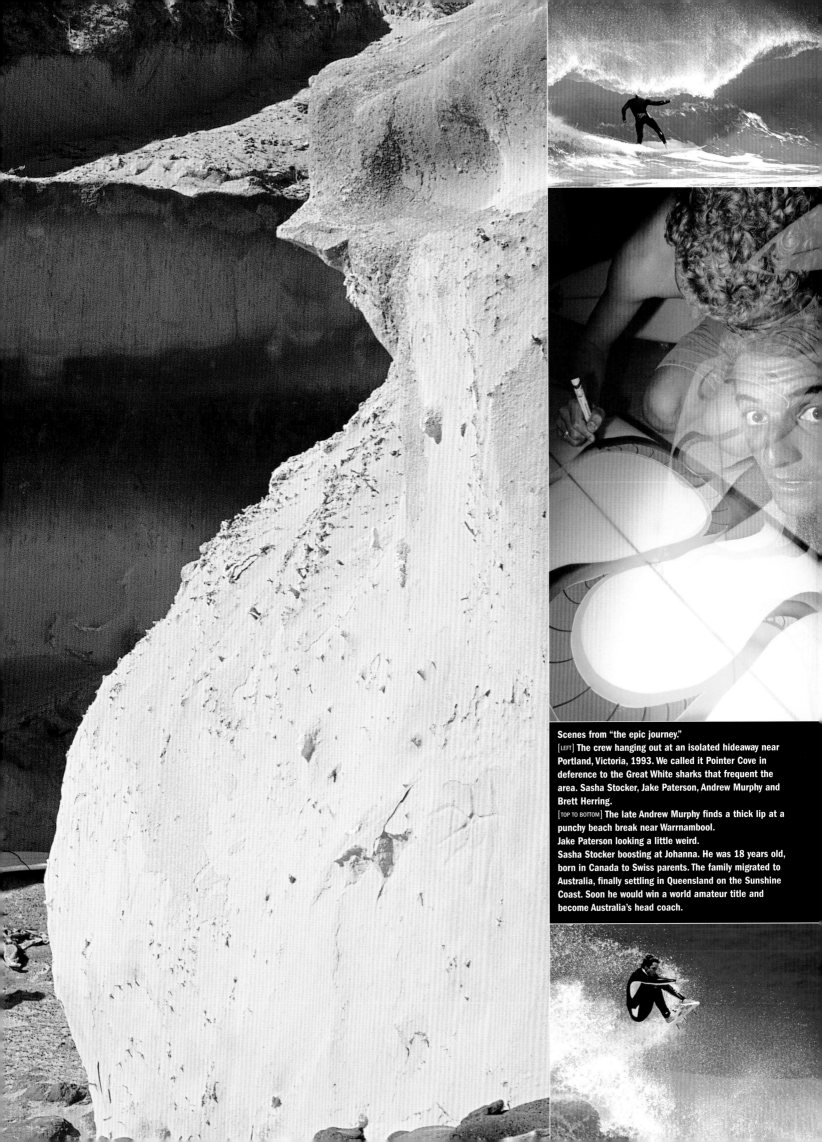

Scenes from "the epic journey."

[LEFT] The crew hanging out at an isolated hideaway near Portland, Victoria, 1993. We called it Pointer Cove in deference to the Great White sharks that frequent the area. Sasha Stocker, Jake Paterson, Andrew Murphy and Brett Herring.

[TOP TO BOTTOM] The late Andrew Murphy finds a thick lip at a punchy beach break near Warrnambool.

Jake Paterson looking a little weird.

Sasha Stocker boosting at Johanna. He was 18 years old, born in Canada to Swiss parents. The family migrated to Australia, finally settling in Queensland on the Sunshine Coast. Soon he would win a world amateur title and become Australia's head coach.

A South West Victorian travelog.
[LEFT] Jake the Snake on a playful left near the South Australian border.
[TOP TO BOTTOM] Brett, Sasha and Jake and a Pointer Cove overview.
Murph air at Princetown, not far from the 12 Apostles. Murph was then Quiksilver team manager, a guy who had grown up in Cronulla with Occy and Jim Banks as contemporaries. Quiet, artistic and stylish, a great loss.
Brett Herring, composure under heavy lip pressure at Warrnambool. Just 17, Herro was emerging from big brother Shane's shadow with his own unique blend of punch and poise.
Sunrise at Winki Pop, Bells Beach's nextdoor neighbor. An appropriate visual sign-off.

Toward a Global Quiksilver

Quiksilver president Bernard Mariette and CEO Bob McKnight at Huntington Beach HQ, September 2003.

Signing the Na Pali acquisition in Paris. Left to right, Darrigrand, Hakman, Winship, Hodge, Randy Herrel.

By 1986 boardshorts, Quiksilver's core product, represented only 35 percent of the American business, while tee shirts and walk shorts had reached 40 percent. This represented significant diversification for a brand that called itself "the boardshorts company" with justifiable pride. And, with the 1985 acquisition of Pro-Lite, a small manufacturer of surfboard bags, Quiksilver USA had made its first baby steps into the lucrative accessories market.

At the same time, sales distribution had spread from coastal surf shops to a nationwide mix of 1,300 surf, specialty and department stores, with some 30 representatives servicing the accounts. From a quiet beginning at Liberty House in Hawaii in 1984, department store sales had jumped to nearly 20 percent of the company's $18.6 million revenue for 1986. Whichever way you looked at it, Quiksilver USA was leading the brand into a brave new world.

Meanwhile, Quiksilver Australia posted just under $5.5 million in sales in 1986, now representing less than a quarter of the brand's global sales. With the American market on fire and the European looking very promising, it was clear that growth in the future was going to be driven from the northern hemisphere, and yet many of the decisions governing those growing markets would be made by a small licensing company in Australia.

So when the Quiksilver, Inc., team flew down to Melbourne, Australia, in September 1986 to seek approval to take the American licensee public, they also had a secondary agenda— to buy the trademarks for the USA and Mexico. While they were initially taken aback, Green and Law soon realized that selling the trademarks was a necessary step in the growth of the brand, and one which, as a pleasant byproduct, would make them both rich.

When the initial public offering was completed on December 16, 1986, and the stock quoted on the NASDAQ exchange, Quiksilver became the first publicly traded surfwear company. The first board of directors of Quiksilver, Inc., consisted of the four working partners—president McKnight, 33; vice-president and chief financial officer Larry Crowe, 34; vice-president Randy Hunt, 35; vice-president Charles Crowe, 31—and two external members, Arthur Crowe, 63, and Robert G. Kirby, 61.

In summer 1987 Quiksilver, Inc., moved another step closer to the kind of professional management it felt the shareholders required with the recruitment of May's department stores executive John Warner, who started as vice president of sales but was CEO and chairman of the board by the end of the year. Warner was to be the first of several professional managers brought into the company to help steer it through phases of extraordinary growth, creating a mix of executives that came to be known as "the salts and the suits."

Warner's first years with Quiksilver were not easy. First, he had to instill a new management discipline befitting a public company answerable to its shareholders, including instituting quarterly reporting, board meetings and annual shareholder meetings. Then he presided over the settling of internal frictions that led to the departure of Larry Crowe, and finally he orches- trated the acquisition of Na Pali SA, the French licensee of Quiksilver Europe.

In 1990, while Quiksilver USA continued to ride high on booming sales of surf's "neon" look, Harry Hodge and his Quiksilver Europe partners approached Warner with a proposal that the U.S. company invest in Europe. The idea was a good one, but neither Warner nor McKnight were interested in a minority position. As negotiations ensued through the summer, it became clear that there was only one positive outcome as far as the Americans were concerned. Hodge recalls: "It was a difficult decision for all of us at Na Pali, but I guess I was better prepared than my partners because I'd already had to consider the various possible outcomes. But the bottom line was that (selling) was the right thing to do for the growth of the company and for us personally."

On October 3, 1990, Quiksilver USA announced its purchase of Quiksilver Europe for $10.5 million dollars, plus an injection of $5 million of working capital. The deal was signed in Paris the following February, with the four Na Pali partners agreeing to a two-year earn-out period, during which time Hodge would be the boss and the others would maintain their old roles. So for Quiksilver Europe, there was no immediate or earth- shattering change. For the Quiksilver brand, however, the balance of power had shifted forever.

[TOP] **Harry and Bernard, the dynamic duo.** [ABOVE] **Alan Green and Bernard Mariette.**

While the acquisition of Na Pali made Quiksilver USA a licensee again—Green, Law and licensing boss Raymond had no intention of selling the trademarks for Europe—and theoretically should have created stronger ties between the Quiksilvers around the world, the reality was that it began to place strains on the brand's entire licensing strategy. Since the 1986 IPO, Quiksilver USA had been building its business through an aggressive five-year plan that required fundamental shifts in what they made and where they sold it. Boardshorts now accounted for less than seven percent of total sales, while John Warner had opened up new channels of distribution where few surf companies had gone before, and those that dared had suffered the consequences in their core markets.

With American sales heading toward the $100 million mark, McKnight, Warner and their board knew that this diversification was essential, but down in Australia, Green and his key executives saw it as a strategy that was increasingly dangerous for the credibility of the brand. The general feeling, too, was that there was a possibility that America would grow away from the core values of Quiksilver.

Bob McKnight and his team disputed this view, of course, but there was growing dissent within their own ranks too, and John Warner left the company in 1991, just as the American surf industry began to suffer its first serious downturn.

As the summer of 1991 approached, recession hit right across America's retail industry, coupled with a dive in consumer confidence over the deployment of American troops in Operation Desert Storm in Iraq. For the surf industry there was a double whammy, for on top of all this, reports of shark attacks, water pollution on all coasts and new skin cancer concerns made the beach seem rather gloomy, and the new urban/hiphop music, culture and fashion had more appeal to much of the teen market. At the beach, surf would never go out of fashion, but in the 1980s the surf market had expanded beyond the coasts where there was no such allegiance, and fashion was fickle. When the neon fad began to fade, its effects were felt across the industry.

Overnight 30 percent of Quiksilver's retail account base disappeared, with domestic sales plummeting from $91 million to under $60 million. While the financial analysts who had sung the brand's praises in the '80s now began to write epitaphs, McKnight stepped into Warner's CEO role and introduced a new president of the company.

Hiring Shaheen Sadeghi seemed a master stroke. Not only was he an aggressive merchandiser who could be expected to re-ignite retail, but he was a star player at Gotcha, still leading Quiksilver in sales but experiencing the same difficulties. Quiksilver's gain would be Gotcha's loss. And Sadeghi had plenty of ideas about diversifying the brand that would one day be adopted, but when he stood up at a Quiksilver international summit meeting and backed the common thinking of the time, that surf was "dead," everyone in the room realized that the company strategy, and some of the team, would have to evolve.

After Sadeghi's departure, McKnight took on the role of president as well, but he also promoted Warner hire Randy Herrel to the dual roles of chief operating and financial officer. Herrel had proven to be a hard-nosed operator in tough times, and McKnight thought he saw in him a future president of the company. Together they presided over some harsh cost-cutting measures, including the laying off of 50 employees, several of them top managers and close friends. "It was the toughest time of my life," McKnight recalls. "But I knew it had to be done.

Post-acquisition meeting at Na Pali, 1994.

We had to cut 20 percent from our operating budget or we were not going to survive.

In September 1992, Quiksilver, Inc., reported a 74-percent plunge in profits for the third quarter of the year, which was bad news but hardly shocking. It was the fifth straight quarter the company had reported sliding figures. With a basic survival plan in place, McKnight and several of his team then flew off to France for an international meeting of Quiksilver executives that had been dubbed the "Global Directions" meeting. Never had the brand needed a global direction more, but the preamble to the meeting had been a long exchange of differing views.

Since Quiksilver USA had bought the trademarks in 1986, the glue binding the company to its Australian parent had been called a "sharing agreement." It called for a free flow of ideas, product designs and marketing concepts, and relied on the good will of a small group of friends who from the beginning shared a philosophy centered on integrity and authenticity. The problem, as the Australians saw it, was that

USA's necessity for growth was destroying its authenticity. The problem, as the Americans saw it, was that the Australians were playing in a very small pond and were not looking at the big global picture.

Although there were many shades of gray presented at the frequently tense French meetings, it really got down to an emotion-charged confrontation between Alan Green, who had founded the brand, and Bob McKnight, whose company made 70 percent of its global sales. This was not a clash between salts and suits, for both men were surfers first, businessmen second. Rather, it was a clash over how to balance the integrity of the brand with the reality of the global marketplace, and, despite the tears that were shed, the meeting resulted in a consensus view that growth and authenticity could live and work together. And the diversification strategy that emerged from the Global Directions meeting provided the blueprint for growth throughout the '90s and the subsequent globalization in the new century.

Mariette and McKnight at work on acquisition plans.

As Quiksilver Europe's two-year directors' earn-out period came to an end, Bob McKnight and Randy Herrel began to look for an operations executive to support Harry Hodge. While Hodge had done a great job in building the European license thus far, his strengths lay in marketing and product design, not in steering the operations and finance of the fastest-growing arm of a public company.

Quiksilver found Bernard Mariette, the enterprising young manager of Timberland France who had a strong previous track record with L'Oreal, the cosmetics giant. Mariette knew nothing about Quiksilver (or surfing, for that matter) but over an extended courtship in both France and California, he was seduced by the company lifestyle and what he saw as the limitless opportunities for the brand in Europe. In October 1994, he signed on as director general (finance and operations) at Quiksilver Europe.

Although Mariette was clearly not a surfer, his adventurous approach to snowboarding and his bonhomie soon won over his new colleagues, and he and Hodge formed a powerful management alliance that saw Quiksilver Europe deliver outstanding results through the mid-1990s (including 48 percent growth in 1995). After the departure of Randy Herrel in 1996, McKnight formed an "office of the president" to share his workload, but already he was looking to the young Frenchman to play a global role at Quiksilver.

As Hodge began to ease out of the day-to-day running of Quiksilver Europe in preparation for his eventual return to Australia, Mariette became European president, and then, amid the retail reverberations of September 11, 2001, McKnight and the board of Quiksilver, Inc., pressed him into service as president of the entire company, working a grueling beat between Saint Jean de Luz and Inc.'s giant new complex at Huntington Beach.

By the late '90s, Quiksilver, Inc.'s, twin engine rooms in California and France were churning out annual sales of more than $300 million and growing consistently at 25 to 30 percent a year. It was becoming increasingly obvious that the company was reaching a size in its mature markets where it would have to look to acquisitions to maintain its long-term growth at the same rate. The most logical of these were from within the Quiksilver family of companies, but since this involved the Australians effectively "selling the farm," the issue was clouded with emotion. But Alan Green and John Law both realized that the future prosperity of the brand would have to be built around one global company, and over time the arguments against selling grew less vocal.

The first step in the globalization process was the purchase in 2000 of the global licensing company, Quiksilver International. Bruce Raymond's Sydney-based operation relinquished its licensing role to corporate headquarters and stepped up its orchestration of global marketing initiatives, such as the Quiksilver Crossing. The second step was the 2002 acquisition of the original founding operating company in Australia and the other Quiksilver licensees in the region, Indonesia and Japan, to form a new Asia Pacific division.

After knocking back an approach in 2000, in 2003 Quiksilver again looked at the thriving DC Shoes company for its first large-scale external acquisition. A $150 million deal involving stock, cash and earn-out was hammered out in May 2004. Six months later, as the fiscal year closed, DC had integrated seamlessly into Quiksilver and was plugged into Quiksilver's global sales and marketing platform positioning itself for its second $100 million in sales.

Truly global at last, Quiksilver looked toward its next milestone—achieving a billion dollars in sales and extending its reach from the boardriding sports to the entire outdoors sector.

Quiksilver moves to the New York Stock Exchange, 1998.

Quiksilver Hits the Big Board

After a dozen years trading on the NASDAQ, Quiksilver made the move to the "Big Board," the New York Stock Exchange, in June 1998. CEO Bob McKnight, in New York to celebrate the debut, described the listing as "an important milestone in the growth of Quiksilver."

And the years have proven him right. Being on the Big Board created a whole new level of awareness of Quiksilver stock, prompting greater analysis and a much more diverse range of customers. By the mid 2000s, more than a million Quiksilver shares were being traded each day.

Quiksilver board returns to the NYSE, 2004. Left to right: Quiksilver board members Franck Ribout, Bernard Mariette, Charles Crowe, Tom Roach, NYSE chairman Grasso, Bob McKnight, Bill Barnham, Bob Kirby, Harry Hodge.

Kelly Slater shows an appreciative crowd how to surf Pipeline.

Quiksilver in Hawaii

[ABOVE] **Waimea Bay lineup.**

Quiksilver's involvement with Hawaii, spiritual home of the surfing culture, is almost as old as the brand itself. In 1974 a new pro surfing event, the Coca-Cola Surfabout, joined the existing Rip Curl Bells Pro to create an Australian pro tour that offered more prize money than any other. A large Hawaiian contingent flew Down Under and very few of them came back without a few pairs of Quiksilver boardshorts. As well as Jeff Hakman, surfers of the caliber of Gerry Lopez, Rory Russell, Reno Abellira, Larry Bertleman, Buttons Kaluhiokalani, Owl Chapman and Barry Kanaiaupuni became walking billboards for the new shorts.

Even more importantly, contest judge and Lightning Bolt founder Jack Shipley smuggled a couple dozen pairs home inside his board bag and sold them so quickly from his Honolulu store that he started to import them legitimately. Shipley recalls: "We sold mostly surfboards but we were always looking for real high quality stuff to put in there too. Quiksilvers were simply the best boardshorts I'd ever seen, so we had to have 'em. To be honest, seeing what could be done with real quality is what got us started down the track of doing Lightning Bolt clothing. We were just moving in that direction when my best shaper joined Quiksilver."

Tom Parrish was a shaping legend when he became Quiksilver's first Hawaiian sales rep. A close friend of Hakman's and a new friend of Bob McKnight, he might have become a partner had he been available early in 1976 when Quiksilver, Inc., was founded. Instead, by the end of the year he was selling the new American product to his other boss, Shipley, and a small list of surf shop accounts. Parrish worked hard at building the brand in Hawaii, but by the beginning of the 1980s, as Quiksilver's product offering began to expand, he found that running a sales office and warehouse, however small, was not what he was cut out for.

In the spring of 1982, Glen Moncata, the Hawaiian sales rep for sportswear brand Fila, got a call from his old school friend Terry Fisher who was an independent sales rep based in the Rockies and selling, among other things, Quiksilver. "Quiksilver's rep in Hawaii just quit," Fisher announced. "Might be an opening for you." Moncata, who had run ski shops in Southern California before moving to Hawaii, knew snow, surf and selling and considered himself well equipped for the job, but it took him five trips to the mainland to convince Bob McKnight. The main reason was that McKnight and Hakman both felt that a "haole" who had

[TOP] **Glen Moncata.** [ABOVE] **Makaha car park musicians.**

only recently arrived might not be accepted by the surf community. But Moncata and his wife, Meredith, were an engaging and persuasive duo, and within a few months they had given up Fila to sell Quiksilver full time.

The Moncata MO was—and still is—to build brand loyalty through community involvement. Says Glen: "If you make a statement here, people never forget it." Quiksilver began supporting small, grass-roots clubs, associations and events on

Titus Kinimaka.

Hanalei Bay.

all the islands, paying particular attention to the depressed Westside of Oahu, where the brand helped Rell Sunn and the Keaulana family with kids meets and charity functions.

As surf brands began to realize the importance of sponsoring athletes, Quiksilver's Hawaiian "dream team" of the mid 1970s was eroded somewhat, but two of the best competitors on the pro tour, Dane Kealoha and Michael Ho, flew the flag into the next decade, when they were joined by hot new talent Marvin Foster and Mickey Neilsen, as well as big-wave charger Ken Bradshaw, longboard champion Rusty Keaulana, and later Johnny Boy Gomes, Derek Ho and Sunny Garcia.

In the early 1990s Glen Moncata was approached by a group of Honolulu businessmen who had been following the growth of the Quiksilver brand and wanted to create a dedicated Quiksilver store in Waikiki's International Market Place. Although the idea of a Quiksilver-specific store was not new—Alan Green and John Law had opened Quiksilver Custom Surf Shorts in Torquay in 1976 and there had been a Quiksilver store in Biarritz since 1985—Bob McKnight was initially skeptical of licensing the name to an unknown retailer. The solution was to call it the "Boardriders Club," a name that Danny Kwock came up with. Decorated with classic surf photos and Hawaiiana by Steve Jones, the Waikiki store was an immediate hit, spawning Boardriders Clubs all over America.

Glen Moncata saw opportunities for more Boardriders Clubs in Hawaii too, but he was anxious to ensure that it didn't look like a corporate takeover, alienating long-established surf

shops. So he offered partnerships to the most respected families in Hawaiian surfing. At Haleiwa on the North Shore, Barry Kanauipuni opened a Quiksilver Boardriders Club, followed by a Rusty Keaulana store at Ala Moana and, later, an Eddie Aikau store. Dane Kealoha, who had managed the first store in Waikiki, opened a new one on Maui.

Although Hawaii is a thriving market for Quiksilver today, the basic nature of the business has not changed since Glen Moncata took over from Tom Parrish almost a quarter century ago. He says: "I had about 20 accounts when I started, I've got 28 now. But that's a lot of doors. What's happened is the retailers have grown with us. When I started; Local Motion and HIC had a couple of stores each. Now they've got six or seven."

And the secret to doing good business, Moncata says, is still to be a good neighbor and be involved in the community. As well as sponsoring a host of small events, ranging from menehunes to paddling to outrigger canoes, Quiksilver's big-ticket Eddie Aikau memorial big-wave event underlines the brand's commitment to the soulful roots of Hawaiian surfing, and the 2003 Makaha Masters brought international pro surfing back to the Westside for the first time in decades.

In 2006 Sunset legend Barry Kanaiaupuni will plant the Quiksilver flag in North Shore Central when he opens the BK Sunset Beach Boardriders Club on the site of Kammie's Market. Says Moncata: "It's a great fit—a legendary location, a legendary surfer running the store and the all-time legendary surf break right out in front."

Contestants line up at the Eddie opening ceremony.

Eddie Aikau Sunset drop, 1974.

In the summer of 1984 Bob McKnight had a phone call from Eddie Rothman, one of the more controversial characters of the Hawaiian North Shore surfing fraternity. While having no Hawaiian blood himself, Rothman had been resident long enough to claim honorary bloodlines and in 1975 had helped the true locals found Da Hui, or the Black Shorts, a sometimes-intimidating organization that sought to uphold the rights of native sons during the annual invasion for the big-wave season. Now he asked for a meeting next time the Quiksilver boss was in Hawaii.

Says McKnight: "I wasn't so sure about getting involved with Eddie, but he'd already met with Glen Moncata, and Glen convinced me that he had some interesting ideas. Danny Kwock and I were on Oahu a few weeks later so we arranged to have dinner, and Eddie shows up at this steakhouse in Pearl Ridge with the entire surviving Aikau clan. So we listened to his proposal, noted how much Pops Aikau was behind it, and it seemed to make sense."

Rothman's proposal was for a tribute event in honor of Eddie Aikau, the leading Hawaiian big-wave rider of the 1970s who had disappeared at sea in 1978 while paddling his surfboard to get help for the stricken canoe *Hokule'a*, listing in heavy seas off the island of Lanai. Rothman's idea was for a simple affair, conducted over just one day, with no heavy commercial trips interfering with the intended spirituality of the occasion.

Ho'okupu ceremony at the Eddie.

He recalls: "Eddie was about two years older than me, and when I started surfing Waimea, he was the man, you know? He would see me paddling for a wave and he'd be like, 'Go, bra, go!' Or he'd go, 'Yo! Let's go!' And we'd take off together. We became real good friends, and after he passed, every time I would paddle out at the Bay, I'd turn around to take a wave and hear his voice, you know? 'Yo, let's go!' I wanted to make sure people never forgot about Eddie, and Pops agreed with me."

McKnight and Kwock saw Rothman's memorial idea as an opportunity to tie the brand to the very core of the Hawaiian surf culture. They accepted the offer.

The first "Quiksilver Eddie Aikau Invitational Surfing Classic" was held at Sunset Beach in December 1984, with local surfer Denton Miyamura winning the $5,000 first-place check. Despite the small memorial ceremony for Eddie, it was just another surf contest at Sunset Beach, and McKnight and his team resolved to make it special or make it go away. They consulted with George Downing, the respected big-wave rider and contest director who had come up with the objective scoring system that had revolutionized competitive surfing in the '70s. Together they decided that the contest had to be moved to Waimea Bay, and that it should only be held when conditions were so good that "Eddie would go," to quote the bumper sticker slogan that soon became famous.

George Downing

COLOR	SURFER	BEST 4 WAVES				TOTAL	FINAL PLACE	COLOR	SURFER	WAVES			TOT	FINAL P
HAW	NOAH JOHNSTON	89	84	67	74	314		HAW	KEONE DOWNING	41		53	41	176
HAW	BROCK LITTLE	67	82	60	53	262		USA	PETER MEL	15		74		173
USA	KELLY SLATER	83	71	78	87			HAW	ROSS WILIAMS	56	4			219
HAW	BRADEN DIAS			67	46	25		AW	DEREK HO	36				178
HAW	MYLES PADACA		52	76	56	232		HAW	PANCHO SULLIVAN	39				454
AUS	TONY RAY		88	71	78	3			ELIJAH YOUNG	56				
HAW	CLYDE				66				CLARK-JONES	49				
AUS	PAUL		2	89					MONIZ	73			04	
HAW	JOHN		60	60					MALLOY	24	3		66	
HAW	JAMIE		8	56	24				BRIAN KEAULANA	15			26	
HAW	RUSS		52	64	2				AVE YESTER	26			4	
HAW	KEONI		5	73	55	2			ARRYL VIROSTKO	40			8	

IN MEMORY OF EDDIE AIKAU

THE QUIKSILVER in memory of EDDIE AIKAU big wave invitational

$55,000

Pay to the order of KELLY SLATER

fifty five thousand dollars

1st place

WAIMEA BAY, HAWAII • DEC 1 2001 - FEB 28, 2002

EDDIE AIKAU waimea bay hawaii

QUIKSILVER

Kelly Slater claims the win.

Downing devised a two-round format that gave the invited big-wave specialists three hours to pick off three high-scoring rides to take the winner-take-all prize money. He also decreed that the contest would only be held when the bay was deemed to be over 20 feet, so the event was given an extended waiting period, from January 1 to February 15, 1986.

On the first day of the waiting period for the re-named "Quiksilver in Memory of Eddie Aikau," the illuminati of Hawaii and of world surfing gathered at Waimea for a moving *ho'okupu* ceremony in honor of Aikau. Then, when a swell topped 20 feet a few weeks later, Eddie Aikau's younger brother Clyde, 36, won the inaugural Waimea event on a fourth-wave countback, riding his brother's favorite Waimea gun.

Aikau had dominated the final, but in the last minutes fellow Hawaiian Mark Foo scored a perfect 20-point ride to tie the scores, forcing the judges to look at the fourth best scores of each surfer. As if scripted in heaven, "The Eddie" became part of surfing's folklore, and its sponsor became forever associated with "authenticity" in surf events.

Subsequent Eddies, in 1990 (when Quiksilver raised the prize money to a record $55,000), 1999, 2001, 2002 and 2004, further fueled the legend, with perfect giant waves ridden fearlessly by the best surfers of the day, and some, like Eddie Rothman himself, who were elected to the pantheon by peer poll. While the event has only been run six times in 20 years, Quiksilver has made a major celebration out of it each year. Says Bob McKnight: "We honor Eddie every year, then we wait for a big day—it's a great marketing vehicle. We didn't plan it that way, we just got lucky. But the reason that people are still interested in the Eddie is that we don't compromise it. We wait until it's big and perfect, however long that takes, and then Eddie goes."

[TOP] **Ross Clarke Jones negotiates a wild drop.**

[LEFT] **Moment of truth for Flea Virotsko, December 15, 2004.**

[ABOVE] **Kelly with the power behind him.**

JIM RUSSI

HANK

JOU

Poster Art *for the* Eddie

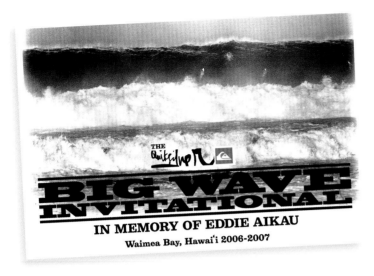

IN MEMORY OF EDDIE AIKAU
Waimea Bay, Hawaiʻi 2006-2007

1986-1987

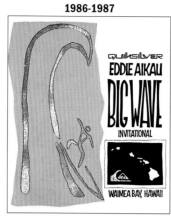

1986-1987

1991-1992

1992-1993

1993-1994

1994-1995

1998-1999

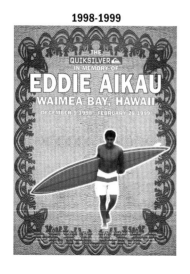

1999-2000

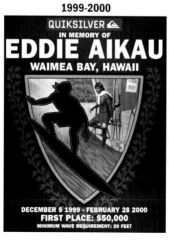

2000-2001

2001-2002

1987-1988

1988-1989

1989-1990

1990-1991

1995-1996

1996-1997

1997-1998

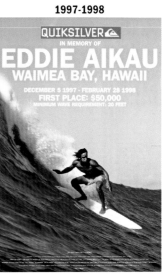

2002-2003

2003-2004

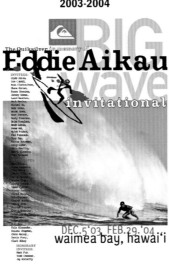

2004-2005

2005-2006

Quiksilver Events

[ABOVE] **Quiksilver's judging tower brands one of the world's great surfing lineups, G-Land, Java, Indonesia.** [RIGHT] **Reef judging tower, Tavarua.**

From its inception, Quiksilver's brand image relied on its close association with the best exponents of the sport, but surfing's popular heroes back in the early 1970s were not necessarily the contest winners. In fact, the more soulful surfers dismissed the events, with their perceived regimentation, as uncool.

Nothing exemplified this lack of cool better than the forced march of competitors down the main street of the western Victorian town of Lorne, Australia, in the opening ceremony for the fifth world surfing championships in 1970. Joe Sweeney, a member of the organizing committee, recalled: "The Americans and the Japanese dressed nicely in their team uniforms, but the Aussies...were a bloody disgrace. Full-on hippies." Several of the hippie surfers, including Nat Young and Wayne Lynch, bowed out of future competitions in disgust, and returned only when the marching had stopped and the flow of prize money had begun.

Surfing wasn't about uniforms and marching—it was about sun in your face and salt in your hair, about freedom! And no one knew that better than Alan Green. Even when his Rip Curl partners Doug Warbrick and Brian Singer ushered in the professional era in Australia with sponsorship of the Bells Beach

JOLI

event in 1973, Greeny scowled. In fact it was not until 1976, when Rip Curl and Quiksilver had finally split into two companies, that he agreed to sponsor an event, the Quiksilver Trials.

When Bob McKnight and Jeff Hakman established the brand in the American market, they too eschewed event sponsorship. One reason was lack of money, but McKnight, like Green, felt that surfing was about more than competition. Surfing's professional tour was just starting to take off, but it was dominated by Australians, Hawaiians and South Africans, so in California the backlash against competition continued, even into the 1980s.

JEFF HORNBAKER

Jay Moriarity at Mavericks.

The Quiksilver world titles, Newquay, England, 1986.

In 1982 Ocean Pacific introduced the Op Pro at Huntington Beach, with $35,000 in prize money and a mid-summer time slot guaranteed to produce a huge crowd. It soon became known as the "Super Bowl of surfing" for the media attention and final weekend crowds it attracted. The Op organization milked the event for all it was worth, schmoozing media and clients in hospitality tents, parading its stars in front of the spectators, and generally doing whatever it could think of to underline the brand's supremacy. Surf event marketing had arrived in California.

But Quiksilver hung back. Unable to afford an Op-style extravaganza (with a 1982 marketing budget of around $150,000) and unwilling to embrace the hype, McKnight and Danny Kwock instead invented the Echo Beach Challenge at Newport Beach, the first of a series of low-key regional "fun" events.

Two years later McKnight was contacted by Hawaiian surfing identity Eddie Rothman with an idea that would forever change Quiksilver's approach to promoting events. (See "The Eddie," page 140) But despite the enormous success it has enjoyed

Quiksilver Slopestyle, Les Arcs, France, 2003.

over the years, The Quiksilver in Memory of Eddie Aikau has remained an event steeped in the brand's soulful tradition and its respect for authenticity. Nothing was ever more soulful or authentic than the great Hawaiian big-wave rider who lost his life trying to save others.

Meanwhile, Quiksilver Europe made its first foray into events with the 1986 world amateur surfing championships, held in Newquay, England. It was a big expenditure for the two-year-old company, but a major marketing coup, helping break the brand in the United Kingdom. However, Harry Hodge and Jeff Hakman soon realized that the best return on event investment was going to be in their number one market, France, which also happened to have the best waves.

Through the late '80s, Quiksilver Europe became the major sponsor of the midsummer Lacanau Pro, which soon became Europe's "Super Bowl of Surf," with more bikinis than waves. In the '90s, following the arrival of the Rip Curl Pro at Hossegor, Quiksilver created its own tour event, the Quiksilver Surfmasters, in neighboring Biarritz.

Quiksilver Bowlrider, Marseille, France, 2004.

Quiksilver Pro G-Land, 1997.

Perfect day at Cloudbreak for the Quiksilver Pro Fiji.

Quiksilver Europe also led the way with events in the snow, helping build the bridge between surfing and the new snowboard market with its Quik Cup, a crossover event in which competitors had to show their prowess in both sports. Then the only such event in the world, the Quik Cup quickly developed a reputation for its innovation and its high-voltage party program.

By the mid '90s the Association of Surfing Professionals, professional surfing's governing body, was starting to see that its future lay in made-for-television events, which had the potential to increase a sponsor's exposure a thousandfold, while at the same time enabling the events to be held in remote and exotic locations rather than mass-market beach breaks. The major surf companies, led by Quiksilver, Billabong and Rip Curl, had already begun to build their image arsenal with video clips of their surfers riding perfect reef breaks framed by palm trees, making footage of events at Huntington Beach or Sydney's Manly Beach appear lame.

During the Hawaiian contest season of 1994, the ASP's

Webcasting from a mobile site, Quiksilver Pro France, 2003.

managing director, Graham Cassidy, mentioned this new mindset, plus the fact that there was a tour event opening available, to Quiksilver's Bruce Raymond. Raymond, who had previously been opposed to sponsorship of ASP tour events, immediately thought of two things.

The first was his recent conversation with the sports marketers who'd paid more than $3 million to buy the naming rights to the Australian Open tennis tournament for the Dutch brewers Heineken. Raymond knew that Heineken's Australian sales did not justify such a sum, but, as the marketers pointed out, it gave the company a branded event that would play on television all over Europe, at a much cheaper price than, say, the French Open. Lightbulb moment! It didn't matter where it was held, what mattered was where it was seen.

Raymond's second thought was of his many surf trips to the G-Land surf camp at Grajagan, on the southeast tip of Java, and of one in particular, during which he and colleague Rod Brooks had fantasized about holding a surf contest in G-Land's perfect waves. He phoned Brooks and told him to fly to Java to

investigate the possibilities.

The first Quiksilver Pro G-Land in 1995 was a logistical nightmare. The remote location trebled the cost and the time involved in doing everything, but Raymond was insistent that if made-for-TV was going to work, every last detail had to look right. A huge tower was constructed on the inshore reef, affording judges and photographers an incomparable view of proceedings as the waves peeled down the reef. Industrial designer Ray Smith (who had reshaped the Quiksilver logo years earlier) was flown in from Los Angeles to apply the cosmetic touches to all the branded structures.

But the most important element was the "Mosquito Express." On each day of the event, a video-taped highlights package destined for television sports desks around the world would be ferried across the reef on an ancient *prahu*, powered by a sputtering outboard, to the village of Grajagan, where a kamikaze motorcycle courier would take delivery and race for several hours to Denpasar airport and the first available flight for Singapore, from which point the package would soar to Heathrow,

Quiksilver Pro Gold Coast, Snapper Rocks, Australia.

then motor to the British Telecom Tower in London, where it would be beamed via satellite to television sports desks across the world.

Won by reigning world champion Kelly Slater in thrilling and perfect waves, the event was hailed by contestants and surfing media as the best ever, but for Raymond the jury remained out until the global television coverage had been calculated. When the figures came in, viewership of the G-Land event had surpassed that of all others in the surf realm, with the bulk of the audience unfamiliar with surfing's image factory.

In other words, rather than preaching to the choir, which was often what surf contests did, the Quiksilver Pro G-Land had been a Trojan horse, taking the brand message across cultural barriers around the globe.

Political unrest in Indonesia eventually forced Quiksilver to find a new home for the Quiksilver Pro in the Pacific paradise of Fiji, but in the new century, as the company completed its globalization, it made more sense to establish major events in each of its sales regions. The result is that there are now Quiksilver Pros in the perfect waves of Australia's Gold Coast and France's

NATHAN SMITH

les Landes, and Quiksilver-presented events in Japan and at California's famous Trestles break. At the same time, Roxy has expanded its event base around the world with Roxy Pro events and the less formal Roxy Jams held in surf and snow around the world.

Quiksilver's events in surf, snow and skate, for men and women, boys and girls, from novices to champions, all have the same creed—to showcase the best and to teach those who aspire to be the best. Just like the values of the brand itself.

Quiksilver Banner Events

Quiksilver and Roxy Pros Gold Coast WCT
Snapper Rocks, Australia
March

Quiksilver Pro France WCT
Les Landes, France
October

Quiksilver in Memory of Eddie Aikau
Waimea Bay, Hawaii
December-February

Quiksilver Bowlriders
Skateboard Event
Marseille, France
June

Roxy Jam World Women's Longboard Championships
Biarritz, France
July

Roxy Pro Fiji WCT
May

Roxy Pro Hawaii WCT
November

Quiksilver ISA World Juniors
Global

Quiksilver King of the Groms
Global

Roxy Chicken Jam
Global

THE ART OF

Almost from its beginnings, Quiksilver embraced the art of beach culture and has never stopped trying to redefine it. From Polynesian-influenced pareo prints thru geometric grids, harlequins and polka dots to tribal motifs and scenes from the urban jungle, the look of Quiksilver is in constant flux, and it is its artists who have created a rich tradition of the unconventional expression of the board-riding spirit.

Starting from a one-room studio in Torquay, where artist Simon Buttonshaw applied the lessons in fabric print creation he had learnt from surf print guru Walter Hoffman, Quiksilver's creative heart now pulses in studios in Australia, California, Japan and France, where artists like Peter Webb, Francois Lartigau, Martial Crum, the late Thom Chambers, Eric Diamond and more recently Natas Kaupas, Randy Noborikawa, Scott Richards and Steve Fontes apply their own renditions to the theme.

Quiksilver art is meant to be worn, originally as board-shorts, then on tee shirts and eventually on a wide range of garments. But invariably an artistic theme permeates the entire brand story, from ads to point of sale displays and event backdrops and banners. Says Simon Buttonshaw: "It's all about attitude. You don't start from a position of creating a new look. You just think of new ways of voicing an attitude."

And Quiksilver artists have been voicing an attitude ever since Simon's earliest creations, moving seamlessly along the borders between commerciality and fine art, but never forgetting the primary motivation—fun.

Creative conference in Torquay: Peter Webb and Alan Green

QUIKSILVER COUNTRY

"In the first place," says Buttonshaw, "Quiksilver Country was simply our version of the Hoffman Fabrics print. Then, as we went on we put variations on it, such as Sky Palm and Toucan. I played around with flowering gums and other distinctly Australian things, but Alan was always very Polynesian in his thinking. The photos of hibiscus in Tahiti, that was what informed our print making in those days. The real success came when we engineered the print and married the Polynesian theme into the design of the shorts."

**I saw the potential
of bringing the language of art to surfing,
so my main contribution was as a thinker
rather than as an artist.**
—SIMON BUTTONSHAW

A ROUGH IDEA...

Most of the sketches, notes and works in progress shown here have been saved from the trash by Buttonshaw, who says that his boss, Alan Green, never wanted to see yesterday's ideas lying around in the workplace. "He was embarrassed by yesterday, always looking at tomorrow. Unfortunately, that legacy has been handed down through the company, and a lot of our art and design history just doesn't exist anymore. Most of what I have left is more like bootleg out-takes than master copies of the greatest hits."

ECHO BEACH

One day Alan (Green) brought in a bunch of photos of jockeys in their racing gear and said, why can't we do something like this?

—SIMON BUTTONSHAW

The idea may have come from the racecourse, but Echo Beach was also a response to the bold new glam-punk look of bands like Talking Heads in the US and Split Enz in Australia and New Zealand. The rock world was taking notice of the outrageous geometric and harlequin patterned on-stage costumes of David Byrne and the Finn brothers, and Quiksilver's stroke of genius was to take the look to the beach.

Despised by retailers when it was delivered in place of standard print repeat orders in the summer of 1980, Echo Beach was an instant hit with the kids, and has been reprised—not just by Quiksilver—for every generation since. The name was stolen shamelessly from the huge hit of the same name by Martha and the Muffins.

ST COMP

After the outrageous success of the bold and bright Echo Beach look, ST Comp was a set of graphics to go along with the first ever use of stretch fabric on boardshorts. There was a new focus on pro surfing, and Quiksilver riders like Tom Carroll, Marvin Foster and Willy Morris were at the forefront. ST Comp was based on the look of Formula-1, and it was all about performance.

EVOLUTION OF THE LOGO

I went to a place called Cash's, a big label company in Australia, and they showed me a bunch of designs, including a swan. It looked like a duck to me. I didn't pay much attention to it until we'd made a couple of hundred pairs of boardshorts with a frickin' duck on them! That's when I thought, we have to be able to do something better than this. —Alan Green

Greeny drew the outline of a breaking wave, with a few droplets of foam hovering around the lip. Then, for good measure and balance, he added a tiny snowcapped mountain underneath it. Though the images were unconnected, Greeny felt that together they represented nature's A List.

I took the existing cartoony logo and saw an opportunity to streamline it and give it a more engineered look. So I played with the geometry of the two elements and tried to tie them together more. I also came up with a new squashed font to go with it. The symbol was actually secondary to the logo type, but it turned out to have greater longevity than the type.   —Ray Smith

The original Roxy logo was highly derivative, with Polynesian and Balinese influences. No one was satisfied with it, but it wasn't until a designer at Quiksilver's Turkish licensee put two Quiksilver logos together to make a heart that the penny dropped.

GHETTO DOG

Peter Webb's offbeat humor and urban sensibilities were reflected in much of the art that came out of the Torquay studio in the 1980s. From the irony of using primitive motifs to tell the story of a modern urban tribe, to the quirky fun of Ghetto Dog (who barked louder than Mambo's), Webb imbued Quiksilver with the look of a changing world.

"The whole surf world was changing visually, getting more street oriented. My response to that was half cartoon, half grafitti.

—PETER WEBB

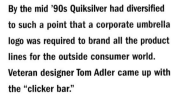

By the mid '90s Quiksilver had diversified to such a point that a corporate umbrella logo was required to brand all the product lines for the outside consumer world. Veteran designer Tom Adler came up with the "clicker bar."

Quiksilver's constantly-evolving men's clothing range featured classic designs, prints and fabrics, no matter what it was called. As the name changed from Silver Edition to Quiksilver Edition, the stylized version of the original mountain and wave continued to identify it.

The ground-breaking visual effects employed by Tom Adler and David Carson to give Quiksilver's advertising a makeover in the late '90s required a restructuring of the mountain and wave logo. The simple, understated oval seemed to sit perfectly with the use of bold copy lines and photo blow-ups employed at the time.

Designer/skater Natas Kaupas began experimenting with his stylized freehand script while working with David Carson. With new applications for it being found all the time, the Natas script changes almost as quickly as the work of the taggers that inspired it, with Natas keeping one step ahead of the designers across the board sports industry who have copied it.

DAVID CARSON

Graphic designer David Carson's out-of-frame images were the classic example of an advertising concept that spilled into product. The in-your-face action inspired a raft of imitators around the world, as well as creating a new ethic about the use of logos, and just how much could be left to your imagination. When magazine covers began to look like pieces of a jigsaw puzzle, it was time to move on. Carson's graphic sensibility also informed his use of rather oblique Jeff Hornbaker images, notably of Kelly Slater, nicely understated at a time when Slater homage was peaking. Likewise, when everything had to look like a website, Carson's touch rendered the cliché new and different.

Tom Adler was the inspiration for Quiksilver's bold fonts and copy-driven images from the mid-'90s forward. When the message had begun to get clouded by a mess of Polynesian warlords and crazy dogs, Adler created simple, bold statement imagery.

TOM ADLER

QUIKSILVER ART HONOR ROLL

So many people have contributed to the art of Quiksilver over so many years it is impossible to name them all here. The people we have nominated have usually led a team of contributors responsible for the final product, be it fabric design or event poster. Quiksilver's approach to its artists has always been to give them plenty of rope, plenty of freedom in which to create, and that policy has paid huge dividends in creative results.

SIMON BUTTONSHAW

The original Quiksilver artist. An uncompromising graphic tactician who continues to put his stamp on the brand.

MARSHALL CRUM

Picked up the Polynesian thing where Simon and Greeny had left off, master of design by xerox. Marshall designed the original petroglyph for the Eddie Aikua contest.

PETER WEBB

Simon's partner in crime at the beginning who went on to create a totally contemporary look for the brand, and give it a fine art sensibility for the first time.

FRANCOIS LARTIGAU

Former French surfing champion who joined Quiksilver Europe in its infancy and is still there, creating a European core feel in his beach-based graphics.

NATAS KAUPAS

After the solid, structured look of the Adler big type, and the weird off-the-page imagery of the Carson era, the pendulum had to swing back, and former skate star Natas Kaupas was there to implement it. The graffiti-style script is the most noticeable feature of Natas' offhand, streetwise approach, but the visual style that belies it is deceptively complex. Almost singlehandedly, Natas has created a new visual motif that translates from boardriding culture to another, with its message being, loosen up, don't take anything too seriously... even making an ad.

STEVE JONES

Like a curator at an art gallery, Steve has collected, directed, assembled and created for decades. No one has been closer to the implementation of the Quiksilver look.

PETER SCHROFF

California avant garde artist and shaper who contributed much to the surf cultural interiors of Quiksilver Boardriders Clubs.

THOM CHAMBERS

Quik's first US-based artist, a sensitive potter who dragged the art department kicking and screaming into the computer age.

RANDY NOBORIKAWA

Huntington Beach-based Randy is one of Quiksilver's "new school" artists who uses collage to fuse urban themes such as environment and racial harmony into a board sports context.

SCOTT RICHARDS

Like Randy, Scott is an exhibiting artist in Southern California whose contemporary social themes and art technique are pushing Quiksilver forward into new realms.

Quiksilver in the Snow

Sam Luebke gets upside down.

First ski-wear advertising, 1987.

In 1970, when Alan Green first scribbled a logo to replace the initial "duck" that he had selected from a label-maker's catalog, a snow-capped mountain sat next to a breaking wave more for balance than from any real sense that the two sliding games were somehow related.

"Torquay surfers had just started going to Mount Buller (a ski resort four hours away) to ski," Greeny recalls. "But it was only a few weekends a year, so even though we could see there were similarities between surfing and skiing, surfing still absolutely dominated our lives. So when I started drawing this thing, I wanted the mountain really tiny, but it didn't work, so we ended up with a mountain that was way ahead of its time."

Throughout the '70s and into the '80s, Greeny continued to ski at Buller and resorts around the world with Torquay friends like surf retailer Terry "Speaky" Lyons and Rip Curl's Doug Warbrick and Brian Singer, while Jeff Hakman, even as he worked toward establishing Quiksilver USA with Bob McKnight back in the mid '70s, spent many winter weekends skiing with Duke Boyd at his chalet in the Rockies. But it was not until the mid '80s that anyone at Quiksilver considered adding snow wear to the brand's fast-growing product range, and then it was out of economic necessity, rather than the belief that the two cultures belonged together.

Quiksilver Europe had firmly established itself on the beaches of France by 1986, but its founders had become increasingly aware that surfwear was going to be a hard sell through Europe's eight months of winter. In December 1985, Harry Hodge and Jeff Hakman took a detour while returning from a Paris trade show to visit guru skier Thierry Donard in the French Alps. Although the visit was purely for pleasure, both Hakman and Hodge were struck with the simplistic construction and rather dull look of the skiwear they saw in Chamonix and Courcheval. They looked at each other and nodded in agreement. Here was a way out of their endless winters of discontent.

Hodge recalls: "We thought we could take surfwear to the mountains, but we really had no idea about the technical aspects of skiwear. We produced the "Dead Inventory" ski jacket in boardshorts fabric that we coated with waterproof spray! Not exactly technical, but people loved it."

In fact Quiksilver Europe sold fewer than 800 of the Dead Inventory jackets, but their influence resonated throughout the market. Just as neon was illuminating the beaches of California, the bright, bold colors of Quiksilver Europe's first technically incompetent offerings shone like beacons in the rather drab fashion world of Europe's ski slopes.

The required technical expertise came in the person of Jean Afanassieff–skier, adventurer, film-maker, designer and the first Frenchman to climb Mount Everest. Afanassieff advised the Na Pali partners on the many technical aspects of snow-wear design and choice of fabrics, and helped them establish Quiksilver Europe's first snow team, the Black Diamonds. The Black Diamond skiers planted the brand's colorful surf look all over Europe's ski magazines, but it was the renegade of the troupe who was to have the lasting impact. Although he was an excellent skier, Serge Vitelli had already converted to the new snow sport just starting to take root in Europe—snowboarding.

Snowboarding had its beginnings in 1965 when an American named Sherman Poppen bolted two skis together to make a mono-ski for his daughter. He called it a "Snurfer." Throughout the 1970s, skier Jake Burton Carpenter, skater Tom Sims and surfer Mike Doyle, among others, worked to apply the dynamics of surfing to the snowfields. By the early '80s, Snurfers and other mono-ski variants had given way to the prototype of the modern snowboard, and the new sport had begun to develop its own contests, heroes and fashions.

In Europe, Vitelli and Swiss skater and snowboarder Jose Fernandes soon became the face of Quiksilver in the snow, and by 1990, skiing had been relegated to a secondary focus. With the growth of a snowboarding culture, the clothes changed too. Gone were the gaudy ski suits of 1988, replaced by the boarders' skate-based look of long jackets and baggy pants in more somber, streetwise tones. Quiksilver in Australia contributed

"Dead Inventory" jackets make their debut in the Alps, modeled by top skiers Lionel and Yvon.

a major technical advance with the introduction of new weather-resistant fabrics like Entrant.

Quiksilver USA launched its first skiwear line in July 1988 and promptly sold out. The following year the ski line represented two percent of sales (almost $1.5 million) and, as if to acknowledge the place of new sports in the Quiksilver world, recent team signings, champion moguls skier Joey Cordeau and volleyball legend Karch Kiraly, shared the cover of the company's annual report with surfer Tom Carroll.

The first American line was a hybrid of European ski suits and "all-over print" parkas, and pieces of a small line from Australia. Rockies sales rep John Thompson, who had been developing Quiksilver's seconds (or outlet) stores, was appointed to sell it. He recalls: "I got the gig because I was the only person with any experience selling to the snow market, but Bob hit me with it in June, months after the ski shows. I told him the shops had already bought for the year. And he goes, 'Yeah, but they haven't seen our shit yet.' You couldn't argue with that kind of enthusiasm. Then the samples showed up

and they were really thick and hard. The fabric was called 'shark skin.' It was like wearing a vinyl couch!

"I worked out that the only way I was going to be able to sell this stuff was to do it up in packs ranging from top of the range to cheap. I visited 80 snow accounts in two weeks and I'd just go in and tell them the Quiksilver story, wouldn't even open the pack. And they bought it on the brand story. I got back to Costa Mesa feeling very pleased with myself, thinking my job was done. But then Bob says, 'Now you'd better go make this stuff. We don't know how to!"

As the snowboard culture took hold in the early '90s, Quiksilver's look moved from neon to the more somber, urban tones of the skate-influenced riders.

By the turn of the century snowwear represented more than 20% of Quiksilver's global sales, and the brand's designers in all territories certainly knew how to make their ranges! From technical outerwear to "smart" boarding helmets, Quiksilver and Roxy snow products had carved a solid niche in the market. In addition, the acquisition of the Mervyns company in the mid '90s

By the new century, snowboard clothing had its own distinctive style.

had given the company three respected snowboard brands in Gnu, Libtech and Bent Metal bindings, and the acquisition of DC Shoes in 2003 introduced true quality boots.

But the biggest advance on the slopes has been the 2005 acquisition of Rossignol, the most respected name in Alpine sports. As Rossignol's full range of snow equipment and apparel is integrated into the company's offerings, Quiksilver will be as much about the mountain as the wave...and the street, and the whole world of outdoors.

The 2006 Winter Olympics in Turin, Italy, saw snowboarding elevated to new heights when millions around the world watched the thrilling half-pipe and snowboard cross events on television. Although unlucky with podium appearances, Quiksilver and Roxy athletes made a huge impression, while the Rossignol and Dynastar brands featured prominently in all Alpine events.

Roxy Snow team, Innsbruck, Austria, 2004.

WHITE OUT

When Quiksilver began, the mountain and wave logo represented an ideal rather than a reality. Although plenty of surfers skied, the two playgrounds were not linked the way they are today. But it didn't take long for the brand's visionaries to see the connection, and today the logo is the lifestyle.

[SPREAD] **Kyle Clancy.** [RIGHT] **Jakob Wilhelmson**

TIM ZIMMERMAN

NEIL DACOSTA

DANIEL BLOM

[SPREAD] **Stine Brun Kjeldaas, Arlberg, Austria, 1997.**

[TOP RIGHT] **Hampus Mosesson.**

[RIGHT] **Todd Proffit flies for the US of A.**

Australian Torah Bright
emerged in the 2000s as
one of the best female
snowboarders in the world.
[RIGHT] **Torah flies high at the
Arctic Challenge, Norway, 2004.**

**Tina Birbaum, Arlberg,
Austria, 1997.**

Eric Jackson and Markku Koski were the stars
of a 2004 New Zealand expedition.

Snowboard Hall of Fame

Over more than 30 years, Quiksilver has been associated with some of the greatest names in snowboarding and extreme skiing. Here are just a few.

Craig Kelly	Chris Roach	Bernard Deneuviere
Shaun White	Rob Dafoe	Serge Vitelli
Shawn Farmer	Todd Messick	Candide Thovex
Nick Peralta	Jose Fernandez	Torah Bright

Retail: Let's Call Them Clubs

World champions at the opening of the Quiksilver Boardriders Club on the Champs-Elysées, Paris, 1999.

At the height of the surf industry's neon boom in 1989, 35 percent of Quiksilver's American retail distribution was into department stores and national specialty stores, but by 1992, when the buyers for the majors had (temporarily) decided that surf was dead, that figure had fallen to under 20 percent. As the industry in general, and Quiksilver in particular, began to pick up the pieces and move forward after the recession, Bob McKnight and his management team realized that department stores were fair-weather friends.

In the first phase of recovery, they concentrated on shoring up the core retail market, the tried and trusted surf and specialty stores who had little choice but to stick with their suppliers until the tide had turned, but clearly this alone was not going to deliver the 30-percent growth of the '80s, a halcyon period that the company and its investors needed to return to.

Says Bob McKnight: "We started to realize that the problem went deeper than just pure sales figures. We were making clothes for a lifestyle, and the surf shops were able to illustrate that quite easily. When you stepped up to the next level of volume sales, the specialty stores like Edison Bros, it became that much harder. Then you'd get to the department stores and it got really frustrating, because in many cases they just didn't get it. We wanted to reach the broader market through them, but we also wanted their customers to understand the authenticity of our brand, and we started to realize that we were the best people to do that."

As the Quiksilver management pondered this problem, Hawaii sales manager Glen Moncata was approached by a syndicate of businessmen and lawyers who had observed the growing presence of the brand in the surf shops of Waikiki and proposed creating a dedicated Quiksilver store in the International Market Place in the heart of the tourist strip. Says McKnight: "They had money, they had a lease on a good location, and they were serious. We couldn't ignore it, but frankly the idea of someone being licensed to do a Quiksilver retail store scared us. I mean they were lawyers! They could steal our name for retail right from under us! We brainstormed it and came up with a solution. A Quiksilver store that's not called Quiksilver, and the name we came up with was 'The Boardriders Club.' If they stole the name it wouldn't be so bad, and we liked the feel of a shop that was a club too. We cut a deal and it was an immediate success. The formula was about

Opening of the Anglet, France superstore, 2005. Left to right, Jeff Hakman, Bernard Mariette, Bob McKnight, Pierre Agnes.

70 percent Quiksilver product, the rest coming from locally sourced stuff or things we didn't make at the time, like surf leashes, shoes or jewelry. And the idea we pushed from the beginning was that the shop should establish the connection between the local surf culture and our brand."

In fact the lawyers' money (at a time when cash was tight) enabled McKnight and his team, led by Steve Jones, to experiment with retail concepts on someone else's dime! A laboratory/studio was set up at the Costa Mesa office and walls were painted and repainted, bamboo was dragged in and dragged out, and countless combinations of memorabilia and photos decorated the space. For months before its opening, and then again for months after, the retail concept was fine-tuned first at the lab, and then to perfection at the Waikiki store.

The success of the Waikiki Boardriders Club soon spawned a chain of licensed stores. Within a year of its opening there were Boardriders in Seal Beach, Santa Cruz and Laguna Beach in California, and Park City and Orem in Utah, and the following year another five stores were added in the U.S. and two in Europe. The idea of a Quiksilver concept store was not new —Alan Green and John Law had led the way in 1976 when they opened Quiksilver Custom Surf Shorts in front of their Torquay factory, and Quiksilver Europe had opened the first stand-alone Quiksilver store in Biarritz in 1985, managed by Jeff Bradburn —but the Boardriders Clubs were the first to present the brand in its surf cultural context. Flying in the face of conventional merchandising, entire walls were given up to surf memorabilia and photographs, while windows promoted surf or snow events rather than the latest product offering.

But while the customers were delighted wherever a Boardriders Club opened, existing retail accounts often were not. McKnight and his sales team had to launch a charm offensive, usually based on anecdotal evidence that the opening of a Boardriders Club resulted in better business for everyone. Fortunately, this turned out to be true, and in time it was the surf shop proprietors who were approaching Quiksilver for licenses to open stores near their own.

With fear of failure long gone, Boardriders Clubs became Quiksilver Boardriders Clubs, an increasingly familiar branded image on high streets and shopping malls around the world. At the time of writing (March 2006) there were nearly 500 Quiksilver and Roxy concept stores around the globe, more than 200 of them company-owned, including flagship stores in Times Square, New York, Covent Garden and Carnaby Street in London, Champs-Elysées and Rue de Rivoli in Paris, and in Sydney, Moscow and

Tokyo. Meanwhile in China, Quiksilver's joint venture with a company called Glorious Sun had begun a roll-out of stores aimed at eventually reaching the largest youth market on earth, with the first Quiksilver Boardriders Club opening in Shanghai late in 2004. In 2005 sales through Quiksilver's own proprietary stores accounted for 18% of total sales, and retail experts like Carol Kristofferson and Gregg Solomon in the U.S. and Chris Athos in Asia-Pacific continued to grow the brand.

As Quiksilver's family of brands continues to grow, company-owned multi-brand stores are expected to mark a new phase in retailing. The first of these, a Quiksilver/Andaska store separated by a health food café, opened in mid 2005 in Anglet, near Quiksilver's European headquarters in southwest France.

Says McKnight: "We stumbled into retail, but now it's a clear focus for growth, a vital third arm of distribution and a great statement about who and what we really are." Quiksilver president Bernard Mariette agrees: "Anglet is a perfect example of where we are taking retail. With a healthy restaurant in between, the Quiksilver and Roxy side features all our boardsports brands, a junior skatepark, a shaping room and a DJ, while the Andaska side features equipment and lifestyle apparel for other outdoor sports, such as skiing, hiking, climbing and cycling. The shop environment is an excellent way to communicate the lifestyles that our brands represent, and it's just a fun place to be."

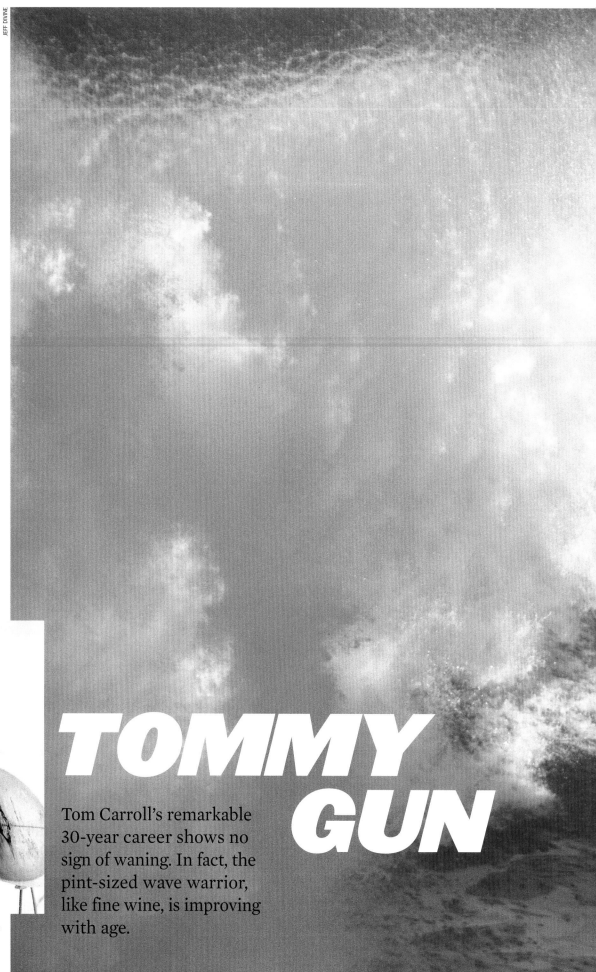

TOMMY GUN

Tom Carroll's remarkable 30-year career shows no sign of waning. In fact, the pint-sized wave warrior, like fine wine, is improving with age.

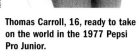

Thomas Carroll, 16, ready to take on the world in the 1977 Pepsi Pro Junior.

[RIGHT] **"The snap heard around the world," Pipeline, December 1991.**

EIGHT EPIC DROP-INS I'VE SEEN MY YOUNGER BROTHER COMMIT

By Nick Carroll

Almost everyone has heard of my brother Tom's amazing propensity for catching the same wave as other people, especially after they've already caught it. What few realize is that he's been doing it for almost 30 years.

August 1978: On me, at Umina Point, Australia, or "Pissing Point" as we knew it back then, as crazy children filled with teenage bloodlust. The 1970s in Sydney was largely a blizzard of big, out-of-control southerly groundswells and winds so foul they turned a man's soul black, and we saw each tempest as nothing more or less than a challenge. The challenge was to find somewhere superheavy yet out of that goddamned wind, and Umina—tucked away inside a big bay, an hour's drive from home—fit the bill. Pissing Point was a merciless ledging right, like turning around and taking off on a house. A set loomed, and I turned—God knows why—and caught the bloody thing and fell directly into the barrel, and watched as my younger brother took off on the shoulder and did his already patented backhand layback. Suddenly, we were in the tube together. We stayed like that for four seconds or so and then hurtled out onto the shoulder, where Tom attempted a cutback, saw me—and we both fell off. Later during that surf, he was hit square by the lip, ripping his anterior cruciate ligament to pieces; in 1981, this injury resulted in major surgery and three months out of the water.

May 1980: On Robert Hale, at Newport Peak. It wasn't very big, probably four feet, cloudy, a typical Peak afternoon session. Robert was an extraordinarily skilled natural-foot, and Tom dropped in on him on a left with the kind of utter noncompunction he'd later reserve for his closest friends on tour. He faded back, and Robert carved a top turn cutback; Tom turned directly off the bottom and caught the nose of Robert's board square in the belly, just like that. *Uggghhh.* Both surfers fell off; Tom came in, complaining of pains in his stomach. We took him to the emergency ward at Mona Vale Hospital and left him there with Helen Porter, a rather sexy nurse. About 25 minutes later, Helen called Robert and me at home. "Tom's got to go into surgery right now!" she said. Robert drove four miles in two-and-a-half minutes to set the unofficial land speed record between Newport and Mona Vale. Tom received surgery from Australia's top endocrinologist, who detected and repaired an internal tear of the stomach lining. Out for six weeks.

November 1982: On me, at Sunset Beach, Oahu. A medium-to-big day from the west-northwest with blustery tradewinds. We were still young and still totally stupid, and Hawaiian surf was all we wanted to ride. Tom was determined to wax me as badly as possible; I didn't care, as long as I was taking off deeper. A super-thick wedge loomed from the northwest, evading all those with enough intelligence to sit farther outside. "This one!" one of us screamed. We turned and paddled into it together—Tom on his Barnfield 7′6″ pintail, me on my Hot Buttered 7′5″ wing pin—and literally fell into the pit of this roaring beast of a wave, Tom delayed his bottom turn just long enough for me to take virtually the whole foamball right on the head. A week later, he won the World Cup.

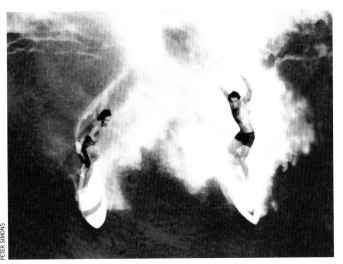

PETER SIMONS

[ABOVE] **On Nick at Sunset** [OPPOSITE] **One Nick didn't see: on Mark Foo at Sunset, 1985.**

July 1988: On Chris Homer, at Grajagan, Java. The sickest day of surf you could possibly imagine, 10-foot and barreling off G-Land's Launching Pad section, and into the unearthly field of dreams known as Speed Reef. Only about 10 surfers in the water and two of 'em were Tom and this bloke Chris Homer from Ulladulla, NSW. Now, Homer is a good man and a skilful surfer, but on this day he made himself unbearable, frantically paddling to the inside every chance he got. It kinda worked with the other eight of us; we'd pull back time after time, cursing as Homer stole the best set wave, but never being cruel enough to retaliate. But Homer didn't know who he was dealing with, and, sure enough, eventually he and Tom crossed paths. An immense and perfect set wave loomed; Homer went to the inside, and Tom composedly ignored him, took off, and got barreled for about two minutes while Chris bounced all over the coral looking for bits of his board. The only deserved drop-in I've seen Tom deliver, but to this day I don't know if he meant to do it.

December 1988: On Todd Holland, at Pipeline. This wasn't really a drop-in, not as we commonly know it, but a "priority paddling interference." It was the round before the quarters at the Billabong Pro. Tom was winning the heat, not by an unbeatable margin; Todd was holding wave priority, which for the unschooled means he had free choice of the next wave, and a nice little eight-foot peak popped up. Tom, who was closer to shore, watched the wave as it approached, turned and began to paddle. Todd saw Tom turn and immediately began to paddle for it, too. Todd caught the wave and went right, scoring a three or some such. Tom pulled back as soon as he saw Todd paddling, but it was too late and the interference was scored. It was the only undeserved interference call I've seen Tom take. It cost him a world title, and to this day I don't think Tom can laugh about it, or even grin.

November 1990: On Taylor Knox, at Off the Wall, Hawaii. Hysterical. It was like a supersession at crap OTW–TC, Pottz, the Fletcher brothers, Archy and a cast of thousands, including photographers everywhere. On the inside prowled Taylor, young and full of piss and vinegar. None of the big guns knew him, and

he wanted their scalps. Go, Taylor! A nice little wave popped up. Taylor sprint-paddled against the rip to the inside slot, called off the pack, and Tom dropped in and shut the whole section down on him. Better still, he did a big backside hack off the end and got a shot run in *Surfer* magazine.

February 1998: On me, at outside Path reef at Newport Beach. By this time, we'd had many conversations revolving around the subject of drop-ins, some of them quite philosophical. "How did it ever become such a crime, sharing a wave?" mused TC, conveniently forgetting he was always the guy on the shoulder, never in the pit. "Human greed is a terrible thing." We discussed how selfish the sport had grown, how there was a duality here between the pure Greek triptych ideal of one person, one wave, one board, and the need for all surfers to learn to share as part of their spiritual growth. With these higher thoughts uppermost, we paddled together out to the outside Path reef, a massive bombing right in the 12-foot range. A colossal, perfect wave loomed only yards away from bare rock, I swung and stroked as hard as I could into its roaring silvery guts, leaped to my feet, and Tom dropped straight in from the shoulder with absolutely no conscience whatsoever.

February 2005: On Gary Elkerton, at Newport Peak. Elko totally deserves to be dropped in on, which makes this occasion so suitable for inclusion. Tom had dragged Gary, his old mate, out of the nonsurf hell of Bondi Beach to Newport in the midst of a classic Sydney easterly groundswell. Earlier that morning, he'd provoked Elko into towing him into solid six- to eight-foot ledging lefts off Newport's southern point to the massed cheers of hundreds of Newport schoolchildren who'd gathered at the other end of the beach to watch. In the afternoon, they paddled out to Newport Peak; a great set of eight-foot lefts appeared, and sure enough, on the second wave of the set, Tom dropped in on Gary, forcing him to do go-behinds all the way to the sand. I was standing on the dune watching this ride next to an old local surfer. At the end of the ride, he looked over and chuckled and said, "That was *completely predictable.*"

So, as you can see, Tom has strung together a great career of dropping in on people. And the good news for his fans is that it's far from over! I'll almost guarantee that come the age of 70, God willing, Tom Carroll will still be out there in the lineups of the globe, a bit gray, sure, a bit wobbly, naturally—but he'll be out there amongst it, and given an ounce of opportunity, he will drop in on you, too.

ART BREWER

One of surfing's finest journalists, Nick Carroll (above, left) is a former Australian amateur surfing champion and former editor of Tracks, Surfing, *and* Deep. *To the best of his knowledge, he has never dropped in on anyone.*

Tom's commitment to wave-riding goes way beyond the normal limits. It's a passion he can't control, and I guess that's what makes him fearless.

—JEFF HORNBAKER

[ABOVE LEFT] **Sunset.**
[ABOVE] **Carving a long line at Safi, Morocco.**
[LEFT] **Mentawais.**
[RIGHT] **Canary Islands training camp.**

"He's always had this ability
to make everything he does
on a wave
look deceptively simple.
—JEFF HORNBAKER

Beer o'clock in the Narrabeen carpark.

[RIGHT] **Pipeline.**

BY RANDY HILD

The Roxy Story

Roxy team on a photo shoot in Namotu, Fiji, during the Roxy Pro.

When Quiksilver started a women's line in 1990, it was a gutsy move. But the company saw the untapped women's surf market as a huge opportunity. Turns out they were right.

In 1993 Quiksilver acquired the Raisins company, where I had been vice president of sales and marketing. The surf market was just starting to rebound, and Bob McKnight was determined to diversify. The strategy at the time—and it's a strategy that still works for us—was to grow through acquisitions and brand extensions. So buying Raisins gave Quiksilver $15 million worth of business and some expertise in the women's market.

Roxy already existed—Bob and Danny Kwock started the concept in 1989—but it floundered when the surf market tanked.

Mel Matsui was already doing some denim and sportswear pieces for Roxy when I came on board. We had one sales rep, and it was pretty slow until we stumbled across the boardshorts thing. Glen Moncata, our Hawaiian sales rep had been saying for a while that he was selling a lot of boys' board-shorts to women and that Roxy should do some, but it never went anywhere. Then Bob was at the Pipe Masters in '94 with Glen and our designer, Sonia Kasparian, and suddenly these two girls walk by wearing men's boardshorts rolled down over their hips to show the thongs of their bikinis. It was very sexy, but athletic.

The timing could not have been better. Lisa won her first title that same winter—she'd been with Roxy since '92, but her star was just starting to shine. She became the face of the whole thing. Lisa just shattered the beach-babe-or-butch stereotype of women's surfing. She was beautiful. She was nice. And she ripped. Kelly Slater stayed to watch her heats. She hung with the guys. They wanted to date her; she wanted to date them. We couldn't have dreamed of a better brand image. She was— and is—one of a kind.

The retailers weren't into the boardshorts at first, but we obviously touched a nerve somewhere; girls wanted them. By '96 they were on fire, and our sportswear was growing. Lisa was well into her title run and had turned into a mainstream media sensation.

I knew in my gut—and Danny agreed with me—that in order for Roxy to become the major fashion brand that we envisioned, we had to have a presence in New York. We decided to do a vibe book for our customers and figured we could use it

Roxy guru Randy Hild.

to drum up some mainstream fashion editorial. But it was really important to us that the girls not look posed. They had to be natural, real. We had this young crew of team riders—VK, Lila, Cristiana, Sanoe, Daize—young, beautiful, fun, lots of personality. It was perfect.

We did the shoot in Hawaii. Jeff Hornbaker shot the girls in the water, and fashion photographer Dewey Nicks did the stills. Dewey had this incredible ability to capture girls in a candid, natural way. So between the two, we had this amazing juxtaposition of surf and fashion. You look at that first vibe book today and you think, oh yeah, everybody does that. But in 1996, nobody had done it yet. Nobody even saw it coming.

It was when people started to see those images that the projections started to go wild, numbers I'd never even dreamed of. I give Bob and the company huge credit here, because when they saw where we were going, the money was there to increase the marketing spend and to produce a photo shoot with fashion photographer Dewey Nicks. They're still the definitive shots, even today.

You know, we had no idea that we were doing it at the time, but we touched on this lifestyle thing that is different from the men's market. With men's, it's all about the sport of surfing and rip and tear and points and world championships. But for women's, it's about the lifestyle of being in and around the water and the beach. We managed to be the first to capture that.

So, armed with this amazing book, *Surf Girl Oahu*, we did our first runway show in New York. We did it in this tiny little showroom with this goofy little runway, and I brought six or seven quintessential Roxy girls. I made sure the editors from the teen magazines were there. We gave them all leis and pareo print bags filled with beach towels, tees and stuff. It blew their minds. *Women's Wear Daily* reported later that these editors wore their

Sofia Mulanovich, on an all-girl boat trip in the Mentawais.

World champ, 2004, receiving her title at the Roxy Pro Hawaii. Sofia became the first South American to win a world title in any sport.

leis proudly to all the other shows. The whole thing got a major buzz going for Roxy. All this was before the surf image became a major trend. It was a really new story for the fashion media at the time. It was something real for a change.

Going to New York with these tan, fit, happy, beautiful girls planted the seed. The girls were so fun, so captivating, you just couldn't help but want to be a part of it. We got a ton of coverage from it. *Seventeen* immediately asked to do an editorial with our girls. And then this surf story thing started to find its way onto the major runways. In '98-'99, Chanel did a boardshort, Dolce and Gabbana did them, Anna Sui did a Hawaiian-print pareo line. These big designers caught that buzz from our vibe book and that first seed we planted in New York.

Our first contest happened right as everything was taking off, in '95. Graham Stapelberg was at ASP at the time, and he called and convinced us to sponsor a Hawaiian event. It made perfect sense for us. We started out small, and over the years it has grown and grown and now it's the longest-running women's pro contest with a prize purse reaching $100,000.

But the contest I'm most proud of is the Roxy Pro Fiji. It was 1998, and Lisa Anderson, Rochelle Ballard, Layne Beachley

[ABOVE] **2005 world champ Chelsea Georgeson on the same boat trip.** [INSET] **Roxy's first boardshort.**

and Megan Abubo were the pack at the top of the tour. We had all become friends over the years, and I asked them what their dream was for the sport. They said they wanted their own event, because they were tired of losing audiences and waves to the men. I thought it was a great idea. It took a couple of years to find the financial support, but I'm so proud that we listened to the girls. We created a historic moment in the sport of women's surfing. Every year we take over two islands, Tavarua and Namotu, and there's this great feeling of camaraderie that the girls don't have anywhere else. It's become their favorite event, and ours too. We now sponsor four pro events and a series of regional amateur contests and camps. The core exposure is great, but what we value most about the events is our ability to support the girls and promote the sport.

As we got more confident, we moved into other markets. Snow seemed like an easy transition for us, because the lifestyle was so close to surf. This again was the late '90s. We had already expanded our apparel into outerwear. We developed some hardgoods. Roxy Europe was having a ton of success, and with such an established snow market there, they sponsored a snowboarder, Stine Brun Kjeldaas, who silver medaled in the 1998 Olympics.

We really thought it was going to be easier than it was. We showed up at the Ski Industry of America trade show that first time, in 1998, and we were laughed at. The market just wasn't having any of it. We didn't have credibility. Our hardgoods were a joke; we didn't have a real team. The lesson we learned there was that it wasn't enough to have brand recognition. So we partnered with Mervin Manufacturing to do our hardgoods, built up our team and continued to refine our outerwear offering. The end result, eight years later, is that 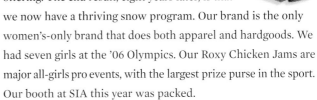 we now have a thriving snow program. Our brand is the only women's-only brand that does both apparel and hardgoods. We had seven girls at the '06 Olympics. Our Roxy Chicken Jams are major all-girls pro events, with the largest prize purse in the sport. Our booth at SIA this year was packed.

Roxy Ski is the next step in our success on the mountain. Quiksilver purchased the Rossignol company in 2005, and Roxy was the first test of the merger. Ski is an old industry whose youth market got taken over by snowboard 10 years ago. Now you're slowly seeing kids coming back into skiing, but the big traditional

[ABOVE] **Veronica features in Roxy's first ski advertising, 2005.** [FACING PAGE, CLOCKWISE FROM TOP LEFT] **Groms with leader of the pack Carissa Moore; Chelsea in the Mentawais; Heidi Drazich at the Roxy Pro Fiji; Malia Manuel; team rider Missy Gibson; snowboarder Amber Stackhouse; Veronica Kay, early days photo shoot at Newport Beach, CA; the Roxy girls.**

ski retailers don't know how to connect with them. So here we are, this strong youth brand, and we've paired it with the technical savvy of Dynastar. We've opened the door to the younger girl audience, and it's been a huge success. It all comes down to the right brand and the right product. We want to continue to build on the success of the brand, but continuing to support all of the established categories as well. We're going to expand our footwear product, continue developing Roxy Room (home décor), our line of waterproof and fashion watches, toddlers, accessories, luggage, fragrance, wetsuits, surfboards, snowboards, and the list continues to grow.

Ultimately, it's our idea of the Roxy girl that guides us. She's a high-schooler, active and inspired by the coastal and mountain lifestyle, whether she actually boards or not. We describe her as fun, alive, naturally beautiful, daring and confident. That's who the girl is. We try to let our decisions within the company be steered by the idea of this girl. We don't say surf, skate, snow specifically—we are all those—but really it's about the feeling, the casual lifestyle that happens at the beach and in the mountains.

But no matter how much we grow, our core will always be surf. Lisa's now our Global Ambassador, really nurturing the

team and representing us in the sport. We've never had stronger talent. Lisa pointed Sofia Mulanovich out to me at the U.S. Open when Sofia was only 14. She ripped. We signed her, and five years later (2004), she was the first Peruvian world champ of any sport, ever. A similar thing happened with Chelsea Georgeson. Lisa and Bruce Raymond spotted her in Avalon, just north of Sydney. She had skill beyond her years, so we signed her really young. Again, her fourth year on the pro tour and she wins the title. Right now, nobody comes close to either one of them. They'll be keeping each other busy chasing titles for a while.

There's this younger generation of girls, these "tween" girls who are unlike anything the sport has ever seen. Carissa Moore is the leader of the pack. These girls have talent that's just crazy for their age. And there are so many of them, even beyond our company. There have to be at least a dozen girls right now aged 10-14 who have world title potential. It's amazing. You look at these girls, and they have no idea where all this even came from. They're living the lifestyle, so beautiful and healthy and having fun. And really, it all started with that book, and Lisa Andersen, and Bob and Danny's vision in 1989. I think if we have anything to be proud of, it's these girls. We paved the road for their future.

ESSAY BY
JASON
BORTE

LISA IN WONDERLAND

The '90s was the decade of surfing's reinvention —from Kelly Slater's New School uprising, to hellmen towing into unimaginably mountainous waves, to the pro tour's shift from bleachers and beachbreak slopfests to Internet feeds from exotic locales.

But in terms of sheer numbers of lives affected, none of these came close to the rebirth experienced in women's surfing. After years of sitting on the beach holding their boyfriends' towels, women charged the lineup in force and turned what had become a hostile battle zone into a happening party. And the person who (unintentionally) pioneered this transformation? Lisa Andersen.

This improbable scenario was the furthest thing from Lisa's 16-year-old mind when the Ormond Beach, Florida, she-grom set out for California, leaving a note to her parents claiming, "I'm going to become world champion." She'd only been surfing for three years, and she honestly wasn't sure such a thing as "world champion" existed in women's surfing.

But Lisa knew she loved surfing, and that her parents, who blamed the sport for her late nights and poor grades, didn't. That was obvious when her dad, in a rage, dragged her board into the living room, jumped on it, and busted the fins out. Like Kelly Slater's, Lisa's was a tumultuous and broken home, and she resolved to get as far away as possible, even if it meant sleeping on floors or under piers.

Having been the lone girl on her Little League team and her school surf team, Lisa was used to competing against the boys. In California, pitted against her own gender, she flourished, running unchallenged through the National Scholastic Surfing Association, then returning to Florida to win the U.S. championships. She learned there was indeed a female world champion, and she set out to become it, turning pro and catapulting up the ranks.

Like the rest of her generation, she wanted to surf like Tom Curren. And damned if she didn't. She reeked of potential, combining feminine grace with sports-car cornering, but an inability to fully focus left her short of her goal. Great surfer, horrible competitor. She was too busy trying to show the boys she could surf to worry about heat strategy.

Women's surfing, meanwhile, was floundering. Whereas the fairer sex had enjoyed equal status in the water dating back hundreds of years in Hawaii, and was reinvigorated by the 1960s Gidget boom, a girl's role by 1990 had become nothing more than bikini filler. Power surfing was the rage, and it was hard to sell the idea of brutish chicks gouging vein-popping cutbacks. Sponsorship was scarce, and life was anything but glamorous. The best female surfers in the world were indistinguishable from the middling dude at any random beach.

In 1993, Lisa's life, and that of women's surfing, took a most radical turn. First, Lisa got pregnant. And rather than trade in her ASP card for a PTA membership, after the baby, she went straight back to work. Parenthood was a kick in the ass, providing a distraction from her distractions and sharpening her focus immediately. On the inside she was all woman, but her attire said otherwise. Bikini bottoms weren't cutting it in the heat of competition, so she donned men's trunks and felt like a clod. As the first athlete signed to promote an anemic new girls line called Roxy, she was sporting almost all Quiksilver garb. She complained, but no one listened to a lowly female surfer. So she complained some more, and this time someone listened. In search of a feminine, yet functional, pair of trunks, Lisa entered a brainstorming session with the design department and emerged with boardshorts for women. The notion of short, snug trunks was simple (Tom Carroll's been wearing 'em forever) yet revolutionary.

The fact that Lisa hit her stride at the dawn of the juniors' fashion craze was a stroke of pure luck. Here was Lisa—tanned, blonde, a genuine goddess. Motherhood became her mojo. She'd rock up in her little Roxy boardies, with baby Erica in one arm and a Merrick thruster in the other, slay the entire field, and inspire hordes of chicks to chuck their pom-poms and take to the surf. Girl power blindsided the industry and lurched it into mainstream consciousness.

For Lisa, the accolades rained down—a quartet of world championships, Surfer magazine poll wins out the wazoo, only the second woman to appear on the cover of *Surfer* in the mag's 40-year history (with the startling but accurate cover line, "Lisa Andersen surfs better than you"), named one of the "25 Most Influential Surfers" and "Top 100 Female Athletes of the 20th Century," and the only woman to appear in Activision's Kelly Slater ProSurfer video game. If that wasn't enough, Warner Brothers planned a biopic entitled Andersen in Wonderland.

Despite all of this, clearly Lisa's greatest contribution to the sport was in the precedent she set: Manly surfing could be executed with womanly elegance; hot chicks could rip! On her personal quest to prove herself to her parents, she laid the foundation for girls the world over. By the time she stepped down from competition at the end of 2002, it was a whole new world.

Talk about leaving something better than you found it, Lisa carried women's surfing from a bleak Kansas nightmare to the wonderful world of Oz. Then, since there's no place like home, she gracefully clicked her heels and was back in Florida as if it had all been a dream. With two children, a current role as Roxy global ambassador, and an off-the-top that still sends shudders through the girls on tour, she hasn't quite woken up yet.

Former pro surfer Jason Borte is the coauthor of Kelly Slater's autobiography, Pipe Dreams.

DEWEY NICKS

ROXY LIFE

When Quiksilver launched its young women's brand in 1989, there were a lot of different ideas about how to capture the girl surf market. Was it just like the guys? Could girls really surf? And what did they really want?

The answer to the first question was no. The answer to the second question was check out Lisa Andersen. The answer to the third question was girls just wanna have fun.

No one has captured the fun aspects of Roxy better than photographers Jeff Hornbaker and Dewey Nicks, and both were in top form for a series of late '90s photo shoots that helped set the tone for Roxy right around the world.

JEFF HORNBAKER

JEFF HORNBAKER

DEWEY NICKS

[ABOVE] **Left to right: Lisa Andersen, Daize Shayne, Sanoe Lake, Veronica Kay, Lila Metzger, Roxy team riders, 1998.**

[FAR LEFT] **Australian Torah Bright, Roxy's snowboarding phenom.**

[FAR LEFT] **Cristiana Janssen, one of the original Roxy girls.**

[RIGHT] **Surf team photo at the 2005 Roxy Pro Fiji.**

JEFF HORNBAKER

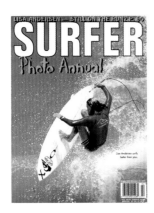

[FACING PAGE] Lisa focused.

[FAR LEFT] Lisa's landmark *Surfer* cover.

[LEFT] With the Quiksilver team at G-Land, 1997.

[BELOW] Looking for the barrel, North Shore, Hawaii.

[BOTTOM] World champion Sofia Mulanovich off the top at the Roxy Pro France.

**"When I first started shooting Lisa
she seemed to run hot and cold.
Some days she was amazing;
other days she'd fall off
just as I was about to get the shot.
Then she became so focused
it was scary,
and she became an incredible surfer,
controlled aggression
with flashes of pure brilliance.
She started to smile a lot more too.**

—JEFF HORNBAKER

DEWEY NICKS

[ABOVE] **Missy Gibson, Roxy team, 2003**

[FACING PAGE] **Daize Shayne, Makaha, 2002.**

"We were at Pipeline
when this sexy girl
and she's go
rolled down over
with her

We just looked

[TOP LEFT] **Daize Shayne, North Shore Hawaii.**

[TOP RIGHT] **Torah Bright, Lake Tahoe, 2004.**

[ABOVE] **2006 Roxy snowboard and ski team.**

[RIGHT] **Veronica Kay, Waikiki, 1996.**

[FACING PAGE TOP] **Paddling out in Fiji.**

[FACING PAGE] **Surfing Waikiki style.**

watching the contest
walks by
a pair of men's boardshorts
her hips
bathing suit thong
        up above the shorts.
t each other and went, aha!"

—BOB MCKNIGHT

PORTFOLIO

Bruce Irons had taken this wave from behind the boil in the Waimea Bay takeoff zone. It was the biggest wave of the day during the 2004 Quiksilver Eddie Aikau Big Wave Invitational. I figure the judges had already given him the perfect 100-point score that he got before he zig-zagged his way through the middle of the Bay trying to make it into the shorebreak.

From his days as a
Quiksilver marketing man
20 years ago, to his forays
around the world with
team riders, Peter "Joli"
Wilson has tracked the
fortunes of the brand.

JOLI'S TOP 10

This was shot during the filming for *All Down The Line*. Paul Witzig had lined up a red convertible for the party scenes being shot around Byron Bay. Surfers left to right, Jake Spooner, Carwyn Williams, a very young Danny Wills.

This was shot in the Bells Beach car park one Easter (around 1980) during the Quiksilver Trials and the Rip Curl Bells Beach Easter Classic. In the foreground is the late Peter Crawford, who was shooting photos for a Quiksilver ad campaign featuring the "new" Echo Beach range. Left to right, Gary Elkerton, Rabbit Bartholomew and Tom Carroll.

This shot was taken on the back deck of the Quiksilver International office at Collaroy, Sydney. Tom Carroll is signing a historic five-year, $1 million contract. This figure was unheard of in the surfing industry at the time. L to r, Tom's manager Peter Mansted, Tom, Jeff Hakman and, with camera, Tim Bonython.

This sequence redefined Pipeline surfing. I shot 12 frames as Tom ripped this snap. For more than two years during the early 2000s these originals, having been sent to a company for advertising consideration, were missing, presumed lost, before finally being found and returned to me. The company shall remain nameless!

Tug of war at the Lennox training camp. Tom was in charge of one team while Rob Rowland Smith was in charge of the other. There was always a fierce rivalry between the two for the tug of war championship. In the background of this shot is a very young Chelsea Georgeson.

This trip to Easter Island took place in June 1993. We'd spent two weeks in Tahiti before Ross Clarke-Jones, Sasha Stocker, Jake Spooner, Chad Edser and I moved further into the South Pacific to the most isolated island in the world, Rapa Nui, or better known to the world as Easter Island. We arrived during the filming of Kevin Costner's *Rapa Nui,* and when the director saw all these guys surfing the raw, powerful waves, he enlisted them as extras for the film. If you check the credits of the film, these four guys' names appear somewhere in the fine print.

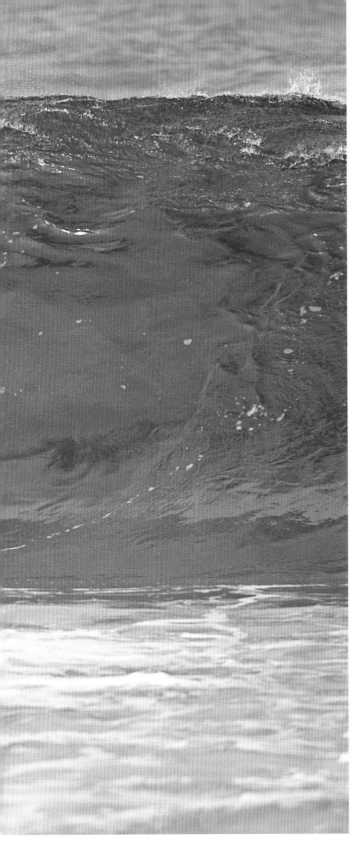

**Lisa was the first female surfer
to really get in the barrel at Off The Wall.
I know she wouldn't mind me saying this:
She had real balls out there,
just pulling in and going for it.**

—JOLI

Lisa's Thanksgiving barrel. Most of the pro surfers celebrate Thanksgiving in Hawaii due to the contest schedule. The funny thing is that, despite the quality of the surf, the lineup empties around lunchtime and will stay empty for most of the afternoon. Turkey dinner takes precedence over the waves. Mid afternoon Lisa called me and said she was going out at Off The Wall. I'd only just set up my cameras when Lisa pulled into this barrel. I fired off about 12 frames as she disappeared and reappeared a few seconds later. This tube sequence was one of the first real barrel rides recorded of a girl at Off The Wall.

Mike Newling cracked everyone up with his acceptance speech after he won the Quiksilver Trials at Bells in 1982. A big, likeable pom from Newport in Sydney, he was a powerful young surfer who gave up competing quite early to concentrate on a photography career.

Kelly's First WCT win. He had just finished high school and had joined the WCT in France at the end of the summer. The hype around him was already running high and it didn't take long for him to live up to expectations, winning the Rip Curl Pro at Hossegor.

Mini Gun

At the same time the Australians were taking surfboard design in a new direction, innovations were also coming out of Hawaii. Dick Brewer's "mini-guns"—scaled down versions of big-wave boards—were designed for the specialized art of tube-riding. Mini-guns featured racy pointed noses and radically drawn-in pintails but were also characterized by a new rail configuration. Where in the past rails had been rounded up from the bottom and later became more egg-shaped in profile, Brewer gave his design a "down" rail, very different from those that had gone before. While the early mini-guns' rails had a hard edge running almost the length of the board from tail to nose, the profile soon rounded and softened to a tucked-under edge that reduced the tendency of the board to "track" and allowed the rail to "release" making direction changes easier. Down rails quickly became the standard for all surfboards.

Lopez Bolt

Nowhere did the quest for better performing surfboards during the mid 1970s have greater impact than on surfing's embryonic international pro surfing circuit. Top-flight contest surfing has driven surfboard design ever since. Several of the first generation of top professionals were shapers themselves, supplementing their still meager prize money earnings by making surfboards and promoting their skills as craftsmen with their contest results. Two-time Pipeline Master Gerry Lopez epitomized the surfer-shaper-pro, and images of him casual and relaxed deep in the tube on his finely-tuned Lightning Bolt speed shapes have become icons of the era. The mid '70s were also notable for the realization among competitors that a broad range of sizes and shapes of boards was needed to deal with widely differing surf conditions they encountered on the circuit. Touring pros began traveling with a "quiver" of boards that would handle any type of surf likely to be served up.

Vee Bottom

For almost three decades almost all the significant advances made in surfboard design and construction had been coming from California. That all changed in 1967 When Australian surfer-shapers Bob McTavish and Nat Young came out with their wide-tailed, vee-bottomed "plastic machines," setting the stage for what would become known as "the shortboard revolution." In addition to their deep vee on the bottom in the tail area, the boards featured a major advance in fin design from George Greenough, an eccentric Californian kneeboarder living part time Down Under. His wide-based, deep, rakish, carefully tapered and foiled fiberglass fins delivered not just stability and steering but real thrust and drive, helping achieve the carving turns and pumps of speed that blew minds when they put the new design through its paces in Hawaii during the winter of '67-'68. So began a period of experimentation in design that would change surfboards dramatically.

Lynch Evolution

In the nine-foot range, the boards that fomented the shortboard revolution—the early vee bottoms and the early mini-guns—were not themselves much shorter than the average longboards of the mid '60s. But things quickly changed after their 1968 debut as average board lengths tumbled from 9′6″ into the seven-, six- and even five-foot range, before settling in the mid '70s to between 6′4″ and 7′2″. It was a time of wild creativity and experimentation energized by a proliferation of under-ground board-builders or "backyarders" and some truly innovative surfing mostly inspired by the Australian "total involve-ment" school. Nobody better represented the new style of riding in, under and around the curl of the wave than 16-year-old Wayne Lynch, who added the element of vertical surfing to the mix just for good measure. Lynch's performances on an elliptically-outlined 7′1″ board in the 1969 Paul Witzig movie Evolution set bench-marks for the new approach.

First Foam

The Chip and Pig designs represented major progress, but the supply of light-weight tropical balsa from Central America was inconsistent. Some batches were so dense they produced boards as heavy as many planks. Sometimes the wood was simply not available, every stick having been scooped up by the busiest surfboard shops of the mid '50s such as Hobie or Velzy and Jacobs. A breakthrough came in 1956 when Santa Monica surfboard maker Dave Sweet produced a surfboard blank from yet another plastic material refined in the aerospace industry—polyurethane foam. At 25-30 pounds in weight and quite durable, foam and fiberglass boards were easier to manage by surfers and easier to shape than wood, throwing open the door to vastly increased production numbers.

Noserider

Another example of how years of trial an[d] error in the shaping room and the waves le[d] to a specialized body of design knowledg[e] can be seen in mid-1960s noseriders. Surfers were obsessed with noseriding [at] the time, especially on the U.S. mainlan[d] and riding a wave while standing on the front of the board—hanging five and ten [—] had become the ultimate maneuvers in small-wave surfing. Shapers responded b[y] making boards specially adapted to mak[e] noseriding easier and to maximize time on the tip. The boards reverted to a mo[re] parallel outline and featured a wide, roun[d] nose, often with a teardrop concave are[a] on the bottom beneath it and exaggerate[d] rocker in the tail. Professional surfing's humble origins go back to 1965 when Tom Morey, later the inventor of the Boogie board, organized a timed noseridi[ng] contest that offered $1000 in cash for the winner.

The Pig

In 1954 SoCal shaper Dale Velzy came up with a design that turned the conventional wisdom about surfboards literally on its head. Velzy used the front end of a template to create an outline for the tail and the back end to create the nose, blending in the mid section to make a board with its widest point aft of center, pronounced "hips" through the back third and a narrower nose than surfers were used to. Velzy reckoned the board looked like the profile of a pig as seen from above and he named his new design accordingly. Hewn from balsa by now with an electric power-planer, fiberglassed and fitted with a large quarter-round fin, The Pig was revolutionary for its improved maneuverability. It quickly became the standard design for West Coast "hot doggers" and soon found favor in Hawaii and Australia too.

Early Guns

The surfboard industry boomed during the 1960s and as the number of experienced shapers increased—most of them expert surfers themselves—board performance progressed steadily. Surfboards became increasingly specialized for different kinds of waves and individual styles. For the giant winter waves of Hawaii, shapers made longer streamlined boards that became known as guns after big-wave hellman Buzzy Trent quipped that "you can't shoot an elephant with a BB gun." Guns, usually in the 10-12-foot range, featured pointed noses, narrow tails and plenty of heft for the paddling power needed to launch a surfer into 20- and 30-foot waves. The origin of the distinctive gun outline can be traced back to Hawaii in the mid 1930s when Fran Heath, John Kelly and Wally Froiseth cut down their planks to create the "Hot Curl" design.

A Century of

One hundred years ago the era of modern surfing began with a revival of interest in the sport on the beaches of Waikiki. Surfers of that time would have been astounded if they could have seen the equipment being ridden by today's top pro shortboard surfers—diminutive, fragile,

CLARENCE MAKI

Blackout Whaley in hot curl trim, circa 1950.

pointy-nosed "potato chip" boards of foam and fiberglass in the mid-five-foot range, weighing five to seven pounds inclusive of their three fins, and with a life expectancy of just a few months' hard surfing.

The pioneers rode varnished solid-wood, finless "planks" modeled after the pre-contact boards surfed by the ancient Hawaiians. The boards were virtually bullet-proof, but they were also hard to paddle and almost impossible to maneuver. Surfers either rode straight toward shore or took a slight angle across the wave's face by dragging a foot over the side to coax the board into a direction change. Almost a quarter of the 20th century passed before any major advances were made in design and construction and, even then, improvements in performance were hard won and slow in coming.

World War II interrupted the evolution of the surfboard as surfers and board builders in both Hawaii and California were swept up in the conflict. When they got back to work and play at the beach in the post-war years, changes came rapidly—especially in Southern California—as new space-age materials like fiberglass and polyurethane foam became commercially available just in time for surfing's first big boom in popularity during the late '50s and early '60s. Despite that, surfboard building has remained a largely hand-crafted industry ever since its earliest days.

The past 20 years has been mostly a period of refinement rather than revolution in surfboard design. In fact, the biggest changes of late have been mostly due to advanced technology in materials and construction. Shaping machines with computer numeric control and computer assisted design (CNC and CAD) software can be found in most of the high-profile surfboard shops today, resulting in more consistently accurate boards for consumers, often in the form of models exactly like those ridden by the top pros. Standard fiberglassing has begun to be challenged by

Pre-Contact

The ancient Hawaiians classified their boards according to their size and shape. Most were made from native woods, ulu, koa or wiliwili. The *alaia* were the shortest—in the seven-foot range—while *kiko'o* could be 12-16 feet and *olo* as long as 22'. Those made of the dense koa wood weighed in at a whopping 150-200 pounds. All had round noses, wide, square tails and parallel outlines. Bottoms were slightly domed with rails rounding up to flat decks. After shaping, a process that likely involved charring the wood and scraping it with stone tools in the era before Hawaiians had iron or steel blades, the raw wooden boards were saturated with kukui nut or coconut oil to waterproof them and prevent decay. With neither stabilizing fins, curve in their outline or any edge in the rails, they were probably limited to slow, rolling waves.

thermal compression lamination, with epoxy resins and a variety of hi-tech composite fabrics being used to make a more durable skin. The changes are viewed by some traditional manufacturers as a threat to the entire craft and culture of custom surfboard building, as machines and technology replace manpower and surfboard industry jobs are outsourced to plastics factories overseas.

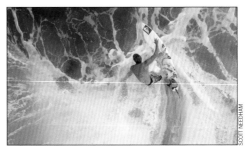

SCOTT NEEDHAM

Danny Wills airborne, circa 2000.

But for surfers themselves, there have never been more choices available for reliable boards that will deliver great performance at every level of surfing skill.

*Paul Holmes has worked as a surfboard shaper, surf magazine editor (*Tracks, Surfer*) and surfwear marketer (*Gotcha, Bear, Hang Ten*), and is the author of* Dale Velzy is Hawk, *2006 by the Croul Family Foundation.*

Surfboards

BY PAUL HOLMES

Blake Hollows

In 1926 while in Hawaii, Tom Blake, a surfer, lifeguard and champion swimmer, figured that surfboards and paddleboards would be easier to handle if they were lighter, so he drilled hundreds of holes through his 4-inch-thick olo-style board, sealed the openings with a thin sheet of wood veneer, thereby reducing its weight from 150 pounds to a mere 110. On such a board in 1928 he won the first Pacific Coast Surfing Championships. Ultimately he patented a hollow board design, made of plywood that was glued and screwed to a wood-framed skeleton. He licensed the design to several companies over the next two decades. The boards varied from 10-14 feet in length and weighed 45-85 pounds. They were notorious for leaking, forcing surfers to paddle to shore to drain them.

Malibu Chip

In the post war 1940s, fiberglass became commercially available and surfers quickly adapted the new material to board building. Fiberglass added strength as well as water-proofing so that lightweight tropical balsa could be used as a surfboard core. Santa Monica-based Joe Quigg turned out a state-of-the-art series of balsa and fiberglass boards in the late '40s that were intended for a group of young women surfers at Malibu. The boards featured added rocker, flatter bottoms, more egg-shaped rails and a larger fin or "skeg." At around nine feet, lighter and better performing, the scaled-down Malibu Chips were quickly adopted by some of the local male surfers and opened a new chapter in the way surfers rode waves characterized by pivot turns, cutbacks and noserides. The easier-to-manage boards were also much more suitable for surfing at fast-breaking beachbreaks, increasing the range of surf spots that could be successfully ridden.

Redwood Planks

By the start of the surfing revival in Hawaii, redwood imported from the West Coast began to replace koa or wiliwili as the raw material of choice for surfboards—its long, straight grain and absence of knots making it easier to shape with hand tools such as the adze, drawknife and blockplane. Varnish became the preferred method of sealing the wood. As surfing took hold in California during the early 1920s, redwood "planks" were standard equipment there too. All surfboards of this time were either self-made or passed along by the few who knew how to make them to those who had neither the skill, confidence or patience to do it themselves. In terms of design, the early redwood planks offered little in the way of improved performance and they still weighed a gut-busting 100-150 pounds.

Balsa-Redwood

California became the main center of surf-board design and construction during the 1930s. Hard-core surfers made their own boards. In addition to hollow boards, plank boards became commercially available. Pacific System Homes, a pre-fab housing manufacturer, launched its "Swastika" models in the early part of the decade. Beautifully crafted out of redwood and sugar pine (and later from redwood and balsa under the "Waikiki" label) the boards were aesthetically pleasing, varnished for a high-gloss finish and often enhanced with alternating dark-and-light strips of wood in laminated stringers, noseblocks and tail-blocks. Pete Peterson and Lorrin Harrison, noted surfers and board makers, were hired to design and shape some of the boards. But in standard 10-, 11- and 12-foot models, they were little different from most other planks of the time.

Surfboards courtesy of the Surfing Heritage Foundation, San Clemente, California.

Slater-Merrick

Nowhere were the benefits of the new era more evident than in the longstanding relationship between Santa Barbaran shaper Al Merrick and record-breaking six-time World Champion Kelly Slater. While Slater's phenomenal talent is self-evident, it was Merrick's ability to provide him with consistently superior surfboards that helped him win year after year in a wide variety of surf sizes and wave types all over the world. As a result, Merrick's Channel Islands Surfboards has become one of the most successful surfboard brands of all time, and three Slater surfboard models are now being produced using traditional methods and materials, one using the latest hi-tech Tufflite technology.

Tow-in

During the 1990s surfers found that by being towed by a 200-plus-horsepower personal watercraft they could ride waves twice as big as any that had been caught under paddling power. Soon a handful of super-fit daredevils were riding waves of 50 and 60 feet, and the quest was on to conquer a 100-foot wave. The boards used, like this of Maui's David Kalama, range from six to seven feet, are around 16 inches wide and weigh 10-20 pounds. Foot straps keep the rider attached and the heft of the board helps prevent spinning out of control when hitting surface chop at high speed

Tommy Gun

Guns became highly specialized during the 1980s, with three-finned versions of the big-wave boards adapted for specific surf spots such as Waimea Bay, Sunset Beach or Pipe and a handful of shapers making a specialty of creating finely tuned designs. Two-time World Champion Tom Carroll won the Pipeline Masters in 1990 on such a craft shaped by Pat Rawson, one of the leaders in this Hawaii-based movement toward more sophisticated and refined equipment being developed through feedback from the most accomplished surfers. It is still the model for surfboard innovation.

Andersen-Merrick

Is there any difference between boards designed for men and those ridden by women at the top echelon of pro surfing? In her winning-streak years 1994-99, Roxy team rider and four-time world champion Lisa Andersen worked with a string of the world's best shapers and rode boards borrowed from top men professionals to discover that the answer was both yes and no. Andersen settled on a design much like Kelly Slater's—narrow, thin and just under six feet long. But she also found that less rocker and a slightly wider tail helped her catch waves earlier and get more power from her turns, both key factors in her winning edge.

| 1970 | 1980 | 1990 | 2000 | 2010 |

MR Twinnie

Twin-fin surfboards were not a new concept when Mark Richards began using them on his way to four world titles starting in the late '70s. The eccentric "mad scientist" of surfboard design, Californian Bob Simmons, had put two fins on his boards fully 30 years earlier, and the "twinnie" had been just one idea explored in the creative aftermath of the shortboard revolution. But on his winged swallow-tail boards Aussie surfer-shaper Richards took twin-fin surfing to an entirely new level with swooping bottom turns, extreme cutbacks and snaps under the lip that paved the way directly to today's high-performance pro tour style.

DK Polka Dot

By the early '80s both pro tour prize money and contestants' sponsorships had grown more lucrative. As a younger generation began to eclipse the established stars, fewer of them relied on their own skills to make boards that delivered a winning edge. Instead they collaborated with proven shapers and became their test pilots—their contest results promoting the design gurus' knowledge and creativity. Increasingly, surfers developed distinctive, easily recognized color schemes for their quivers that also showcased their sponsors' logos. Rookie pro Danny Kwock's board of the time reflects both his association with shaper Lance Collins and with Quiksilver's "Echo Beach" line of boardshorts.

Hollow WAVE

Although Peter Townend was a shaper himself, he was sufficiently intrigued during 1974-75 to ride futuristic, hollow molded boards being produced in California by the innovator Karl Pope. Made with a composite skin of aluminum honeycomb and fiberglass saturated with epoxy resin, the Hollow WAVE designs were created by leading shapers such as Ben Aipa and Dick Brewer but structural flaws in the intitial production runs combined with rapid changes in mid-'70s surfboard design and high tooling costs doomed the concept about a year before Townend became the world's first professional surfing champion in 1976.

Tri-Fin Thruster

Dissatisfied with the lack of drive he was getting from single-fins and perturbed by the tendency of twin-fin boards to skitter and slide, Aussie shaper Simon Anderson designed a sleek, low–area pointy-nosed board with a wide tail featuring a cluster of three small fins. In 1981, on the new design he'd named "The Thruster," he won two world tour events in Australia plus the hugely prestigious Pipeline Masters in Hawaii. The tri-fin soon became stock equipment in nearly every top surfer's quiver and is considered to be one of the most important break-throughs in the entire history of surf-board design.

| PRE-1920 | 1930 | 1940 | 1950 | 1960 |

Quiksilver
On Wheels

Omar Hassan on his way to winning the Quiksilver Bowlrider in Marseille, one of Europe's top skate events.

Back in the mid-1980s, Quiksilver's signing of stylish skater Christian Hosoi was a first for the brand and a first for a major surfwear company. In skate's pioneer days in the 1960s and '70s, teams and events were often sponsored by surf shops (the Z Boys in Venice Beach being the classic example), but a decade or so later skate had drifted away from its surf roots and created a culture of its own. Hosoi and the young Tony Hawk helped bring it back.

As the '80s came to a close Quiksilver added another first to its growing collection, with the release of *Mondo Xtreme Experiment*, the first surf/snow/skate video. Throughout the '90s the brand increased its involvement with skate, particularly after the acquisition of snowboard company Lib Tech, which introduced a revolutionary skateboard deck in 1998. By the end of the decade (and century) Quiksilver had a growing global skate team too, featuring stars like Omar Hassan, Stefan Janoski, Dylan Rieder and Reese Forbes.

Meanwhile in Europe, skate became a major growth area for the company, particularly after the introduction of the Quiksilver Bowlrider event, held in one of the skate hotspots of Europe, Marseille in France. Usually enjoying hot, Mediterranean weather in late spring, the Bowlrider attracted huge crowds and widespread media coverage. And Quiksilver's European skate team flourished, with top riders like Marc Haziza, Javier Mendizabal, Conhuir Lynn and Daniel Cardone making their mark around the world.

When the pioneering surf/snow cross-over event, the Quik Cup in France, introduced a third element—skate—at the end of the '90s, the connection between all forms of boardriding was further underlined.

Then in 2000 came a liaison with Tony Hawk, the most successful skateboarder of all time. Quiksilver took over Tony's apparel line, Hawk Clothing, and he became a Quik team rider. Tony Hawk's impact on youth culture can never be over-stated. A generation older than the kids who idolized him and turned his PlayStation game into one of the biggest sellers of all time, the thirtysomething Hawk could appear at a celebrity poker tournament one day and open a skatepark for disadvantaged kids the next. The Peter Pan of skate, he took Quiksilver's involvement in the sport to a new level.

In the summer of that same year, 2000, Bob McKnight and Danny Kwock were approached by the two young founders

CHRIS ORTIZ

The legendary Christian Hosoi.

of DC Shoes, Ken Block and Damon Way, who wanted to gauge Quiksilver's interest in their brand. As it turned out, it was considerable, and when the acquisition was finally completed in 2004, DC became an important link to the world of skate.

The re-signing of Christian Hosoi as part of the Quiksilver legends team in 2005 was a significant recognition of how much skate history is interwoven with the brand. Writer Jamie Brisick said of Hosoi in his 2004 book, *Have Board Will Travel*: "Part animal, part athlete, and full-blown aerialist, Christian Hosoi embodied the spirit of skateboarding with a style and flair that was pure rock 'n' roll. In 1986 he set a world record with an air upwards of ten feet, and in demos, contests and free sessions Hosoi turned the world on to what skateboarding could be..." And twenty years later he was still blowing minds.

Skater Tim O'Connor says of Christian: "Christian Hosoi was my hero. I would never have imagined I'd end up on a team with this cat."

Today's Quiksilver skate team includes such riders as the above-mentioned O'Connor, himself a veteran wildman, and young hottie Dylan Rieder, of whom O'Conor says, "Dylan seems to be progressing like a mo' fo' at all types of skating. I'm a prickly bastard and I don't back too many people in the skateboard world, but I'm backing Dylan."

STREETWISE

Born of the surf culture, skate developed a life of its own in the late '70s. In the 1980s and early '90s, street moved even further away from its roots until one man brought it all back home. Tony Hawk was the *uberskater* of his generation, and a youth culture icon whose work as a Quiksilver team rider and founder of Quik affiliate Hawk can never be under-estimated.

MIKE O'MEALLY

[ABOVE] **Omar Salazar.**

[FACING PAGE] **Tony Hawk.**

[BELOW] **Danny Way.**

CHRIS ORTIZ

BLABAC

[ABOVE] **Tim O'Connor**

[BELOW] **Stefan Janoski**

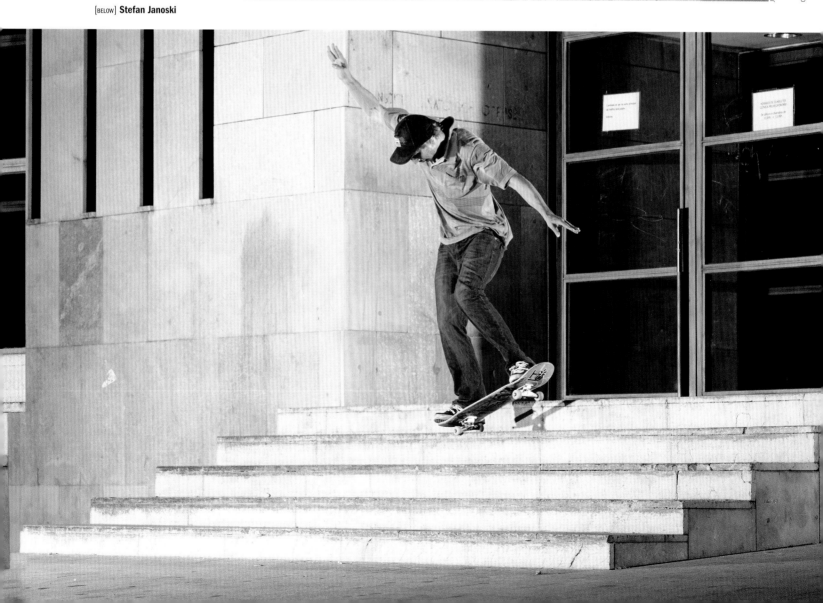

[ABOVE] **Arto Saari.**

[LEFT] **Reese Forbes.**

BY BEN MARCUS

THE WAY DYNASTY:
DANNY HUCKS THE GREAT WALL

The Great Wall of China is all about going big. Built, razed, relocated and rebuilt over 19 centuries by the Qin, Han, Sui and Ming dynasties, the Wall is a 4000-mile long defensive barrier designed to protect China's northern borders from Mongol and Turkic raiders. A long wall with an even longer history, over the centuries it had been assaulted, scaled, bombarded, breeched and burnt by everyone from Genghis Khan to a mountain biker (deceased), but no one had ever successfully jumped it without the aid of a motor.

By the early 21ST Century, Quiksilver was a juggernaut, sweeping up companies large and small and passing $1 billion in sales, with a bullet. Quiksilver had manufacturing loyalties and retail ambitions in China and wanted to thank the People and brand their brands in an unforgettable way: a thoroughly modern, very Western skateboard leap over the ancient and impenetrable Great Wall.

Skater Danny Way and the event team had the unenviable task of negotiating the minefield of government red tape and protocols. Thanks to their expertise and connections and the support of Quiksilver, Danny was able to bring the world's largest skateboard ramp to the world's largest manmade structure.

Building the Megaramp™ was no small undertaking. Sixty laborers toiled in 110° weather to turn 60,000 screws to attach 410 sheets of plywood and 200 sheets of 'Skatelite' surface panels to a frame of 4,000 joists.

The whole effort cost close to $500,000, but it created one of the Seven Wonders of the Action Sports World: the Beijing MegaRamp™

The MegaRamp™ was constructed at the Juyongguan gate, about 30 miles from Beijing. This is the most important part of the Great Wall and is the third most important cultural site in China. The Gate is an imposing fortress sitting in a steep valley by a river with sections of the Great Wall going off in all directions. In leaping over the 70-foot gap Danny would roll down the largest landing ever built to hit a 32-foot x 48-foot-wide quarter-pipe. Both new height and distance records beckoned.

To assist the TV crews making a two-hour live broadcast on the day of the event, Danny decided to do a practice run. That run almost ended his life. With almost 90-percent humidity, the air was thick and the pre-jump tension was thicker. As Danny rolled down the ramp for the first time it became clear his takeoff speed was not what he had calculated.

Losing his board off the takeoff ramp he proceeded to do what may be the longest long jump ever recorded and came crashing into a flat-top portion of the landing ramp where no one had ever anticipated he could or would hit. He landed feet first at 45 mph with a thud no one there will ever forget; he then cartwheeled to the bottom of the ramp. A small audience of crew, friends and family rushed in to find Way alive but shaken and with a broken ankle.

After all that, the jump was off, until Way had a say.

The miscalculation was caused by air density due to the intense humidity, which had slowed down Danny's airspeed to an almost fatal degree. While Danny was rushed to the hospital in Beijing he gave instructions to his team to raise the height of the roll in by about five feet and close the gap by about ten feet. Danny asked the first-rate doctors in Beijing to strap up his ankle, forget the X Ray and give him some drugs to reduce pain and swelling. The world was waiting for Danny to jump the Great Wall and, broken ankle or not, he was not about to walk away defeated.

Danny Way jumped the Great Wall of China not once but a total of five times and created what is probably the most famous image in skateboarding. Newspapers around the world carried (many on their front pages) photos of Danny front-side 360-ing over the Wall. TV news coverage was the largest ever for an action sports event. In the top 5 TV markets and nationally in the US alone coverage of the jump ran to over five hours of TV news time. In giving the Chinese TV station their largest ever audience for a live sporting event he also exposed millions of young Chinese to action sports in the most unforgettable way.

To the Chinese, jumping the Great Wall was the equivalent of going over Niagara Falls in a barrel, or BASE jumping the Lincoln Memorial. The Q was branded forever on the psyche of this imense nation as the coolest action sports brand.

[ABOVE] **Record busting Danny Way.** [OPPOSITE] **Way's Great Ollie over the Great Wall, July 9, 2005.**

MIKE BLABAC

MIKE BLABAC

Explorations

Interested onlookers watch as Troy Brooks shreds an unknown Pacific point break.

Since its very beginning, Quiksilver has always been about chasing dreams. The company founders made boardshorts to fund their surf travels in remote parts of the world. They're still doing it today.

It started out just talking business in the car on surftrips down to Johanna or up to The Ranch. Then, as soon as Quiksilver got big enough to have international meetings, they happened at surf camps in G-Land and Tavarua, with the meeting agenda set to fit in between surf sessions. Apart from what designs would sell well for the coming season, most of the meetings centered on where the next surf trip would be justified by bringing along a couple big-name team riders and a photographer and calling it marketing.

But the surf trips to exotic locations did much more than give the management surf junkies a coral reef fix; they actually helped define the brand. From the use of Tahiti as a backdrop to the introduction of Quiksilver Country back in the '70s, through the Quiksilver Crossing's incredible voyage of discovery to the radical extreme surf and snow trips of today, the adventure of travel has been the lifeblood of Quiksilver.

By the time the idea of staging major professional surfing contests in remote locations began to take form, Quiksilver had been using them as photo studios for more than a decade. Taking the pro tour to G-Land seemed like a logical extension, but even as that first thrilling event was being held, Quiksilver International's Bruce Raymond had an even bolder use of the "Trojan horse" of marketing in mind.

In 1993 he'd met a former salvage boat skipper named Martin Daly, an ebullient Aussie who had made his 75-foot, steel-hulled vessel, the *Indies Trader*, available to a few surfers to sample waves he had discovered along the Mentawai chain of islands west of Sumatra. Although Daly was horrified that having photographers on board would expose the location of the secret reef breaks he and an elite club of adventurers had found, he eventually agreed to allow Quiksilver photo shoots under strict secrecy provisions.

Daly and Raymond soon became friends, and in December 1994, while Raymond was conjuring up the G-Land Pro at the Quiksilver team house on Oahu's North Shore, Daly flew in to make a joint presentation to Quiksilver and Rip Curl. His concept, that the *Indies Trader* travel the oceans of the world

TED GRAMBEAU

Captain Martin Daly.

in search of new surf spots, and that the two brands share in the spoils, was never going to fly. Ten years earlier, it could have been considered, but the two former Siamese twins now had their own global marketing machines with separate agendas.

Disappointed, Daly flew home. But he continued to work with Quiksilver, and after the last-minute cancellation of the G-Land event in 1998, he and Raymond again discussed the idea during the long voyage across the strait from Java to Bali. By the time they reached Benoa Harbor, they had laid out a plan for the greatest surfing adventure ever and went off for a celebratory dinner at the Four Seasons Hotel. But for Bruce Raymond, the hard work was still ahead.

The sheer magnitude of the project Raymond and Daly had christened "The Crossing" made Quiksilver management nervous. They could see a major marketing cost blowout that went on and on...for an entire year in fact, for that was the audacious plan, to lease the boat and its skipper for a year and cross the equatorial Pacific in search of undiscovered surf. Both Alan Green, the chairman of the International Promotional Fund (that controlled licensees' one-percent levy), and John Law were initially against it. Bob McKnight sat on the fence until one night, as he and Daly sprawled on the roof of the *Indies Trader*, drinking rum and Cokes and watching the star-splattered Sumatran sky, Martin Daly explained his vision. Says McKnight: "What it really boiled down to was, wouldn't it be great if we could do this all the time? And Marty explained that we could. I was sold."

At the end of 1998 Bruce Raymond presented his full plan for The Quiksilver Crossing, by now a finely tuned mix of commercial and cultural objectives. Green and Law remained skeptical; the American marketing team felt it was too far away to be relevant, but The Crossing was given the green light regardless.

JEFF HORNBAKER

Tavarua global meeting.

Painted ship upon an ocean.

Martin Daly drove the *Indies Trader* down through the Indonesian archipelago to the port of Cairns at the northeastern tip of Australia, where Quiksilver artist Peter Webb directed a dazzling Polynesian motif paint job, the boat was given a complete overhaul and new satellite navigation equipment was installed. In March 1999 The Crossing began, striking out into the South Pacific to search for surf. On board were surfers, photographers, film-makers and a scientist, because, in addition to its obvious missions of finding surf and creating stunning visual images for Quiksilver, Raymond and Daly had decided to imbue The Crossing with a more serious purpose.

Bruce Raymond had been following the work of an environmental agency called Reef Check, which examined fragile coral reef systems around the world and advised on how to best protect them, so now he offered them a berth on the Crossing. Promoted around the world on extensive website pages, The Crossing's involvement in Reef Check gave it a legitimacy for study in schools and colleges, and thus began a link between Quiksilver and environmental and scientific causes that is still

JEFF HORNBAKER

Heart in mouth time—Dylan Graves.

growing today. The Crossing's other altruistic mission was to promote understanding and empathy for the various cultures that the boat passed through. Raymond had done enough surf exploring in remote places to know that the arrival of surfers could sometimes have an adverse effect on a primitive community. By treading lightly on their territory and treating them with respect, he wanted The Crossing to set an example for young surfers.

For all its lofty ideals, however, The Crossing soon revealed that it could also make its way in the commercial world. Raymond was able to demonstrate that the "floating photo shoot" produced better images at a cheaper price than many of the one-off shoots in exotic locations. And, to add even more spice to the recipe, The Crossing encompassed many side adventures, such as a seaplane surf safari in Nova Scotia. It soon became obvious to all that The Crossing could not accomplish all its goals within the allotted year. The contract was extended to three years, then five, then six.

The boat looped through the Pacific, then through Southeast Asia and into the Indian Ocean, across to South Africa,

JEFF HORNBAKER

Reef Check.

The Crossing takes to the air, Canada, 2004.

Veronica Kay barters for food in North Africa, 2002.

then through the Mediterranean to the Atlantic coast of Europe, across to Brazil, then north the length of the Americas, back down the Mississippi to the Gulf of Mexico and the Caribbean, before heading up the American west coast, then across the Pacific to finish in Hawaii in December 2005. In six-and-a-half years, the Quiksilver Crossing traveled almost 100,000 nautical miles (five times the distance around the equator), discovered more than 100 new surf breaks and carried almost 400 guests, normally eight at a time for a two-week duration. It attracted tens of millions of visitors to its website, with school students around the world following the boat's program.

While very few marketing campaigns go on forever, The Crossing managed to keep delivering on Raymond's promise because it was so much more than a marketing tool, and yet it was so simple. Wherever the boat went, it spelled out Quiksilver's authenticity and the brand's ongoing commitment to the quest of the surfer: to find the perfect wave.

The Crossing is over but the quest continues in myriad ways, with boats, planes and buses pulled into service as required. In fact, Quiksilver now has so many adventures happening around the world that it has set up Quiksilver Travel to coordinate them, and to make them available to the broader Quiksilver family.

Sam Cornish winding up in Latin America.

> "Six years and 90,000 nautical miles later, we remain driven by the mystery of what's around the next headland."
>
> —BRUCE RAYMOND

Over more than six years of its global voyage, the Quiksilver Crossing changed perceptions about where a marketing exercise began and where a lifestyle statement ended. But The Crossing has not finished, despite the fact that its official mission concluded in Hawaii in December 2005. The idea lives on, even as the boat takes a well-deserved rest. The spirit of The Crossing is the inspiration for a whole new generation of Quiksilver adventures.

JEFF

One moment can change an entire life. An event, an observation, an experience introduces us to who we are. The art of surfing cuts through this mystery somehow and we become much more intent in our personal expression. Showing this genuine freedom of spirit through images has always been one of my desires. The call of the ocean, along with the voice of your free spirit, is what separates the initiates from the mass. I encourage everyone to explore both—Ocean and Soul.

HORNBAKER'S TOP 10

If we commit ourselves, we live half our life in the ocean and half out.

Megan, Costa Rica. To me this is one of the most sensual surf shots ever taken. Raw power and feminine energy is everywhere.

The Roxy Branding was so strong it allowed for the abstract expression of surfing to be conveyed without need to hard sell anything but the truth of the moment.

Along with the re-introduction of a women's surfing movement came fun, smiles and positive vibrations. Veronica Kay was this all in one body.

Lisa, the warrior maiden, spearheaded the renaissance of women's surfing.

Being a champion does not necessarily make you a leader.
 Through the years,
  Quiksilver has nurtured several of these chosen few,
 like Tom Carroll, Kelly Slater and,
   on the feminine side, Lisa Andersen.
  By just following her dream,
   Lisa spearheaded a renaissance of women's surfing
 and became the poster child of girl power the world over.

—JEFF HORNBAKER

Much like Tom Curren, her grace speaks louder than her words.

On the road again...the cast at work and rest, sea-planing to Canada, 2004.

Rusty and Buff. The knowledge of living a life devoted to the ocean is passed on from father to son. This character radiates from them both.

Strider. Surfing is spontaneous. Those who are in the water usually are that on land as well.

BY
BEN
MARCUS

GROWING UP QUIKSILVER

Quiksilver began to bubble as a company at about the same time I started surfing. From the early '70s to the '80s I was a teenage high-school surfer, then a traveling surfer through most of the '80s, and then for 10 years I was an editor at *Surfer* magazine. So as Quiksilver evolved as a brand, so did I as a person, from grom to serious surfer to surf media scribe—from outsider to insider. And Quiksilver has been there for my ride all along, through the punky '80s, the New School '90s and into this strange, new 21ST Century.

To be honest, Quiksilver didn't initially make much of an impression on me. I was from Santa Cruz, which was at the time the land of black wetsuits and staid surfboards. All that Echo Beach jive—the neon colors and polka dots and funny haircuts—that was all SoCal style, sound and fury from the other side of the Hollister/ Bixby line. Santa Cruz clung to the puka shells and bushy bushy blonde hairdos of the '70s. North was north and south was south then, and life above the line was very different.

But the line began to dissolve in the '80s, for the surf world generally and for me personally. When I got hired at *Surfer* in 1989 I moved deep into enemy territory. It was all a strange new world, but it was at *Surfer* that I began to develop an appreciation of Quiksilver—an understanding that there was more to the brand than this year's neons or last year's polka dots, that in fact the brand encompassed a lifestyle.

From my 10 years at *Surfer* there are a million images immortalized in the media center in my brain. Photos, ads, videos, film, TV...many of them are Quiksilver's: Kelly Slater demolishing Lowers to win the PSAA contest in the '90s; Kelly eating breakfast in *Kelly Slater in Black and White*. I grew up watching movies like *Free Ride* and *Five Summer Stories* at the Santa Cruz Civic.

Surf movies were a big deal when I was a kid and that big deal began to diminish as video killed the four-wall stars. But Quiksilver stuffed all that big-screen quality into those little VHS boxes, and I appreciated that.

Judging the *Surfer* Video Awards, I watched just about everything you could buy, tried to forget most of it, but some things were unforgettable: Joel Fitzgerald getting impossibly pitted at G-land during one of the first Quiksilver events there; Lisa Anderson paddling out, smiling at the camera, then dropping in and thwacking the lip; Kelly Slater surfing eight-foot G-land as everyone did it in their imaginations—fast, beautiful, stylish; Gary Elkerton doing big, beautiful Hakman/BK fades at Sunset Beach to win a contest there.

While at *Surfer* I went to Tonga with Kelly Slater, Tom Carroll and Todd Miller. We met the King of Tonga and that was cool, but what I remember best was watching from the shoulder as the two best reef surfers in the world took apart a left in the middle of nowhere. Tom Carroll was astounding. So quick and solid, faster and more stable standing straight up in the tube than most surfers are in a full crouch. But the thing that stays with me is a dolphin move by Kelly Slater. He got caught inside a pitching

barrel, duck-dived into the tube, got sucked up to the roof of the wave, got to his feet and dropped in.

What the hell?

Lisa Anderson stayed at my apartment once. This was for the *Surfer* profile "Lisa Anderson Surfs Better Than You." Lisa was nice. She was calm. She had manners. One evening we all looked up at a funny noise and saw a skunk fighting a raccoon in my living room. Most girls would have panicked. Lisa smiled quietly to herself and went back to screwing in her fins.

The thing that sold me most on Quiksilver was that second Eddie at Waimea, in 1990. Amazing. And I wasn't even there, but I know people who were and to this day they all feel special. They saw a once-in-a-lifetime 25-foot-plus dead-solid perfect swell at Waimea being ridden by the best of the second, third and fourth generations of big-wave surfers, from Clyde Aikau to Brock Little. I saw it on video and there are a few waves from that event I'll never forget watching:

Kerry Terukina's headfirst leap from a 20-foot wave, in my mind, is second only to Jay Moriarity's disastrous wipeout at Mavericks in 1994.

Brock's barrel set the pace for a lot of monster tube-riding to come, even though he didn't make it. And there is that huge wave he didn't make—still one of the biggest waves anyone has ever paddled into. Brock achieved immortality that day, with that wave. What the world saw was sheer, unadulterated courage. Can't fake it. Can't buy it. He had the nerve to want that wave and the skills to catch it and get to his feet. Not to mention the lung capacity and the experience to survive the wipeout.

And there is a wave from that event that a lot of people have never seen and don't remember. That was Richard Schmidt's sideways fall down the face on a monster. He took off, his fins came up, he skittered sideways down the wave—parallel to the face of a 20-foot-plus wave—and then he made it. Astounding. Impossible.

Quiksilver has made it because, at the core, they're surfers, running a company that must have seemed a harebrained idea to some, once upon a time. A couple of surfers who wanted to create a business that would let them bend time to the tides, allow them to be productive without getting in the way of water time, keep them out of suits and in their wetsuits. And it has worked. Big time. They've made it beyond their wildest dreams by making a lot of our wild dreams come true.

Malibu-based freelance writer Ben Marcus was an editor at Surfer *magazine for 10 years. His book* Surfing USA *is published by Voyageur Press, and he is now working on a history of surfboards.*

In 2003 I was sent on a mission: to travel around the world, visit Quiksilver events and try to capture on film the moments and feelings that would explain the excitement, camaraderie and intense commitment that always seems to be present. The assignment was very open-ended—all I had to do was use my camera to illustrate the spirit of the places in the world of Quiksilver.

And so I packed my small bag and traveled first, of all places, to Makaha, that wonderful homeland of the surfing spirit and a location and community I already knew quite well, and more importantly for my assignment, I was known quite well too. The occasion was the Quiksilver Masters, a perfect matching of soulful surfing and the original home of international surfing and of the aloha spirit. And, of course, renewing my acquaintance with the Keaulanas and the rest of the community was a blessing in itself.

Next, I went to Australia's Gold Coast for the Quiksilver Pro, and once the event was over I took an unforgettable road trip from Noosa in the north to Ulladulla in the south. Traveling alone with my camera on the passenger seat, meeting champions and legends and just anonymous surfers in love with the life, going from the solitude of a lonely sunset in the bush to the busy streets of Sydney at night...a dream of a journey.

A YEAR IN THE LIFE

PHOTOGRAPHY AND TEXT
BY MAURICE REBEIX

Buffalo Keaulana had a visit from an old friend. It looked like the meeting of King Kamehameha and the Hemingway character from The Old Man and the Sea. This time no royal formality or literary airs, however: just smiling eyes and laughter, Makaha style.

The pride of a father, the dedication of a son. A truly Hawaiian legacy, under the swaying palms and gentle breeze of Makaha. Need I say more?

Big board, long leash, huge smile. A small kid in a gorgeous place, Noosa, where the points are perfect for longboarding and the whole family gets in on the act, from grandpas to groms, golden Gidgets to teenie wahines.

Young Quiksilver team rider Dale Richards from Coolangatta, pictured at Snapper Rocks. There are increasing numbers of Australian indigenous surfers and Dale is one of the most promising. He was a little intimidated to be photographed, but so was I to snap the beauty of a people who have struggled to survive against the cruelty of cold hearts.

In the late summer it was on to California for the Boost Mobile Pro, presented by Quiksilver. After the contest I again took to the road, meeting surfers as varied as the late and legendary Dale Velzy to rising star Dane Reynolds, from print pioneer Walter Hoffman to young radical Greyson Fletcher, and visiting everywhere from San Diego to Santa Cruz in a journey through surfing itself.

Then in the fall it was home to France for the Quiksilver Pro France, held in les Landes and the Pays Basque. And again I had to be thankful for the nature of my commission. I was free to follow my nose and eye in search of a good picture, so whether it was a night of Spanish booze with Kelly Slater, or grooving on an Indian summer evening in Guethary with Malik Joyeux, the experience was fresh and rejuvenating, as I hope my pictures show.

What is evident in all these places is that a Quiksilver event brings all kinds of people together, from the old guy who has surfed all his life, to the tiniest grom who is only just beginning his...or hers. I think there is also a spirit of Quiksilver that hangs over the place, creating those happy, smiling faces. At least that is how I see it.

This portrait of veteran surfer Rusty Miller was shot exactly where I met him—sitting on the beachfront at Byron Bay. It took about two minutes! When your story is told in your face, you don't need to pose. A former USA surfing champion, Rusty came from California to settle in this place a long time ago. Looking at his serenity, on this day I felt I wanted to do the same.

Moments from the Quiksilver Pro Gold Coast: a suite of pictures that for me shows so many emotions, whether it is joy to be competing in the event, solemn contemplation of the conditions or simple pride in one's family. From left to right: Troy Brooks, Luke Munro, Lisa Andersen, John Shimooka and family, Danny Wills.

I asked Rabbit Bartholomew if this was his home town. "Yeah, mate," he said. "Had me first beer across the street and played pinball every day just down the road."

Four-time world champion Mark Richards seemed amazed (even dubious as to my intent) that someone could be interested in taking his portrait. We went to Merewether, a beachside suburb of Newcastle. The salt-water pool behind him is where he learned to swim, and the break beyond that is where he learned to surf. Of course I had him sit on number one!

Veronica Kay knows the camera very well, and it loves her. I wanted to do some pictures that would show her how she is, relaxed and unaffected by her fame as the face of Roxy.

Greyson Thunder Fletcher in an indoor skatepark at night, looking like a Boticelli angel with a silver skull around his neck. A young man with lineage and graced with charm and manners.

A larger than life surfer, cowboy and hotrodder, the late Dale Velzy posed outside his home in San Clemente with a hotrod in the background, a Velzy Surfboards tee shirt on his back and a cowboy hat on his head.

Dane Reynolds is poised to be the next big thing in American surfing. In hometown Ventura he's just another grom on Main Street who's run out of phone minutes.

Strider and Lily Wasilewski caught in a tender moment along the Malibu shore.

After a day passed in his studio, Herbie Fletcher emerged in the late afternoon light, holding a portrait of his Cherokee grandmother in full regalia. Herbie's full regalia, on the other hand, consisted of trunks and slaps.

People who seem to have little or no interest in having their photo taken are among the best subjects to capture. On this morning, Basque surfer and rising Quiksilver executive Peyo Lizarazu was still waking up while looking at beautiful waves rolling into Hossegor. I did not give him time to react and captured him as he was. The portrait of a natural.

In this suite of photos I see the same sense of inner peace and satisfaction, despite different origins and different destinies. From left: sisters Brigitte and Maritxu Darrigrand at the family farmhouse in Bassusarry; big-wave surfer Malik Joyeux, to die tragically at Pipeline just two years later, at Guethary; waterman and surf instructor Christophe Reinhardt outside his Guethary headquarters.

Windsurfing champion Iballa Ruano Moreno resisted my lens for quite a while, with a disdain that only fiery Hispanic women can demonstrate. In the end, on the beach at Seignosse, she surrendered with a smile. A sweet victory to the photographer.

TEAM RIDERS
1990s

The 1990s was the decade of diversification for Quiksilver as an increasingly global company. Conversely it was the decade in which one team rider dominated brand exposure. The high-cost signing of 18-year-old tour rookie Kelly Slater in 1990 came after a fierce bidding war. Many thought the price was too high. Fifteen years and seven world titles later, no one thinks that any more.

But Kelly was not alone in propelling the brand through a decade of incredible growth. In fact in the mid '90s Quiksilver and its new women's offshoot, Roxy, could boast an embarrassment of champion athletes. Underpinning the men's team were twice world surfing champion Tom Carroll and multi world windsurfing champion Robby Naish, while through the decade longboarder Rusty Keaulana continued to amass world titles, and in 1998 Quiksilver surfers Kelly Slater, Mick Campbell and Danny Wills finished 1, 2 and 3 on the WCT. The hot support cast included Californian Jeff Booth, who finished a career-best fourth in the world in '95, Australia's Jake Paterson, hot young Hawaiians Andy and Bruce Irons, guitar-playing Jack Johnson, charger Strider Wasilewski, aerialists Christian and Nathan Fletcher and East Coaster Ben Bourgeois. And as the revival of big-wave riding heralded the age of tow-in surfing, Quiksilver's Ross Clarke-Jones, Peter Mel, Dave Kalama and Titus Kinimaka led the way.

Meanwhile Roxy grew on the delicate but strong shoulders of Lisa Anderson, who won four world titles in succession and staked her claim as one of the greatest women surfers of all time.

In the mountains the focus moved from skiing to the new sport of snowboarding, with star team riders Serge Vitelli in Europe and Shaun Palmer in the United States.

❂ Spencer Hargraves

Spence exploded onto the scene in 1989, winning both the British junior and men's titles, then went on to take out the European pro title three years in succession. Although his tilts at the world tour were not so successful, Spence was recognized as a power surfer of the first rank wherever he appeared. Since assuming a Quiksilver team management role at the end of the '90s, he has helped groom emerging talent.

↶ Miky Picon

One of France's most exciting surfing prospects to emerge in the '90s, goofy-footer Miky blazed through the junior ranks in Europe, but seemed to choke at the highest levels of competition. A late bloomer, Miky is finally attracting the attention he deserves a decade after his dynamic arrival.

↻ Rizal Tanjung

Born within a salt spray of Bali's fabled Uluwatu breaks, Rizal was Indonesia's top surfer of the '90s and a valuable asset as Quiksilver expanded its business in the region. A fearless tube rider, Rizal excelled at Pipeline and G-Land.

↻ Matt Hoy

Tattooed warrior from working-class Newcastle, Australia, "Hoyo" went full-on at everything—from WCT surfing (5TH in 1997) to apres-contest beer drinking marathons. A committed team man, Hoyo has tamed his wild ways since leaving the tour and works with Quiksilver's Australian promotion and staff training teams.

↑ Rusty Keaulana

Three-time world long-board champion (1993-95), Rusty is also one of the most versatile surfers alive, as he proved with consistent performances in the Quiksilver in Memory of Eddie Aikau (including 5TH in '99). Son of Makaha legend Buffalo and younger brother of waterman Brian, Rusty was one of Quiksilver's leading ambassadors in the '90s.

COURTESY NA PALI

⌃ Serge Vitelli

The godfather of French snowboarding, easy-going Serge joined Quiksilver as the lone snowboarder in the Black Diamond ski team. After competing on the inaugural Quik Cup surf/snow events in France, he gave up competition to concentrate on the development of snow equipment for Q-Stix, and on glacier boarding adventures.

➔ Veronica Kay

"VK" may have been "Miss Seventeen" and the face of Roxy for nearly a decade, but it's worth remembering that she was a team rider and a damn hot surfer before that! A stylish shortboard competitor in the mid-'90s, VK soon became a fully-rounded waterwoman, longboarding and canoeing for the cameras, and starring in many *Crossing* adventures.

COURTESY ASP

HANK

⌃ Danny Wills

"Willsy" emerged as a child prodigy in the 1989 Quiksilver-sponsored movie *All Down The Line* and in the '90s became one of our most consistent WCT performers, threatening to steal a world title from Kelly Slater in '98 until an exciting Pipeline showdown. Danny remains a tour standout.

⚲ Strider Wasilewski

Hard-charging Strider has been a leading light of the Quiksilver surf team for a decade now, and he's still charging! The goofy foot powerhouse has put together some of the most exciting sessions at Pipe and Teahupoo in recent years, giving the photographers plenty to smile about.

HANK

JEFF HORNBAKER

⚲ Nathan Fletcher

While older brother Christian was surfing's most radical aerialist of the '90s, and one of its most controversial personalities, Nathan soon emerged from his shadow and proved to be a truly exciting surfer, snowboarder and skater.

⚳ Jack Johnson

Before he dominated the air waves with his surf-based funk, Jack was a red-hot surfer on the North Shore, making the finals of the Pipe Masters trials in '92. Part of a surfing dynasty, Jack is still in the Quiksilver family, in recent years joining friend Kelly Slater on The Crossing.

THE TEAM

Australia
Tom Carroll

Ross Clarke-Jones

Wayne Lynch

Gary Elkerton

Danny Wills

Mick Campbell

Dave MacAulay

Matt Hoy

Sasha Stocker

Shaun Brooks

Kate Scarratt

USA
Kelly Slater

Jeff Booth

Andy Irons

Bruce Irons

Shaun Briley

Miles Padaca

Timmy Reyes

Braden Dias

Jon Rose

Lisa Anderson

Megan Abubo

Daize Shayne

Tim Curren

Scott Farnsworth

Johnny Boy Gomes

Brock Little

Veronica Kay

Ben Bourgeois

Peter Mel

Shaun Palmer

Todd Proffit

Omar Hassan

Dave Kalama

Rusty Keaulana

Bonga Perkins

Keoni Watson

Christian Fletcher

Todd Morcom

Taj Burrows

Darrick Doerner

Europe
Miky Picon

Serge Vitelli

Peyo Lizarazu

Spencer Hargraves

Miki Dora

Gabe Davies

Markku Koski

Stine Brun Kjeldaas

Antoine Albeau

Robert Teritehau

Iballa and Daida Moreno

Fred Robin

Candide Thovex

ESSAY BY JASON BORTE

KELLY SLATER SEES THROUGH WALLS

Have you ever had a conversation with a dog?

Obviously it would be one-sided, but Rover is enraptured nonetheless. He sits stock still, his head tilted to one side. In his struggle to translate your words into woofs and barks, his eyes rummage through your soul, practically turning it upside down and shaking its contents onto the floor.

Kelly Slater has those eyes. When you're telling him something, he gets that same look. Only Kelly is far more advanced than some mangy mutt. He speaks our language, and he'll probe until he gets precisely what it is you're saying. He doesn't strap some concoction to your head that sucks the thoughts from your brain, like aliens do in movies. His methods are more sophisticated. He probes and prods until he's satisfied. And when it comes to grasping the intricacies of standing atop a wave on a slab of foam and fiberglass and putting himself in positions no human could imagine, he's not too bad either.

Truth be told, the best person to ever ride a surfboard is human. He's insecure, he's balding, he failed as a rock star, and he still gets zits. But his ability to tune into the radio station that is surfing, while the rest of us get mostly static, is extraordinary.

Our mind-surfing fantasies are his everyday labors. Is it learnable? Is it explainable? Is it fair? No, dammit!

But beware what you wish for, for being Kelly is no day at the beach. Unfathomable pressure is heaped upon every wave choice, every pump down the line, every turn. It's no wonder he invents outrageous flips and spins, at least then it's OK if he falls. Sign this. Pose for this. Say something about this. Show up for this. Wear this. Stand right there. Put your arms around her. Wait a minute. Let me get this lens cap off. How does this stupid thing work? OK, now smile.

Believe it or not, all that outside pressure, it's nothing to Kelly. He never set out to please anyone but the man in the mirror. He sought perfection because it was all he could do to avoid his demons.

Alcoholic parent. Overbearing brother. Broken family. Crap waves. Little money. Fear of reef poundings. Endless doubters. Public scrutiny. Jealousy. Leeches. Like anyone else would've done, Kelly hibernated. Thankfully, though, he didn't run. He chose a drug as his refuge, a drug called surfing. All his troubles, rather than being hindrances, were converted to fuel—superpowered turbo freaking jet fuel. Here was a hurt kid who managed to avoid the lure of the dark side, with a burning desire to use his supernatural talent for good. He donned his blinders and refused to be stopped.

From his eyes came a laser focus that allowed him to dissect the sport like no one before him. He became a mad surfing scientist, breaking it down, studying every frame, and figuring out how to do it better. He wasn't content to be the next Carroll, Pottz, or Curren, but the amalgamation of all who came before him, and more. The secret, of all things, was golf. He turned to this tirelessly analyzed act for guidance. You just stand over the ball and swing toward the hole, right? Hah! And you think surfing is as simple as hopping up on a board and ripping.

Kelly devoted his entire existence to riding waves perfectly, from the moment his hands hit the water until he stepped foot back on the beach. He became...well, he became Kelly Slater. The international mug of surfing. Seven-time world champion. Indestructible, indefatigable, almost inhuman. Almost.

Throughout his reign, Kelly has worn nothing but his best face before an audience. He became the greatest for himself, but he never forgot that his success was tied to that of the sport. Could it be merely coincidence that in 1992, the year of his first world title, surfing was languishing in its own neon-infused hangover? As Kelly's star grew, so did that of the industry, the activity, and the game itself.

Everyone questioned Kelly's motives when he showed up on *Baywatch*, but in hindsight it wasn't him being pulled into the mainstream as much as him pulling the mainstream into surfing. For as much as he likes to hang with famous actors, musicians, and prime-time athletes, he's still one of the boys. Highfalutin' he ain't. He's from Cocoa Beach, for goodness sake. No matter how many trophies crowd his mantel, or how many zeros adorn his bank account, he remains a Southern gentleman, just a good old boy, never meanin' no harm, as the song goes.

Even as he was light years ahead of his peers, he didn't think, or act like, he was better than any of them, or any of us. Trash talk and end-zone dances never made it into his repertoire. It's all about competition. Doesn't matter if you're a Yank or Aussie, black or white, old or young, goofy or regular. Kelly craves a challenge. Always has, ever since his big brother beat him to the front seat of the car. In the heat of battle, those disarming eyes fill with fire. Not aimed at his opponent, but at himself, to perform, lifting the entire pursuit as a result.

History will count Kelly among our greatest ambassadors because he refused to acknowledge any lines. He isn't a Floridian, or an American, or a New Schooler, or even merely a surfer. He is a human, a superior one because he asks questions and finds answers. Upon mastering the fundamentals of riding waves, which took the five-year-old prodigy perhaps all of a single, scorching Florida afternoon, he immediately began to wonder where else he could take it. Why can't I go faster? Why can't I slide it all the way around? Why do I have to grab my rail when I pull in? Why can't I win the title my first year out? Why not high-five my opponent in the biggest heat of my life? Why can't surfing be analyzed the way golf is? Why shouldn't I break every record there ever was? Not only did his futuristic method rocket us into the new millennium, but he vehemently squashed the stereotype of surfer as space cadet. Nearly a century after Duke Kahanamoku took surfing public, Kelly did it again. But he's not happy to merely journey outside the boundaries. He lives there.

Jason Borte is a freelance writer and the coauthor of Kelly Slater's autobiography, Pipe Dreams. *He is also a former pro surfer and a friend of Kelly's, which explains how he can get away with comparing him to a dog.*

OUTSIDE
THE BOUNDARIES

Scenes from Kelly Slater's world

"Is he the most
Not really—
doesn't try to surf
What's the point?
But does he
against which all
and of what is
regardless of how

nfluential (surfer)?
the greater surfing world
Like he does or even be like him.

set the standard
other surfers are measured,
possible,
you surf, and what and where?
Absolutely."

—SURFER MAGAZINE, 2002

"When I was a kid I had this idea that every wave
could be ridden perfectly for what the wave is...
Your body positioning has to be right,
you need the right equipment and
you have to approach it with the right speed.
There is a perfect line for every wave out there;
it's all about trying to tap into that."

—KELLY SLATER, *WATER* MAGAZINE

JEFF HORNBAKER

"Slater is the best
        bodysurfer in the
                world today.
He just happens to
    bodysurf standing up."
—SURFER MAGAZINE, 2002

BY BOB MCKNIGHT

QUIKSILVER NOW

A snapshot of Quiksilver today

Quiksilver Rossignol will finish 2006 as a $2.5 billion company with 20 brands—Quiksilver being the biggest, followed by Roxy, Rossignol, DC Shoes and Cleveland Golf. We have about 7,500 employees spread over our five major headquarters—Huntington Beach, California; Saint Jean de Luz, France; Torquay, Australia; Rossignol in Voiron, France; and our sourcing center in Hong Kong—and our offices in Brazil, Japan, London, New York and South Africa, and our retail stores around the world.

Our company has a 35% market share in board sports and a 45% share in snow sports. We have close to 500 retail stores from Tokyo to Sydney, from New York to London, from Paris to Moscow, a network that accounts for more than 18% of our sales. We make 85 million garments and 2 million skis and snowboards a year.

How the company operates

We're set up in three time zones—the Americas, Europe and South Africa, Australia and Asia Pacific—managed from Huntington Beach, Saint Jean de Luz and Torquay respectively. Each has its own president—Marty Samuels in the Americas, Pierre Agnes in Europe and Clive Fitts in Asia Pacific—and key players under him. Each has its own management and shares in global resources for sourcing, logistics, finance and big-picture management. Zone management reports to its president, who reports to global president Bernard Mariette, who reports to me.

At Huntington Beach we also have our global management team, headed by Bernard and myself and including chief financial officer Steve Brink, business and legal affairs head Charlie Exon, and Roxy head Steve Tully. Sydney-based Quiksilver International now focuses on global marketing initiatives and the management of our global athletes, such as Kelly Slater. Finally, Quiksilver Entertainment is represented in all three zones, with direction and policy decisions being made by global management.

How the CEO operates

Managing any large company is difficult, but one with a global reach like ours is a real challenge. One thing that I regard as essential is that we foster an *esprit de corps* that matches the values of the brand but that is also efficient. I want people to be able to walk into any of our offices around the world and feel this friendly vibe, this sense of fun, the feel of a little family company wrapped around a core of energy and discipline that can deal with the business of business.

As Alan Green used to always tell me, we're in the fun business. We make stuff for people who want to hang out in the outdoors with smiles on their faces. With those dual objectives in mind—fun and efficiency—we really encourage individual growth within the company. We encourage people to be innovative and to take risks, and we reward them for their accomplishments. My door is always open. I want people to feel comfortable coming in and giving me their input, whether they're warehousemen or managers.

I used to have a sign on my door that said "Director of Groovology," and I still feel that's my role. Keeping your team feeling good about what they do is the number one job of any CEO. My personal style might be the opposite of what you'd find in any book ever written about being a CEO, but it works for me and it's

worked for Quiksilver. And looking after your people goes beyond their salary packages. It's about listening to their problems and trying to help them through them.

I also believe in pushing authority down and sideways. I believe that people have to be allowed to grow in their jobs, to make decisions and to make mistakes and learn from them. And I want the best people we can get to work for our brands. We pay them well; we give them plenty of free time, but we expect efficiency and we expect results.

What it means to work at Quiksilver

Working at Quiksilver means parking your ego at the door. No individual is ever solely responsible for our successes. Each of us needs to wake up in the morning, look in the mirror, remember who we are, then come in here and kick ass as part of a team.

We have always had entrepreneurs within Quiksilver who have helped create what we have today, but we've also learned that entrepreneurs alone cannot run a multi-billion-dollar company. We've learned that we need professionals working alongside them.

We need our people to stay relevant to the market. That means going to the beach or the snow, visiting schools and colleges, listening to new music, reading magazines, visiting websites, watching youth channels, staying in touch. Many decisions we make need a broad range of views from people with their eyes and ears open to what's happening in our market.

The board sports industry

This is now a $5 billion-plus industry, a lifestyle that is here to stay. Everyone loves the beach and the mountains, being outside and having fun. Half the world lives at the beach, the other half wants to. The industry is focused on real board sports athletes, young and old, male and female. These days kids wear the uniforms of board sports year round, every day, all day. The clothes they wear to school or out at night exude board sports. It's in their DNA.

We're in the fun business, and that's why even our old managers are young at heart. No one gets tired of his job. We all live and work a lifestyle that is constantly rejuvenating us.

Where are we going?

To the outdoor market. We want to be the number one company in the outdoor world with a multi-brand, multi-demographic attack. We believe that each of our brands needs to stand on its own with its own mission. As each one grows to maturity it gets consumer permission to extend itself, like Roxy doing perfume or Roxy Room. That's what getting big but staying cool is all about. We're a global brand because of the way we've developed, the way we grew up simultaneously around the world. We've been incubated by small, core companies. And in each place we are locals. In Australia we're an Australian brand, in Europe we're European, in America we're American. And Rossignol has the same history.

Together as Quiksilver Rossignol we are the market leader in the $45 billion outdoor market that encompasses individual sports and adventure in the natural environment, and we are poised to become in that exciting market what Nike is to traditional team or stadium sports. It's a thrilling ride and it's only just beginning.

ART BREWER

Salts and Suits

The first time I went to Quiksilver I wore a hot pink Gotcha shirt. It was 1991, and like the 10 or 15 other lawyers, accountants and investment bankers assembled in the boardroom ("suits" as the author of this book would say) I had been invited to the Costa Mesa headquarters to meet with Bob McKnight and his management team to discuss Quiksilver's pending acquisition of Na Pali (Quiksilver Europe). This was still the era when professionals always wore a suit and tie, but I, like the other suits in the room, had been given the word that it would not be cool to wear a suit to hip, laidback Quiksilver.

Duly warned, I had fished around and found a Gotcha neon woven that my kids had gotten me. The meeting at Quiksilver was typical M & A (mergers and acquisition) talk, but I noted that Bob, for all his easy-going diffidence and charm, was asking some very suit-like and probing questions about the proposed deal. Maybe it was my imagination, but Bob also seemed bemused by the room full of dressed-down suits. For the next 10 years as I served as outside corporate counsel (I joined the Company in 2000), I always wore a suit to Quiksilver. Even in the late '90s when my law firm had gone to the dress-down look, my partners couldn't believe that I would actually dress-up to go to Quiksilver, of all places. I just knew that Bob wasn't interested in how cool I was. Bob was looking to me to be the best suit I could be.

That 1991 meeting led to my traveling to France several times over the next year as we structured and completed the Na Pali acquisition. After that, the "dealmobile" as Bob called our transaction team, passed through Southern California (Raisins—1993), Sydney and Torquay, Australia (Quiksilver International—2000), Torquay and Tokyo (Ug Manufacturing —2001), Park City, Utah (Quiksilver Factory Outlet Stores—2000), Vista, California (DC Shoes—2004) and Voiron and Paris, France (Rossignol—2005). The dealmobile could also accurately be called the "suitmobile" because it's dominated by the suits of Quiksilver—inside and outside the company—strategizing, creating financial models, structuring, negotiating, and closing the deals. Normal stuff, but working for Quiksilver, in general, and in the dealmobile, in particular, is always challenging, complicated and forever fun.

When Bob McKnight asked me to join Quiksilver, he was very direct. "What I like about you is that you know how to get things done with a bouquet of roses, instead of an axe and a pair of pliers." Bob's dad had made the "bouquet of roses" approach part of his business philosophy, and it's obvious that Quiksilver has come to reflect that philosophy—do your job, but do it by convincing, not commanding people. Of course, when Bob hired me, he was undoubtedly telling me he wanted me to be careful about my lawyer's tendency to talk too loud and lecture, but I think Bob was also telling me that he was happy that I did have an axe and a pair of pliers in my repertoire, because without that the bouquet of roses is almost meaningless.

The most important asset Quiksilver has to protect is our brands, and that starts with trademark protection. As of 2006, Quiksilver Rossignol has over 10,000 trademark registrations of our principal brands in over 100 countries around the world. These trademark filings require continuous monitoring. Disputes and conflicts are inevitable. Some result from straightforward bad people who counterfeit our trademarks and products and pass them off as ours. For these people, you need the axe and pair of pliers.

There are also bona fide disputes with bona fide adversaries. In 1999, the Mercury Marine division of Brunswick began selling "Quicksilver" (with a "c") apparel in its marina-located boating stores primarily in the Midwest (but, potentially, all over the world). Brunswick honestly thought that it should be no big deal that Mercury Marine sell some "Quicksilver" boating apparel in Fond du Lac, Wisconsin. How could that hurt surf-oriented, California-based Quiksilver? From our perspective, if Brunswick could sell "Quicksilver" in Fond du Lac, what was to stop them from selling Quicksilver in all of our territories. At the time, (1999) we were a $100 million company (compared with Brunswick's $4 billion plus), but we had to fight.

After a few months of litigating, though, Bob and I sat down with the Brunswick legal team and honestly convinced them of our justifiable concerns. After a bouquet of roses meeting, we ended the lawsuit and came to an agreement covering the world in all the classes of our respective products.

In August of 2005, Quiksilver closed the acquisition of the Rossignol Group, completing the evolution of Quiksilver from a surfing company to an outdoor company. This evolution is marked by the superstars of the Quiksilver business, Alan Green, Bob McKnight and Bernard Mariette, a trio of larger-than-life figures in our company's history that I like to think of as Quiksilver's Mount Rushmore.

The legend of Greeny was around well before I got to know Quiksilver in the late '80s. I had heard all the Greeny stories, but it was obvious that Bob had more respect for Alan than anyone else. Greeny was clearly Bob's mentor, albeit a wild one.

Charlie (right) with Quiksilver founder Alan Green.

But during the negotiations for the acquisition of Quiksilver International I didn't see the wild side. I saw a sophisticated and shrewd negotiator who (along with John Law) was tough, but straightforward in getting the best deal he could for his family and partners, while encouraging the deal to happen because he knew it was the best thing for his brand.

I think only Bob McKnight could have managed the growth of Quiksilver into the New York Stock Exchange global powerhouse that it is today. Bob's business philosophy and success is founded upon his ability to listen to and manage a multitude of people and points of view (Quiksilver's global legacy!) and make tough decisions that always reflect his commitment to Quiksilver and our shareholders.

The third person on Quiksilver's Mt. Rushmore is Bernard Mariette. Bernard was the guiding light in Europe in the second half of the '90s, working with founder Harry Hodge to grow Quiksilver Europe from a small surf brand in southwest France to the leading lifestyle brand throughout Europe. During that time, Bernard was also quietly cultivating a relationship with Laurent Boix-Vives, the iconic head of the Rossignol ski business in the French Alps. Bernard had come to realize that for Quiksilver to continue to grow, we had to grow our pond from the $4 billion surf industry to the $50 billion dollar outdoor market where we could develop a global lifestyle brand. While Mr. Boix-Vives courted Bernard as a future Rossignol chief executive, Bernard fantasized about the possibility of Quiksilver acquiring the French "Nike." Over the years the fantasy became reality. Quiksilver Europe's annual sales went from $100 million to nearly a billion, while Rossignol's stagnated at $500 million. With Bernard's persistent assurances, Mr. Boix-Vives began to share the vision of a Quiksilver/Rossignol leading the global outdoor market.

When Bernard first came to the States to become president of the company, there were doubters. How is this French guy going to pull this off? How? By asserting his leadership through his intelligence and charisma. Alternatively, challenging and charming, Bernard is a confident natural leader. The Rossignol deal is still filled with challenges and hard work, but the good part for me is that I get to be part of the Bernard show and watch the transformation of that great old brand into a great new re-energized brand. —Charlie Exon, *Huntington Beach, CA, June 2006*

It's All About the Team

The first time that I ever heard of Quiksilver was in 1977. I had moved from Brooklyn, New York to the San Francisco Bay area in 1972 and surfing to me (like millions of other "kooks" in the US) meant the Beach Boys, Gidget and Moondoggie. I was working as a buyer at Mervyn's and my boss gave me responsibility for the surf category. We were a large—if not the largest—customer for brands like Ocean Pacific (Op), Hang Ten, Hobie and Lightning Bolt so I really thought I knew what was going on. My boss had grown up in Southern California and he said to me: "The stuff we carry is okay, but if you really want to know what's cool, then check out the surf shops in Southern California; Quiksilver is cool!"

In 1986 I moved from Mervyn's to a chain of stores in Southern California called Miller's Outpost. There I became general merchandise manager. We had over 300 stores and Quiksilver, which had just gone public, was letting us carry their products in 11 of them. The guy who was selling us Quiksilver was a soft spoken surfer named Tom Holbrook. I couldn't understand why he would only sell us in 11 stores; every other supplier we were dealing with was begging to get as much business as possible. Tom attempted to educate me about the sensitivities of the surf industry and the "core" shops. It all seemed a little strange to me, but we tried to be understanding and Tom urged us to be patient. Quiksilver wouldn't let us carry any boardshorts and I always found it a little funny that while Tom assured me that he was showing us the rest of the product line, every season I would find a whole lot of cool stuff in the surf shops that somehow we had never seen.

In 1988, besides Tom, we began to work with the new national sales manager, Steve Tully and eventually our patience paid off and we were allowed to carry Quiksilver in all of our stores. We became one of their largest customers. During those days I met Bob McKnight, John Warner, Randy Herrel and many other Quiksilver folks. I have to admit, I was a bit envious that they always seemed to be having more fun than other people I knew in the business. I remember really being impressed with Bob when he found out from Tom Holbrook that I was a big Oakland Athletics baseball fan and presented me with an autographed Reggie Jackson baseball. Bob wasn't just a surfer, he loved sports and athletes. I had a little different experience the first time I visited Quiksilver's head office in Costa Mesa. Tom had invited me many times and I was excited to finally see the place where all the cool stuff happened. He took me around and introduced me to people like Charles Crowe and Randy Hunt who received me the way a big customer would expect. I was a little shocked when I met the head marketing guy, Danny Kwock. It seemed like he could barely stand shaking my hand and mumbling hello, like he couldn't wait to get rid of me. I guess I was just the "kook" from Miller's Outpost. Oh well!

By 1996 I was working for No Fear in Carlsbad, California, and while it had grown four-fold in sales on my watch, I was becoming disillusioned. Then, the best thing that ever happened to me in my business life occurred. I received a phone call inquiring about my interest in interviewing for the job of executive vice president of sales and national marketing for Quiksilver. I felt like I had just won the lottery, but I tried not to let on how excited I was.

I began working in Costa Mesa headquarters on December 30, 1996. While I knew some of the guys—Tom Holbrook was now VP of Quiksilver sales and Steve Tully was EVP of the women's swimwear business Raisins—there were many new people to get to know and much to learn. Probably the guy who helped me most, besides Bob, was the guy who had given me the "stink-eye" back in the '80s, VP of core marketing, Danny Kwock. D.K. would spend hours showing me the history and culture of Quiksilver and surfing, and no one can talk story better than Danny. He shared his passion and his knowledge and taught me about marketing to the "core." I owe D.K. a lot for helping me to fit in and I will always be grateful and value his advice and friendship. Quiksilver was a family and even though the sports that we were part of were all about individual effort, Bob had created a work environment that was all about teamwork. I really felt like I had found a home.

During 1997 we realized that surfing and the boardsports lifestyle were really starting to explode. Roxy grew from $12 million to $28 million that year led by Randy Hild, head of sales and marketing and his team. We felt there was an opportunity to grow faster than Bob's existing plan to double sales in five years if we got more aggressive with marketing, product and inventory. We code named the project "ER", which stood for Early Retirement if it worked and Emergency Room if it didn't. With Bernard Mariette and Harry Hodge rocking with Na Pali in Europe, our company grew sales and earnings

Bernard Mariette, Bob McKnight and regional presidents Pierre Agnes (Europe) and Marty Samuels (Americas), Waimea Bay, 2006.

in 1998 and 1999 by 40 percent. We doubled the size of the company in two-and-a-half years instead of five. By the way, nobody retired early; we were having too much fun.

In 1999, we bought Hawk Clothing from Tony Hawk and his siblings and signed Tony to a Quiksilver sponsorship. We were now getting serious about not just surfing and snowboarding but skateboarding as well. The Internet was starting to impact our world and things were getting more competitive, complex and challenging, but we were still achieving our goals and making quarters and keeping Wall Street happy. Then, in the middle of our fourth quarter of fiscal 2001, something happened that would change our business and our lives forever—9/11. Needless to say, we were in shock both professionally and personally. Bob and the board of directors decided that the Office of the President—a management decision-making committee instigated in 1997—was no longer an effective way to manage the business (it hurt at the time, but they were right), and Bernard Mariette became global president of Quiksilver, Inc.

Together, Bernard and Bob restructured the way the company was managed. Steve Tully became president of women's, I became president of Quiksilver men's and retail, Bill Bussiere became CFO and Greg Ziegler COO for the Americas. The four of us formed the Americas Executive Committee, reporting to Bernard, and under his leadership the business recovered well in 2002 and we all began to understand Bernard's strategy to globalize the business. In August 2003, Carol Christopherson became president of Quiksilver retail for the Americas and joined the Executive Committee.

There is no doubt that our company is blessed with great brands, great products, great marketing, great athletes, great events and a great lifestyle. But it is the people, "the team" here in the Americas and around the world that really makes it happen. When I joined Quiksilver in 1996 I was lucky to be surrounded by a great team. Tom Holbrook, Randy Hild, Pat DeRush, Tunia Kaawa, Gregg Solomon, Rick Kuhn, John Mills, Vicki Redding, Mark Daly, Greg Macias, Steve Jones, Glen & Meredith Moncata, Rick Banta, Willy Morris, Sandy Schwarzenbach and literally hundreds of others were all here and they still are. Our roots run deep, this is not a job, this is our family. We may not always agree, we may even yell and fight, but it works when you know that your family has your back.

—Marty Samuels, *Huntington Beach, CA, June 2006*

PORTFOLIO

Raimana Van Bastolaer, Teahupoo

Strider Wasilewski, Pipeline.

It's a cliché of course, but as far as Hank (Brian Stephen) is concerned, a photo really is worth a thousand words. Hawaii-based Hank Foto is a thriving business and Brian doesn't get much time to do anything other than keep Quiksilver and other clients supplied with stunning imagery. So we decided to just let the pictures do the talking.

Cheyne Magnussen, boardshorts ad shoot.

HANK'S TOP 10

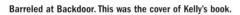

Barreled at Backdoor. This was the cover of Kelly's book.

Coupla champs. Kelly and Rabbit Kekai.

Kelly being Kelly.

Marvin Foster [ABOVE AND RIGHT] and Mickey Neilsen [BELOW],
Quiksilver's leading Hawaiian chargers in the late '80s, early '90s.

Nathan Fletcher and a sunlit baby barrel.

Peace, bro'.

Europe, The Melting Pot

From its beginnings more than 20 years ago, Quiksilver Europe has always been a melting pot, a subtle blend of personalities and nationalities reflecting the image of its founders, Harry Hodge (Australia), Brigitte Darrigrand (France), Jeff Hakman (USA), and John Winship (South Africa.) There have been many changes since then, but the elements that compose Quiksilver Europe's heart and soul are still there: variety of experience, cultural diversity, a passion for our sports...these are what make Quiksilver Europe unique and permit it to continue to grow while maintaining the passion and authenticity of its origins.

At the start, few people would have bet on Quiksilver's success, but they weren't taking into account Harry Hodge and his energy and product instinct. Together with his team, Harry fought to give surf credibility in Europe and to demonstrate that it was a worthwhile activity. It is often said that bankers lend only to the rich. But in 1984 a French banker took the risk of following this little company and of financing its growth. Today the company comprises 1700 employees in Europe.

Following the pioneering work of the initial decade, Bernard Mariette became the head of the company. To say that his vision brought a true business sense to the enterprise would be a huge understatement: Bernard encouraged the blend of the business and surf cultures, surrounded himself with strongly performing teams, and expanded the vision of the brand, thanks to some major initiatives, such as the signing of partnerships, the creation of a true retail presence and the development of women's products. And, backed by the mothership of Quiksilver, Inc., where Bob McKnight held steadfast to the brand's boardriding core, Bernard was given complete freedom to execute his vision.

Pierre Agnes

COURTESY NA PALI

The foundations set in place during the '90s are enabling Quiksilver Europe to remain innovative in comparison to its competitors, as it negotiates its mutation from small Basque country surf company to leader in the boardriding sports. One of the most celebrated examples of Quiksilver's policies from this period remains the opening of the Quiksilver Boardrider's Club along the prestigious Champs Elysées in Paris. People said it was crazy, but Bernard motivated everyone, including the American team, to take the necessary steps. It was a matter of vibrantly displaying Quiksilver's colors in a place no one had ever expected. This became the point of departure in the image transformation from surf brand into true lifestyle brand, a lifestyle attractive to city-dwellers and not exclusively to surfers. For a long time the Boardrider's Club on the Champs Elysées was the largest Quiksilver store in the world, although it has now been displaced by the Times Square store in New York, inaugurated after Bernard's arrival in the USA as President of the Quiksilver Group.

Another characteristic of Quiksilver Europe is its spirit of innovation and creativity, a reality that concerns not only product creation, but also our riders and our competitions. In terms of sponsorship, we were probably the first to believe in our young European surfers at a time when only Australians, Americans, and occasionally Brazilians monopolized the top 44. Today, the breakthroughs made by European surfers are not by chance—they are the fruit of an exceptionally close relationship between our team managers and the riders. Jeremy Florès, European surf champion, Miky Picon, in 2006 the first French national to join the WCT, Joan Duru, Patrick Beven and Marc Lacomar are all proving that the European elite no longer has an inferiority complex and that Quiksilver has largely contributed to this evolution.

And there is just as much to say about the quality of our snowboard and skate teams. We can call to mind Serge Vitelli and his V turn, which marked the beginnings of Quiksilver's existence on the mountain. The new generation of Candide Thovex (winner of multiple X-Games), Mathieu Crépel (world champion 2005/2006 and recipient of a Crystal Globe in 2005), Markku Koski and Kjersti Buuas (bronze medals at the Olympic Games in Turin) and also Bastien Salabanzi (three-time world champion in street skating)...these competitors are all marvelous ambassadors for our brands and our sports. But more than the results of which we are so proud, it is the spirit and the quality of the relationship between our riders and Quiksilver that we take to heart. We undeniably have the best team in Europe, and of this we are all very proud.

Multicultural, innovative, unique—this is the reality of Quiksilver. More than 10 nationalities work at the headquarters in St. Jean de Luz, and quite a few individuals have been with the company for many years, blending their experience with the differing experiences of those more recently arrived. Maritxu Darrigrand, pioneer of the Nuits de la Glisse and of the brand in Europe, symbol of women's surfing and head of Roxy Europe since its beginning, or Jeff Hakman, co-founder of Quiksilver USA and of Quiksilver Europe, as well as a world champion of surfing, and Marketing VP of Quiksilver Europe... these are just a couple of the must-know personalities of Quiksilver Europe. One runs into them in the office, around the traps and at the competitions, proof that talent and passion have no limit.

Quiksilver has never had the ambition to sell a lifestyle, but simply to make it accessible, through the guidance of leaders who know how to manage a business while preserving the dream, the magic of human encounters, the beauty of a spot...Everything has changed, but nothing has changed! The dream, the passion, the magic of a Kelly Slater taking the road toward an eighth world title, the hope of a Jeremy Florès and his audacious talent, the smile of a salesperson in one of our stores, the pleasure of having a garment both super-technical and beautiful, everything is here. We have simply to follow our dreams of bigger and more beautiful projects, and through these to continue to make the younger generations dream too.

—Pierre Agnes, *St. Jean de Luz, France, April 2006*

COURTESY NA PALI

Presidential pigdog.

From Ug to Asia Pacific

There is so much emotion attached to this brand. The first time I placed a Quiksilver decal on the back of my car I was so proud. I had not experienced this feeling before, having spent over 12 years in a corporate environment in Melbourne. I think it's because the company has substance. There's a real story around the founders, and a passion among the people that work and live similar lifestyles.

Even though the Australian operation was small when I started in 1989, the company had expanded to all parts of the globe, and I was in awe of what Alan Green and John Law had started. And today we're in the billions, and they're still involved. True believers.

Craig Stevenson charging at Two Mile, Victoria.

Whether it's a mountain of water or a snow capped slope, you are sitting there on the precipice, your heart is pumping, you're on the edge. You realize this is more than a sport; this is an extreme spiritual and physical experience. You take the drop, you put your board on an edge, you lean over, carve your first turn and look down the line. You're alive...nothing else matters.

—Clive Fitts, Craig Stevenson and Greg Healy
from The New Frontier 2003-2005

In the early days, the presence of Alan and John in the office was integral to the feel and dynamic of the organization; it has always felt right to have that connection to the beginnings of the story, and helped to foster staff loyalty and staff ownership of the push to brand success. Now, the next generation is involved, and so the journey continues.

When I started, I joined a group of 120 employees, mostly made up of machinists. All of Ug's products were either made in Torquay or Geelong. Norm Innis, managing director at that time, employed me because I had the longest hair, and I didn't wear a suit and tie to the interview. My background was not strictly accountancy, but I slotted in as accountant, starting a journey that I feel honored to have traveled.

In 1991 we made the momentous decision to take our product offshore. Even though the Chinese factories were not as technically advanced as Australia at this stage, external conditions dictated that this was the right decision and would lead to higher profitability for the company. This was a very emotional time, as we recognized the effect this would have on the livelihoods of many of our people. It took some time to move our total production offshore, with the ski factory closing in 1996 and the last boardshort line in 1999.

This was the beginning of QSS, Ug's production office in Hong Kong, started in 1994 by Norm Innis and Michael Foyster. It is now the global sourcing office for Quiksilver with offices in Shanghai and Shenzen and employing around 150 people. With Norm in Hong Kong, I took over the reins in Torquay, a year after Craig Stevenson joined the company as the national sales manager. And so began an amazing relationship, the hard-core surfer and the ex-accountant.

The company was returning around 5 percent in those days. I remember at my first board meetings Alan Green asking why we could not return 10 percent, so that was our goal, finally achieved in 1999. We ran into hard times in 1996, and I remember reporting the poor year at the board meeting. It was so bad Greeny said all he wanted to do was go out to the car park and kick his tires. It was a subdued meeting, one that I will never forget, and one that I vowed would never happen again. From that point a recovery plan was put into place that was the start of Ug's growth to where it is today.

Internal changes were made; we acquired the Omareef business—licensees to produce wetsuits and accessories in Australia—which brought all of our products under the one roof, and the most strategic spend was buying back the Roxy trademark for apparel from Gazal. Our first professional three-year strategic plan, Towards 2000, would take the company to $AUS 100 million in sales and a 10-percent return at last. They were big, hairy,

Clive with the Asia Pacific management team, Hawaii, 2006.

audacious goals, and it was time for big change if we were going to meet them. Our company culture had to change from being a manufacturing company to a design and marketing company, and that is where we placed our resources with all of our production requirements now offshore in the hands of QSS managed by Andrew Lau.

It is now well known within Quiksilver that we made the plan easily and in fact achieved the numbers within two years, not the three as planned. During this stage we moved to new premises in Torquay, bringing the whole team under the one roof and creating strong morale amongst all employees.

In 1998, Greg Healy joined the company as the chief financial officer. Craig, Greg and I formed a very strong bond and were dubbed "The Three Amigos" by Norm. This seemed to stick wherever we went around the Quiksilver world. From here the business went from strength to strength, and in 2002 The New Frontier plan was born. In simple terms the plan was to acquire Quiksilver Japan and Quiksilver Indonesia. Both businesses at this time were performing poorly. The plan was well received by the Board; the only problem was how to fund the acquisitions. We took the plan to Quiksilver International, and then on to Bob and Bernard at Quiksilver, Inc., for funding opportunities. They quickly embraced the plan, and instead of Ug going through with the acquisitions, Inc. decided to merge the companies under the Inc. umbrella, to be known as Quiksilver Asia Pacific. Backed to the hilt by Quiksilver, Inc., we were given complete freedom to run Asia Pacific, provided we stuck to the vision. We spoke at length with the Green and Law families about this, recognizing this would be a sensitive issue because the spiritual home of Quiksilver was Ug.

Since the merger both Japan and Indonesia have been performing strongly, and we have been given the opportunity to take on new territories in China and Korea, so the future for Asia Pacific looks extremely exciting and full of opportunity.

—Clive Fitts, *Torquay, Australia, April 2006*

TEAM RIDERS
2000s

If diversification was the theme of the '90s, in the new century Quiksilver's buzz strategy was acquisition, with the parent public company in the U.S. globalizing by acquiring major licensees around the world and further extending its reach by merging with DC Shoes and Rossignol.

Not only did this expand the total athletic team tremendously, but it put greater focus on all disciplines of boardriding—surf, snow and skate—as well as a renewed interest in skiing (through Rossignol) and golf (through Cleveland Golf). Despite the company's overall "outdoors" direction, however, Quiksilver's team focus remains on its core sports.

Interestingly, even as the brand moved forward, it looked back, signing '80s skate legend Christian Hosoi who, along with fellow team rider Tony Hawk, WAS skate 20 years ago. There have also been some left-field signings, such as Huntington Beach surfer Timmy Turner who morphed into one of the great surfer/adventurer/film-makers of the decade. Presently recovering from serious illness, Timmy is supported by Quiksilver.

SCOTT NEEDHAM

↻ Fred Pattachia

Long known as a charger, Fred is now opening eyes on the WCT. His fearless approach to surfing and happy-go-lucky attitude make him a crowd favorite at home in Hawaii and around the world.

↻ Dane Reynolds

Ventura's favorite son and the unofficial Top Gun of the Young Guns, Dane has pulled off impressive performances as a WCT wildcard and can be expected to secure a regular slot on the tour very soon.

BERNARD TESTAMALE

HANK

↻ Chelsea Georgeson

Like her best pal, Sofia Mulanovitch, Chelsea was recognized as a standout early in her surfing career, being spotted by Lisa Andersen at Avalon in Sydney. What amazed everyone when she signed with Quiksilver was the fact that she had just started surfing! Chelsea soon developed into a real power surfer, joining the WCT at 18 and taking out a world title just three years later. Just married, Chelsea is as focused on winning more titles as she is on one day creating some groms to surf with.

JEFF HORNBAKER

⚲ Troy Brooks

The son of veteran Aussie champion Rod Brooks and younger brother of '90s Quiksilver team rider Shaun Brooks, Troy has developed into one of the most innovative aerialists and all-round surfers of the '00s. Finally making the WCT in 2005 after perhaps taking too many chances with radical maneuvers in previous years, Troy was unfortunate to suffer a knee injury late in the season, but he's returned in 2006 surfing better than ever.

⊘ Todd Richards

At 36, Todd Richards is an absolute snowboarding legend, still competing against kids half his age, but also an ambassador and influential spokesman for his sport, providing the NBC commentary for the snowboard events at the Torino Winter Olympics. Since '99, Todd has amassed multiple Vans Triple Crown medals and Winter X-Games golds, and was a member of the first U.S. Olympic halfpipe team. Married with a four-year-old son, Todd and his family divide their time between homes in Breckenridge, CO, and Encinitas, CA.

JEFF HORNBAKER

◖ Sofia Mulanovich

A child prodigy from Peru, Sofia won her first pro event at the Roxy Pro Fiji in '04. For the then-20-year-old, the genie had been unleashed from the bottle. She went on to take three events in the season and wrest the world title from six-time women's champion Layne Beachley. The first South American of either sex to take the title, the diminutive Sofia is a great ambassador for women's surfing around the world.

ARFF

◗ Jeremy Flores

Considered the best junior surfer in France for several years now, Reunion-born Jeremy has been stunning older surfers with his audacious moves since he was a tiny grom. Kelly Slater pronounced him "better than I was at 12." Making the transition to senior ranks is never easy, but while he has sometimes had problems pressing home a natural advantage in contests, his free surfing is never less than amazing. Now showing new maturity and strength, he was European Pro Junior champ in '05, celebrated his 18TH birthday with a flying start in the '06 WQS, and is expected to make a huge impact.

SCOTT NEEDHAM

⊙ Lindsey Kildow

Rossignol skier Lindsey Kildow has become one of the most recognizable sportswomen in America. Despite suffering injury and disappointments at the Torino Winter Olympics, she is regarded by her peers as one of the classiest skiers in the world, finishing top three in World Cup events no fewer than six times in the '04-'05 season.

DEXPORT/VERNON DECK

⊙ Julian Wilson

The youngest gun in an Aussie surf family, Julian emerged as a real talent on both long and shortboards at the turn of the century. Now he's one of the hottest juniors on the planet.

⊙ Omar Hassan

A mainstay on the Quiksilver skate and snowboard teams from the late '90s, Omar was a huge hit in the crossover surf/snow/skate Quik Cup and the Marseille Bowlrider in France, as well as starring in domestic skate and half-pipe events at home in the US.

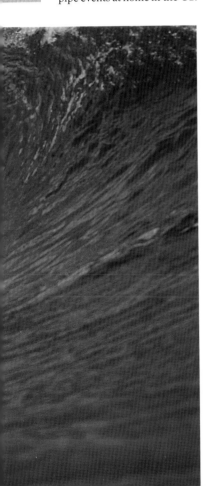

SCOTT NEEDHAM

⊙ Torah Bright

Australia's Torah Bright may have been unlucky to place only fifth at the '06 Torino Winter Olympics, but the 19-year-old snowboarder is on a hell of a roll. With firsts in the U.S. Open halfpipe, the U.S. Vans Cup and the World Superpipe, all in the first quarter of '06, and a second at the Winter X-Games, the Roxy star is set to rewrite the record books.

THE TEAM

Asia Pacific

Luke Munro
Troy Brooks
Ry Craike
Maz Quinn
Julian Wilson
Mar Ohno
Chelsea Georgeson
Jake Paterson
Danny Wills
Ross Clarke-Jones
Wayne Lynch
Mark Richards
Simon Anderson
Martin Potter
Torah Bright
Josh Rouillon
Tristan Walker
Jemma Lenton

The Americas

Kelly Slater
Tony Hawk
Danny Way (DC)
Sofia Mulanovitch
Dane Reynolds
Dylan Graves
Fred Pattachia
Todd Richards
Titus Kinimaka
Dave Kalama
Clay Marzo
Danny Fuller
Jimmy Rotherham
Mark Healey
Reef McIntosh
Christian Hosoi
Tim O'Connor
Eric Fletcher
Omar Hassan
Carissa Moore
Kassia Meador

Europe

Miky Picon
Jeremy Flores
Caroline Sarran
Alain Riou
Marlon Lippke
Mathieu Crepel
Markku Koski
Bastien Salabanzi
Candide Thovex
Teiva Joyeux
Joan Duru
Marc Haziza
Jelle Deschout
Martin Cernik

YOUNG

NATHAN SMITH SCOTT NEEDHAM

We don't get to choose the body we inhabit

here on earth. If we could, instead of being stuffed into any random bag of bones, who among us wouldn't elect to become one of the ace teenage boardriders of surf, skate, or snow? The Young Guns, if you will. To envision maneuvers and be able to accomplish them, to travel as a rock star the world over while your peers are staring at four walls and a chalkboard, and to have a career doing the thing you adore stretched out in front of you like a stacking Superbank wall. The world isn't merely at your feet, but far below, gazing up in awe as you soar above it and tweak for good measure. If there's a more enjoyable way to rattle through one's days, I haven't heard of it. Clearly, the life of the übergrommet waxes all others.

Yet, just as Uncle Ben told Peter Parker, "With great power comes great responsibility." And responsibility, as young Spider-Man discovered, imposes the one law the Young Guns fear: gravity. It's enough to ruin a kid, to send his aerial dreams crashing back to earth.

None of our teen titans—water whizzes Dane Reynolds and Jeremy Flores, street star Bastien Salabanzi, or snow specialists Eric Jackson and Mathieu Crepel—ever set out to achieve such a position. Of the millions of kids who hop on a board each year, very few will ever rise to prominence, and fewer still do so before reaching adulthood. Those that do haven't attained their greatness from any sage instruction or radical training regimen. Sure, they're out there every day giving it a go, but so are heaps of other folks who will never rise above the level of intermediate. The goal of every session, every wave, is mere unadulterated fun, just like for the rest of 'em. The ascent just ... like, happens, which is the true peculiarity of this almost-ready-for-prime-time state. It is a gift.

The Young Guns have inherited one insanely valuable commodity that cannot be purchased in any store for any price. What these kids have is an innate, freakish ability to stand atop a slab of wood or foam and put themselves in ridiculous predicaments without totally losing it. Rather than panic, they relax and let instinct take over. The kids are born with that special something, but it is

only detectable once the human becomes the rider. One day they're fumbling to ride for the first time, be it in a Quiksilver Surf Camp or just kicking around with some bros, and the next they're tapping into some invisible force. From there, the learning curve transitions to vert and punts skyward.

Once these kids get discovered, things don't come as easily. Fortunately, there exists a grace period between uncovering one's talent and becoming a certified Young Gun. This chapter of innocence is shrinking as action sports become bigger business. For Tony Hawk and Kelly Slater back in the 1980s, a few years passed in which they stayed in school, were treated like "normal" teenagers, and were allowed to establish a firm footing before getting sent to the lions. Then, equipped with well-honed teeth, they did all the mauling while the so-called lions tucked tail and ran.

Can the gift be a burden? You're damn right, it can. Many have received this offering of a lifetime yet failed miserably. It is far too easy to mistake the trappings of success for the real thing. The hangers-on, the ego, the pressure—as with child actors, the hardest part is still to come. Carrying the burden into adulthood is no safer than crossing the Bridge on the River Kwai. Can you say Macaulay Culkin? No one escapes unscathed. As a Young Gun, you're expected to achieve bigger and bigger results, or else.

But what about the rest of us, the wannabes who sit on the sidelines and wonder why we were passed over? We lose interest, or we latch our own hopes onto the still-developing Young Gun shoulders and hang on for their ride. They owe us something, those spoiled little larrikins. We're just taking what's rightfully ours.

Given the demands, the continued growth exhibited by these otherwise average teenagers is astounding. Each generation starts younger, improves faster, and goes bigger than the last. For them, adolescent invincibility is no myth, and momentum is everything. They're building up speed for a run at the top. The hard part is coming. Rivals are taking aim. There's no time to think about it. Just put the pedal to the metal and hold on.

Jeremy Flores.

GUNS

ESSAY BY
JASON
BORTE

California's wunderkind, Dane Reynolds,
loving life in the Mentawais.

Luke Munro

SCOTT NEEDHAM

PHOTOS: NATHAN SMITH

[LEFT] **Troy Brooks rooster tail.**
[ABOVE] **Masatoshi Ohno.**
[BELOW] **Ry Craike.**

[TOP] **Julian Wilson**
[ABOVE] **Masatoshi Ohno**
[RIGHT] **Luke Munro**
[INSET] **Everything you need for a day at the beach.**

A Message from Bernard Mariette, President, Quiksilver, Inc.

Quiksilver:
The Past and the Future

When I hear the fantastic story of Quiksilver, I am struck by the responsibility that I and our 2006 global management team have to continue the legacy of this great brand and the people that created it. Even though, now, Quiksilver is just one of our six globally recognized brands, it is our key brand and its spirit and success are the foundation of our Company.

In 1994, when I joined the company, Quiksilver total sales were less than $100 million, and Roxy's were around $3 million. Although Quiksilver products had long before been extended beyond boardshorts and our distribution included non-core specialty stores, we had no common global ownership, hardly any sales to juniors, no company-owned retail stores and a total global staff that numbered in the hundreds rather than thousands. Still, Quiksilver was becoming more and more known and admired outside the surfing community, and in Europe we took Quiksilver's great brand equity and made it our mission to take our lifestyle message to kids in places like Paris, London, Barcelona and Berlin. These are the kids who had never been on a surfboard but who loved coming to our Boardriders Clubs and feeling the Quiksilver and Roxy magic. It was during this transformation that we truly began to identify Quiksilver and Roxy as lifestyle brands whose appeal transcended the surfing world or, actually, by then, the boardriding world, since we were also targeting skate and snowboarding.

Quiksilver's global management team at Waimea Bay, April 2006.

By the late '90s and early 2000s, after unifying the Quiksilver and Roxy brands worldwide, we realized that Quiksilver's real power and authenticity remained in its surfing roots, and that to truly address the skateboarding and snow segments of this boardriding world, we needed brands that were the authentic leaders in those worlds. We were starting to see that our Company could become a major player in what was becoming known as the "outdoor" market. Outdoor is a term used to describe individual sports like surfing, skating, snowboarding, skiing, sailing, hiking, even golfing—sports that you do, not in stadiums, but in challenging, often beautiful natural environments. Our challenge in expanding in a big way into the outdoor world was to remain true to the legacy of the Quiksilver brand, the unquestioned leader of the surfing segment of the outdoor lifestyle market. To carry out our strategy, in 2004 we acquired DC Shoes, the leading brand in the skateboarding market, and in 2005 we acquired Rossignol, the leading and legendary ski brand in the snow/mountain segment of the outdoor market. In the Rossignol deal, we also acquired Cleveland Golf, another one of the leading brands in the outdoor country (golf) segment. Each of these brands, like Quiksilver, has its own history of authenticity, separate and distinct from Quiksilver, but sharing the same outdoor values.

This transformation of Quiksilver from surfing company to lifestyle brand, and now to the anchor brand of the world's largest outdoor lifestyle company, has been accompanied by an amazing globalization process. In the last few years, we have created the global framework upon which our company now stands, with centralized global management overseeing regional headquarters in three geographic zones—the Americas, Europe and Asia-Pacific—while each brand has its own global brand management structure. I am proud to say that we have done all this by creating working environments in the United States, Europe, Asia Pacific and around the world where creativity will thrive.... where people will dream.

When I look back on my dozen years or so at Quiksilver, it is amazing what our company has accomplished in that time. But, just as none of that growth and diversification could have been achieved without the firm foundations of what went before—The Quiksilver Story—we look at our company today and see not just a pinnacle of achievement but a base upon which to build an even more exciting future. For all our success, I am most proud and thankful for the personal relationships that I have developed in the Quiksilver and, now, Rossignol worlds. Over

COURTESY NA PALI

Bernard Mariette, French Alps, 1997.

the years our management teams and employees have been incredibly hard-working and loyal and made my job easy and fun. When I came to Quiksilver (Na Pali) in 1994, I was welcomed into the Pays Basque and respected for what I could bring to the company. The same when I came to Huntington Beach in 2001. My best friends are in Quiksilver.

The legacy of Quiksilver people is not just in the Alan Green and Bob McKnight stories, it's also in the stories of the so-called little guys who have made our business work. Even though we in management like to dream of big strategies and plans, the ultimate success is in the details and the people who execute. The legacy of Quiksilver is not just dreams, but execution. I always love to talk to our people in our warehouses, or our retail stores, or in the accounting department. They teach me what makes our business work. This tradition of taking pride in the details of what you do goes all the way back to Alan Green and Bob McKnight, who inspired the people that built this business. And so does the idea of working as a team. Even though this book is a collection of individual stories, the most important key to Quiksilver past, present and future is team spirit. Just as the Quiksilver founders showed us, our future will be unlimited so long as we transcend our individual egos and work as a team to build and manage our brands. As we continue to grow into the dominant player in the outdoor market over the next decade, I'm looking forward to working with all the new people who will share the love of our sports, our lifestyle and our brands, and who will carry on the Quiksilver legacy. And looking backward, to all the family of athletes, customers, manufacturing partners, board members and, of course, all the talented people that I've had the honor and privilege of being a part of and leading, my deepest thanks.

—Bernard Mariette, *Huntington Beach, June 2006*

Robby Naish

HEROES

Great athletes inspire everyone. Digging into his personal vault, Bob McKnight recalls some special moments

I was sitting in the back of a longboat by myself, heading across the channel, when I saw Robby Naish kite jump over Namotu Island. I couldn't believe what I had seen. That couldn't have happened...could it?

We were in Fiji to celebrate the new millennium. The morning had been incredible. A few of us knew it was going to be on, so we had pulled the plug on the previous evening's kava party quite early. The first boat to Cloudbreak was just past dawn, and perfect barrels awaited us. It was a postcard blue-green morning, not a drop of water out of place. Long rides, clean barrels, swing sets, tower tours, reef cuts, broken boards—the full Cloudbreak experience.

We surfed for four hours, then headed back to Tavarua for breakfast, the salt drying into our skin and hair, laughing and bragging about our rides, exhausted and exhilarated. Later, I crossed the channel to have lunch with friends...and that's when I saw Robby's jump. For no reason, just for the pure pleasure of it. There was no one around. I doubt if anyone else even saw it. But there he was, soaring 40 or 50 feet above the palm trees on his kite-board.

Now, I know Robby Naish is the greatest windsurfer in history—more than 20 world titles, basically invented the sport—but nothing prepares you for a sight like that. It was just amazing.

What can be better than watching great athletes, well, being great athletes? How can one person be so good, so much better than everybody else? Pure skill, hard work, fearlessnessness and a real passion for what they do, I guess. And imagination. How could Robby have even imagined that jump, let alone pull it off!

I think of Wayne Lynch and how he turned my life upside down by getting upside down himself, back in the '60s. Growing up seeing photos and surf movies of Wayne doing this incredible stuff at Bells Beach made surfing my complete obsession. Nobody had done what he was doing. He defied gravity and redefined surfing.

With some buddies I went to MacGillivray Freeman Films and rented *Evolution*, the 1968 movie that starred Wayne. Supposedly it was to do some screenings at school and make a

SYLVAIN CAZENAVE

Jeff Hakman

Wayne Lynch

Emile Allais

JOHN PENNINGS
COURTESY ROSSIGNOL

little money, but our true mission was to take the reel home and watch Wayne's moves a thousand times over. And we did. I never tire of watching a great athlete.

So how lucky am I? And how lucky are all of us at Quiksilver? We get to do this for a living! For 35 years we've been able to share in the achievements of our entire family of great board sports athletes, and sometimes share the mountains and the waves with them too. I remember back in the early '70s, the first time I shared waves with the great Jeff Hakman, at that time the best pro surfer in the world and a true legend of the sport. I was in awe of the way he knew how the ocean moved and made it all look so easy. But best of all, he was as stoked as I was. Jeff soon became my good friend and co-founded Quiksilver, Inc., with me in 1976.

One day last winter I was surfing fun little waves at Makaha with a bunch of our people, and Dave Kalama paddled past, standing on his tandem board and paddling with a graphite canoe paddle. "Hey, hi Bob. Catchin' a few?" Dave is one of the greatest watermen alive and a Quiksilver rider. As I watched him flick his rig around with such ease and catch all the best waves, sharing them with his friends, I couldn't believe how blessed I was to be sharing the spirit of surfing on this beautiful day.

To me, 2005 was the year of the Quiksilver athlete. The incomparable Kelly Slater won his seventh world title, our Roxy girls fought out the women's title, with Chelsea Georgeson taking over the mantle from Sofia Mulanovitch, and skater Danny Way jumped the Great Wall of China. Amazing achievements, all of them. But perhaps we should be talking about Quiksilver-Rossignol athletes, because 2005 was the year we joined forces with the company that has defined winter sports just as we have defined surfing.

JEFF DIVINE

Jamie Lynn

JON FOSTER

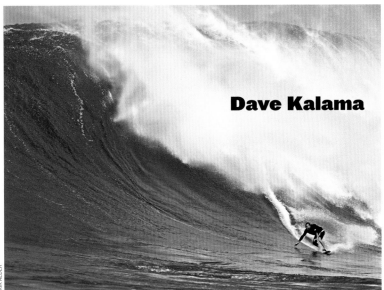

Dave Kalama

ERIK AEDER

Rossignol athletes have won more world championships and Olympic medals than most countries, let alone companies. And the heritage goes back to the 1930s when Emile Allais raced down the glacial slopes of Chamonix to revolutionize downhill racing, imagining and then inventing turns that didn't exist. And this time someone was watching. A man named Laurent Boix-Vives was so inspired by Emile's downhill runs that he bought Rossignol and used it to breathe life into alpine sports, and to create opportunities for thousands of world-class athletes over the next half-century.

Great athletes inspire and transform, and the best moments often come unexpectedly and improbably.

It was at the end of a long day of heli-snowboarding the infinite powder at Tyax in British Columbia's Chicotin Mountains. Down at the bottom of the valley beneath the glaciers, the helicopter waited. I was off to the side watching a group of

boardriders—all friends, some pros, some mere mortals like me—make their last run. Out of their sight, I smiled as I watched my exhausted companions give it their end of the day hurrah.

The last to go was one of our pro riders, Jamie Lynn. Jamie's not only a legendary snowboarder but an artist and musician as well. Wayne Lynch on snow. Down he flies, lugging a backpack overloaded with first aid, avalanche radio and other obligatory emergency equipment. And then, for no apparent reason, Jamie picks out a little rock feature on the flat and launches up and over the handlebars into a full radio flip. Landing it, he just rides away. No one watching, no big deal. Doing it just because he could, and for the sheer hell of it.

I've never talked to any of these guys about this. Just private thoughts and memories. If I ever did, all I could say to them, and to all our other incredible athletes, is, simply, thanks for the memory, and the inspiration.

Quiksilver's Family of Brands

Quiksilver is not just a brand but the name for a family of brands. Each symbolizes the sports it represents and provides people with a connection to the outdoors, beyond sport-related equipment and apparel into everyday sportswear and accessories.

DC SHOES

In the summer of 2000, Bob McKnight and Danny Kwock were approached by the two young founders of DC Shoes, Ken Block and Damon Way, who wanted to gauge Quiksilver's interest in their brand. As it turned out, it was considerable.

Born out of a stable of street/skate brands in San Diego in 1993, and spearheaded by the popularity of Damon Way's skate star younger brother, Danny, DC was firing by the turn of the century, with sales of more than $50 million and an extraordinarily high profile in the very area where Quiksilver was weak. And, like most companies that experience growth at warp speed, DC was struggling to fund it. So the dance of courtship began, but it was over the moment Bob McKnight realized the complex dynamic of DC's top management team.

Towards the end of 2003, DC came knocking on Quiksilver's door again, this time with tighter reins on its operations and a cohesive management team in place. Finance manager Bill Bussiere went down to their headquarters at Vista, CA, and liked what he found, a tight operation controlled by young, enthusiastic and creative people. Quiksilver president Bernard Mariette followed and came back full of excitement about the possibilities.

As Quiksilver reached a billion dollars in sales, its management had identified that acquisition targets needed to be a minimum 10 percent of existing sales. Now close to $100 million, DC fit the bill perfectly, and, following its changes at the top, the company also fit McKnight's three basic criteria of acquisition—products within the core mantra of Quiksilver, operations in reasonable shape (no demolition required) and a cultural fit at management level.

A $150 million deal was hammered out in May 2004. Six months later, as the fiscal year closed, DC had integrated seamlessly into Quiksilver, with DC designers working on improvements to Quiksilver and Roxy footwear, while Quiksilver designers worked on improving DC's apparel lines. And the shoe company had already plugged into Quiksilver's global sales and marketing platform and had positioned itself for its second $100 million.

ROSSIGNOL

With its long history of success in ski racing, Rossignol has developed a reputation for excellence, innovation and technical knowledge that has enabled it to appeal to multiple styles of skiing, including racing, all-mountain, freeride and freestyle. Rossignol covers all of the major product categories of the ski and snowboard markets, including skis, bindings, boots and poles in the alpine category, skis, boots and bindings in cross-country, snowboard boots and bindings and technical outerwear and accessories.

The Rossignol product line is now being expanded into an all-season sportswear and accessories range representing the alpine lifestyle. Since Quiksilver's acquisition of Rossignol in 2005, the company has moved into new North American headquarters in Park City, Utah, and begun a revitalization of its European facility in Voiron, France.

DYNASTAR

With a heritage of racing, trendsetting and performance, Dynastar symbolizes technically specific skis to use in all alpine experiences. Lange ski boots combine its race boot prowess with a commitment to building better, more comfortable boots for skiers of every type. Look bindings have a winning history in alpine ski racing with a focus on producing high-quality, innovative release bindings. Kerma poles complement the offering.

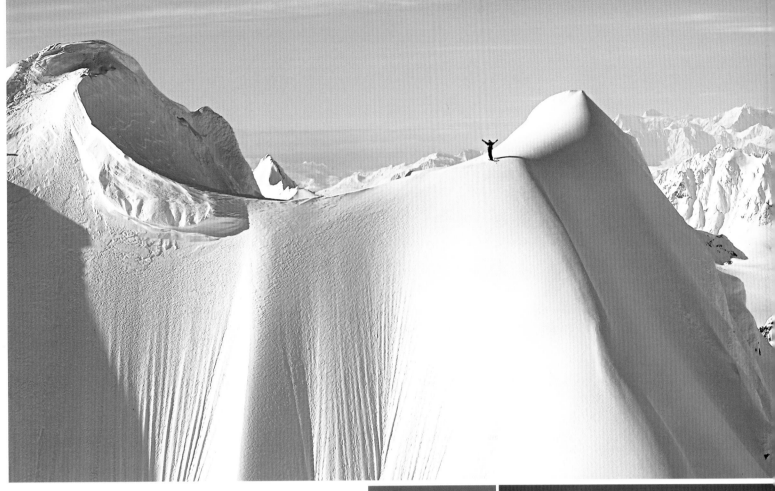

LIBTECH, GNU, BENT METAL

Part of Quiksilver for many years now, Lib Technologies, Gnu snowboards and Bent Metal bindings are feeling the benefits of synergies with the world's leading ski company, as most of Quiksilver's snowboard business is relocated to one large facility in Park City, Utah. The trio's expertise in snowboard hardware now has the backing of a century of technical development.

HAWK

Inspired by skate guru and 12-time world champion Tony Hawk, Hawk targets the boys and young men's skateboard market with a range of streetwise apparel and accessories. The incredible popularity of Tony Hawk through his computer games and television appearances propels sales. In 2005 Quiksilver licensed the Hawk brand in the Americas exclusively to Kohl's, further extending its market penetration.

RAISINS, RADIO FIJI, LEILANI

Since its acquisition in 1993, this trio of women's swimwear brands has not only been an important part of the Quiksilver family of brands, but in the '90s helped position Roxy in the swimwear market too, with technical, sales and marketing synergies. Raisins and Radio Fiji target the juniors market, while Leilani is a contemporary swimwear brand.

CLEVELAND GOLF

For over 25 years, Cleveland Golf has produced high-performance golf equipment. Cleveland Golf strives to make the most technologically advanced golf clubs available. Players of every level and age, both male and female, benefit by using top-quality Cleveland equipment, such as Launcher woods, CG irons and the best-selling wedges in the sport. Cleveland also produces putters under the Never Compromise brand. The brand has achieved a high profile around the world through the sponsorship of such great golfers as Vijay Singh.

Fidra is Quiksilver's golf apparel line.

Berndt Greber

Crew with attitude. Todd Kline, Bob McKnight, Tom Holbrook, Dan Hopkins.

Cute chicks in the car park.

'80s CEO John Warner in the bosses chair.

Bob contemplates his next move.

Bob on the job. Shop opening somewhere, can't remember why the tie!

Mid-'80s sales meeting. Now we got numbers.

Hey, Winship, I hear the kava is quite good around here. Let's make a night of it.

Tiax trip.

Horny on the

Shaheen Sadeghi reassures Bruce Raymond and Simon Buttonshaw that surf is alive and kicking.

Quiksilver founders claim Everest! Okay, Tiax.

My name's Jeff Sweeney and have I got a design for you.

Stylin'.

Hurry up and take the picture before we go blind. Global management in France, 2004.

...chael Owen and Martin Daly share ...rare moment of Bintang clarity.

Hey, we can't eat out every night! On the road with Tom and Bob.

Oh my god, I'm like, I don't believe it... Kelly Slater in our little town!!!

Paparazzi not welcome. The cold hard stare from Pierre Agnes, Poupy Poupignel and Harry Hodge.

My name's Peter Webb and I live for art. And fun.

Bob, Tom Brown, John Sabo.

Blox with stocks.

Sales force USA

Bruce does the rabbit ears again.

USA team rafting on the Kern River. Bring on those rapids.

John Winship and John Law all at sea.

Boardriders Club soiree.

Legends day out in Bali.

San Marino gang at Gaviota Pier. L to R: Hugh Penton, Packy Jones, Bob McKnight, Rob Rebstock.

Quik 20th birthday party, Sydney '89. Shirl Strahan, Harry Hodge, Alan Green, Bruce Raymond, Bob McKnight, Phil Jarratt.

My logo's visible, how about you guys? Peter Bloxham teaches Charlie Exon and Pierre Lalande a lesson in brand exposure.

Mentawais boat trip '04. Back l to r: Daly, Farny, Titus, Lewie, JT. Front l to r: Banta, Rotherham, Hakman, Hempy, Bob.

Windsurfing legend Robby Naish in high disco mode.

Bob and Randy Hunt bro' down with Brutus Beefcake and Hulk Hogan.

Trout fishing in New Zealand. Bob's plastic replica is from the gift shop.

Gratuitous butt shot.

Tavarua Thanksgiving trip. The next generation.

Come this way guys, Randy Hild finds the short way home.

Peter Schroff having a quiet drink.

Yasua.

Taylor, Riley and Marty, party time.

Eureka moment for Murray Boyd, remembered where he buried his car keys.

I'm sorry, m'am, it's gotta all come off. Tom Holbrook judges a beach girl pageant.

And the theme was? Party animals, JT, Mcknights, Hilds, Joneses.

My name's Jeff Booth and have I got a deal for you.

My name's Bob McKnight and if anyone can help me get off this thing right now...JACQUIE!!!

DK and Riley Walton.

My name's Bernard Mariette, and whatever Boothy offers, I will double it.

A Quiksilver

Quiksilver has meant a lot of things to me in my life, but none so important as the sense of family I get from sharing time with the people who work with us all around the world. When we first started in Costa Mesa back in '76, we knew everybody who worked with us; we shared meals, went surfing together and hung out. For the first few years you could count the employees of Quiksilver on the fingers of one hand, then two, then toes as well.

Back in the day, each new hire gave me a great feeling of accomplishment, and it was so cool to watch as new people who had the right attitude made a perfect fit with our tiny operation. Of course many of our first employees were not exactly strangers. Tom Holbrook and I had tended bar and surfed together during our college days; Bruce Raymond, who came over from Australia to work with us, was a surfing buddy; Danny Kwock was the leading grom at our home break, and so on. But most of the people that I first met when they joined Quiksilver went on to become friends, and I'm stoked that so many of them are still friends, and still with us!

ROBBY NAISH   GARY ELKERTON   OMAR HASSAN   MEL PU`U   MARTIN POTTER   MARK RICHARDS   TOM CARROLL   SIMON ANDERSON

GREAT COVERS

Since the beginning of time—well, the 1960s at least—surfing success has been measured not only in contest victories but in media exposure, and the benchmark of success has always been the magazine cover. These days "exposure-meters" track individual and brand exposure. Back in the day, if there was a good surf shot on the cover, the guy was probably wearing Quiks.

When Dan Merkel shot MR trimming in the barrel at Off The Wall in his red Quiksilvers, surf mags cost $1.25 and in the US Quiksilvers were only available at Lightning Bolt (Honolulu) and Vince Troniec's Islander Surf Shop (New Jersey). This April/May '76 *Surfing* was on sale when Hakman and McKnight started Quiksilver, Inc.

By the late '80s, Tom Carroll, Quiksilver's recently-signed "million dollar man" was not just a two-time world champion—he was a true waterman. His benchmark performances at Pipeline wearing a Gath helmet were heavily photographed, but few captured the mastery of his positioning like this "camera board" cover.

During the '80s *Australia's Surfing Life* emerged as a colorful and witty counterpoint to the dominant American magazines. This 1990 cover introduction to the new wunderkind, Kelly Slater, cleverly used a play on *Surfer's* controversial '60s John Witzig article "We're Tops Now" by asking, "Dude! Is America Tops Now?"

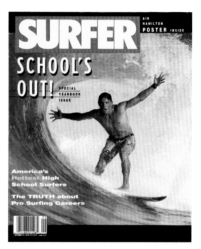

Meanwhile, Kelly was on his way to matinee idol status. Who else could be the cover for *Surfer's* 1991 "School's Out" summer number? The photo shows Kelly measuring the width of the barrel and revealing the latest Gen-X prints to the fullest extent. A marketing man's dream, even at this tender stage.

In the late '90s, Quiksilver was attempting a major push in the landlocked heartland of the USA, where sports like wakeboarding were helping to spread brand awareness. This summer cover of *Wake-Boarding*, with perfectly positioned logo under the masthead, didn't hurt at all.

When *Surfer* magazine decided to devote an issue to the re-emergence of big-wave riding, what better image to put on the cover than the Quiksilver in memory of Eddie Aikau, the world's premier big-wave contest?

With Quiksilver's global sales nearing the billion dollar mark, news and finance media around the world started to sit up and take notice. This photo of Quiksilver founder Alan Green paddling into an Indonesian reef lineup illustrated a surf industry cover story in Australia's national newspaper, *The Australian*.

...arua sales meeting in the ...—deifinitely not a surf trip.

Let me get straight to the point, I am proto-Roxy shell woman.

Last supper in France.

Jeff and Joelle center stage a...

No, seriously, they said if we hung around for the photo, there'd be a free barbeque afterwards.

Bernard and Clive Fitts tete-a-tete.

Clive Fitts, Gregg Soloman share a private joke.

Ah, another sales conference, another fabulous meal. Remember when we used to surf? Holbrook, Hild, Hakman, McKnight.

My name is Steve Tully and I'd really like to sell you some cheap neon.

Taylor Whisenand, Pete Sarry, Steve Titus, Dave Rosenberger.

Smile Clive, or I break your neck.

Team Texas Hold 'Em.

Pinhead talks story. Maritx... and Holby are rivetted.

Pierre Agnes lights the way.

Crammie, Bruce Raymond, Di Lyons.

Love your work, Mark Oblow. Legends and founders at Haliewa Joe's, 2005.

Paul Heussenstamm.

Okay boys, second verse, same as the first. TC whoops it up in France.

My name's Todd and I'll be your server tonight.

Bob claims Bradburn an...

Where's that bloody kava?

Holbrook, McKnight, Sebek, Tully, Farnsworth.

Pin not happy.

The Jim Everett/ St. John Knits Invitational Golf Tournament

La Quinta, Calif.

Holby captains the team at La Quinta.

Harry and Bruce cosy up to rocker Billy Preston.

Greeny and Gracey wine tasting.

Lisa and Bob.

Bob does the blah blah for the evening news.

Promo time. TC and Kelly grin and bear it.

Meribel.

Bob with new Lynchie.

On top of Tiax. Herb Blauer, Bob, Trevor Peterson, guide, Willy Morris.

Legends at the Eddie: Dennis Hopper, Bob and George Downing.

Punkers Bob, Moura Pleas, Charles Crowe, Randy Hunt.

We only look like this very late at night. Marty and Randy.

Peyo Lizarazu.

Design conference, France, 1989.

Eddie opening ceremony, year of the blazer.

Funny hat, Bob. With Harry Hodge and Alan Green at La Ferme Ostalapia.

Damn water hazards!

Tavarua volleyball team.

Bob and Kelly in New Jersey with East Coast sales veteran Vince Troniec.

Sure I tow in... but only in rivers.

Asia Pac's David Toda and Greg Healy with HR heavy Pierre Lalande.

Mark Daly, Jeff Sebek, Greg Macias, Steve Tully, Hall of Famer George Brett, Preston Murray, Danny Kwock, Sandy Schwartzenback.

win in Scotland. Lawo, Greeny think he's joking.

Shawn Fredrick and Tony Wales.

Jeff Bradburn explains to Bob and Greeny that he left his wallet back in the hotel room.

The book factory, San Clemente; Girard and Jarratt.

to McKnight & Mariette

Family Album

It's not possible to know everyone in the company now, but Bernard and I make it our mission to see that the sense of family remains the same. I love going off to France, or heading Down Under, or to any of our other operations headquarters to renew acquaintances with people, cruise around and see what's going on, generally hang out. And it's so great to see the same vibe at our offices around the world. Whether it's Huntington Beach, Torquay or Saint Jean de Luz, I know when I walk in and see people smiling, laughing, cruising the corridors on skateboards or out in the car park getting ready to go for a surf, that we're still doing something right. And for me there is nothing more reassuring than seeing wet wetsuits dripping from their positions on window sills all around a surf company headquarters. May we always make time to enjoy ourselves, no matter how big we get.

This scrapbook shows the Quiksilver family at work and play—probably a lot more of the latter than the former! It's our little indulgent celebration of ourselves to finish the book. And why not? Hope you enjoy it.

—Bob McKnight

MARK OBLOW

CHRISTIAN HOSOI   TITUS KINIMAKA   JEFF HAKMAN   PETER MEL   RAIMANA VAN-BASTOLAER   DAVE KALAMA   ROSS CLARKE-JONES   WAYNE LYNCH

SURFER

SURFER

A WINTER OF HIGH ENERGY SURFING

SURFER

Hawaii; North Shore Action
New England's Quality Waves Revealed
A Day to Remember; Lopez, McCabe Rip Padang
California Portfolio by Mike Moir

By the time the January 1977 issue of *Surfer* appeared in November 1976, with world champion Peter Townend pretty in pink board and matching Quiks in Jeff Divine's gatefold cover, the Australian dominance of the Hawaiian pro scene was reaching boiling point. Rabbit's cover-lined "Bustin' Down The Door" article didn't help.

PT's second *Surfer* cover of the year, a classic soul arch captured by Art Brewer, was his swansong as a Quiksilver rider. He and fellow Aussie Ian Cairns were about to launch their own brand and surf team, The Bronzed Aussies.

Although Mike Moir's cover of Danny Kwock in the March '80 *Surfer* highlighted DK's Rip Curl wetsuit and McCoy surfboard rather than his patchwork Quiks, the cover heralded the 56th Street gang at Newport's "Hottest 100 Yards." That summer, vertical performance and Quik's new Echo Beach boardshorts would explode here.

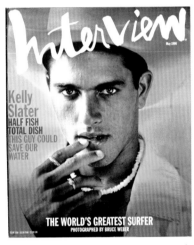

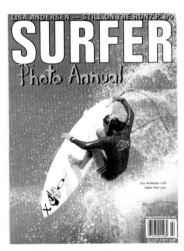

Despite founder Andy Warhol's interest in surfing—he made a surf short in the '60s—New York-based *Interview* magazine had never run a surfer on the cover...until '96 when Kelly's *Baywatch* gig catapulted him beyond cult. Bruce Weber's cover was great for Kelly and great for Quiksilver, but "half fish, total dish"...oh, come on.

"Lisa Andersen surfs better than you" barks the intimidatory cover line on *Surfer's* 1996 photo annual. And it was true, if not very palatable, for about 99.8 percent of the mag's readership. On her third of four consecutive world titles, Lisa was at the top of her game and had singlehandedly put Roxy on the map.

While the global fashion media, based in New York, Paris and London, tended to be dismissive or patronizing about surf, this 1998 cover of the European edition of *Sportswear Magazine* was a major breakthrough for Quiksilver.

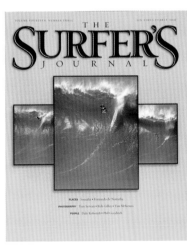

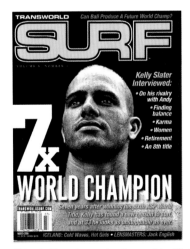

Another cover from the Eddie, this one a classic wipeout sequence of Flea Virotsko, shot by Jim Russi. Branding the cover of the esteemed *Surfer's Journal* has become a major coup.

Older, balder, wiser, and quite possibly still not at his athletic peak, 33-year-old Kelly Slater won a record seventh world title in 2005 and appeared on the cover of almost every surf mag in the world. Few, however, captured the emotional strength of the achievement as well as this March 2006 cover of *Transworld Surf*.

When the *L.A. Times* wanted to show '06 beachwear in their *West* magazine, they had to look no further than Quik team rider Danny Fuller for the cover, photographed with model Cameron Richardson. Jeff Lipsky took the photo.

GREAT ADS

It took Quiksilver several years to get into print advertising. Founder Alan Green initially favored "flowing" free boardshorts to trendsetters, but when the brand did start to buy media, it revolutionized surf advertising. Initially it was Green's homespun philosophizing that attracted attention, then Quiksilver led the way into the striking use of full-page action images.

John Witzig's Sea Notes had a brief life in 1977, and Simon Buttonshaw sent this rough off for the debut issue. The finished ad was still crude, but a distinct improvement.

"Rise above the negative" was part of the homespun Greeny philosophy, and this Bernie Baker photo of then small-wave supremo Peter Townend charging at Waimea illustrated it perfectly. From *Surfing World*, 1975.

This ad was shot on location in Tasmania by Peter Crawford before Echo Beach had a name. The bold new fabrics are modeled here by Nat Young, Wayne Lynch and Maurice Cole.

Jack McCoy shot this striking image of Craig Brazda on a tanning blanket at 54th Street, Newport Beach. The ad would not look out of place in a magazine today, 25 years later.

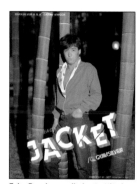

Echo Beach was all about attitude, and proto surf punk Danny Kwock had it to spare. This early fashion-styled ad was "non-core" before the brand even knew what that was.

Did we mention attitude? Here's a full page of it courtesy of the Newport Beach crew. There were many variations on this shot through the early '80s as Echo Beach took off.

Hawaiian team rider Marvin Foster was a charismatic and gifted surfer who had the world at his feet in the mid '80s, and several advertising campaigns were built around him.

In the early '90s surf adventure travel became the flavor of the month, with more and more remote reefs being discovered. The camouflage-influenced Surfers of Fortune theme reflected this new passion.

As part of its diversification strategy in the '90s, Quiksilver led the way with denim, although some of the early advertising seemed to struggle with how to illustrate surf brand jeans.

The 1990 signing of Kelly Slater was perhaps Quiksilver's smartest marketing decision of the decade. This ad, pre-world titles, introduced the kid the world knew was a champion about to happen.

Although they would become standard in the new century, in the '90s double-page spread ads were an expensive indulgence. With Californian Jeff Booth riding high on the pro tour, this one was justified.

The emergence of the Roxy brand in the '90s meant Quiksilver's designers had to find new visual expression. New type styles, softer images etc. By the new century the Roxy look was stylin'.

Roxy icon Lisa Andersen features in this stunning watch ad. While the men's brand moved away from the big letters look, Roxy refined it.

Multiple influences at work here in this spread of Fred Patacchia at Pipe. Designer Natas Kaupas introduced the grafitti-style script and the "impaired" logo, used here to highlight the Neo-Fly boardshort.

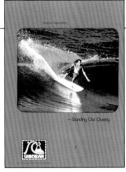

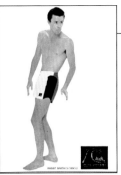

Quiksilver USA was still operating out of a truck and a post office box in Irvine when its first ads started appearing in *Surfing* in early 1977. Partner Jeff Hakman was the logical featured surfer.

Okay, Rabbit Bartholomew didn't land this prototype 360, but the Merkel photo helped cement Quiksilver's growing reputation for using cutting-edge action shots rather than product.

By the end of the '70s, Rabbit was surfing's rock star and Quiksilver's leading team rider. This iconic image rammed home his brand allegiance.

Quiksilver's early advertising philosophy was that nothing surpassed a good surf shot, so although he was little known outside of Australia, this classic Wayne Deane cuttie by Aitionn was seen around the world.

While Quiksilver's early focus was on surfing, surfing and surfing, by the end of the '70s volleyball was coming on so strong in California that it could not be denied.

Following hot on the heels of Echo Beach, ST Comp was about putting the surfing back into boardshorts, its emergence coinciding with the rise of the pro tour. New pro sensation Kong models the stretch fabric.

Marvin Foster didn't need Warpaint to look fierce, but this ad was a classic depiction of the rootsy, tribal feel of the new theme from Quiksilver artist Peter Webb.

Peter Webb's late '80s Gen-X border treatment provides light relief for an ad with a serious purpose—a tribute to California surfer Justin Robertson.

Ghetto Dog was a recurring and ironic theme in late '80s advertising. Here Jamie Brisick "barks at the moon."

The surf boom of the late '80s was built around neon, a beachwear fashion statement that reached way beyond the beach. Unfortunately, when neon went, so did the boom.

Silver Edition (now Quiksilver Edition) was a '90s nod to the older surfers. Who better to feature in this *Surfer's Journal* ad than the hard-charging boss of the brand, Bob McKnight.

Copy-conscious designer Tom Adler's influence can be seen in this Tom Carroll ad from the late '90s, part of a personality series that made a huge impact.

The spirituality of the Quiksilver in Memory of Eddie Aikau touches everyone who experiences it. This photo told its own story.

Designer David Carson introduced some bold new graphic concepts at *Surfer* magazine in the early '90s, then brought them to Quiksilver. These much-copied ads soon influenced editorial pages.

Australian snowboarding sensation Torah Bright also presented a sophisticated side to the Roxy image, used here to great effect.

Torah again, this time in more playful mood as she introduces Roxy's new ski product range. Photo by Fragnol.

A combination of Natas script and the primitive-themed art of Scott Richards make an eye-catching and very different Quiksilver ad.

Back to where it all began? Well, it is a full page product shot, and the product does look a little like Echo Beach, but this ad helped put the new Intervention series boardshort front and center.

GREAT POSTERS

Quiksilver event posters have become valued collector items, and with good reason. The company's artists around the world view each event as a new challenge in distilling its essence into one powerful image. The challenge gets harder the longer the event runs too. Here is a highly subjective sampling of some great poster art for Quiksilver and Roxy.

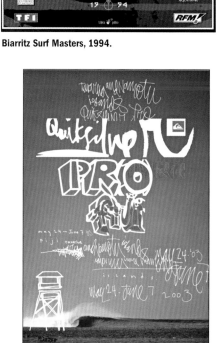

Biarritz Surf Masters, 1994.

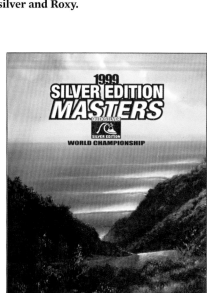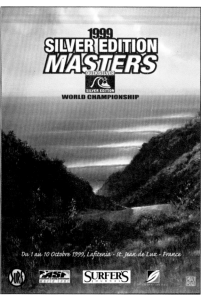

Gothic representation of snowboarding event the Quiksilver Air & Style, Austria, 1997.

Debut of the Silver Edition Masters, Lafitenia, France, 1999.

Classic image for a remote location event, Quiksilver Pro Fiji, '03. Design by Natas Kaupas.

Quiksilver Men Who Ride Mountains, Mavericks, 2002. Design by David Carson.

Quiksilver Edition Molakai-Oahu Paddleboard Race, 2005. Design by Clive Percy.

Roxy Hawaiian Pro, 1997.

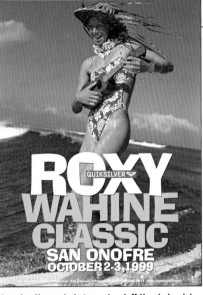

Veronica Kay and photographer Jeff Hornbaker joined forces on this poster for the Wahine Classic, 1999.

Wahine Classic, 2004. Art by Ron Croci.

Roxy Pro Fiji, 2002.

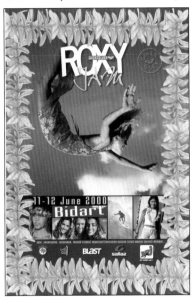

Roxy Jam, France, 2000.

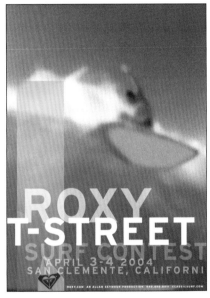

Surf posters meet fine art. Roxy T-Street Contest, 2004. Design by David Carson.

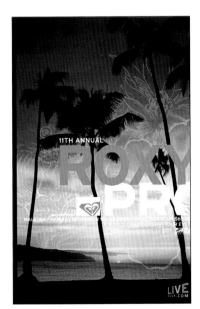

Roxy Pro Hawaii, 2005

Roxy Wahine Classic, San Onofre, 2005. Art by Harry Daily.

Roxy Pro Fiji, 2005. Art by Wolfgang Bloch.

GREAT ATHLETES

The Quiksilver group's family of current team riders.

Quiksilver

SURF

Kelly Slater
Fred Patacchia
Dane Reynolds
Peter Mel
Danny Fuller
Jon Rose
Clay Marzo
Mark Healey
Josh Hoyer
Dylan Graves
Timmy Turner
Anthony Tashnick
Reef McIntosh
Ola Eleogram
Ryan Moore
Frank Walsh
Ralph Bruwhiler
Matt Kechele
David Awbrey
Skeeter Zimmerman
Nico Manos
Ned Snow
Bill Pierce Okana
Gilbert Brown
Ramon Navaro
Jimmy Rotherham
Patrick Castagnet
Gabriel Villaran
Gabriel Aramburu
Magnum Martinez
David Diaz
Colin Saunders
Marcos Goncalves
Jihad Kodhr

Wiggolly Dantas
Alejo Muniz
Caue Wood
Luan Wood
Danilo Rodrigo
Jeremy Flores
Miky Picon
Mark Phipps
Jose Gregorio
Fred Robin
Joan Duru
Greg Pastuziak
Alain Riou
Manu Portet
Spencer Hargraves
Gabe Davies
Tom Butler
Nathan Phillips
Milo Castelo
David Perez
Aritz Aramburu
Gorka Yarritu
Luis Rodriguez
Nicola Brescani
Simone Bali
Marlon Lipke
Travis Logie
Daniel Redman
Jason Ribbink
Mathew Kruger
Stanley Badger
Brandon Jackson
Keegan Nel
Brett Shearer
Kyle Lane
Mathew Moir
Tom Myers

Garrett Parkes
Chris Salisbury
Julian Wilson
Beau Atchison
Richard Christie
Dion Atkinson
Tim Wrench
Luke Munro
Maz Quinn
Nic Muscroft
Danny Wills
Troy Brooks
Jake Paterson
Andrew Mooney
Ry Craike
Jamie Mitchell
Harley Clifford
Tamaroa McComb
Michel Bourez
Wayan "Betet" Merta
Mustafa Jacksen
Masatoshi Ohno
Kenta Hayashi

SKATE

Tony Hawk
Arto Saari
Reese Forbes
Dylan Rieder
Stefan Janoski
Kyle Leeper
Omar Salazar
Tim O'Connor
Eric Fletcher
Otavio Neto
Javier Mendizabal
Daniel Cardone

Conhuir Lynn
Manuel Margreiter
Dominik Dietrich
Jean Postec
Ross McGouran
Jelle Deshout
Alex Giraud
Pete King
Jesus Fernandez
Roman Hackl
Micky Iglesias
Marc Haziza
Jaime Fontecilla
Jesus de Pedro
Sascha Muller
Puddy Zwennis
Inus Wiehahn
Josh Rouillon
Brenton Weihrauch
Tristan Walker

SNOW

Scotty Arnold
Kyle Clancy
Eric Jackson
JP Tomich
JF Pelchat
Robbie Sell
Bryan Fox
Todd Richards
Markku Koski
Chris Sorman
Hampus Mosesson
Jakob Wilhelmson
Fredrik Austbo
Mathieu Crepel
Martin Cernik

Kalle Ohlson
Candide Thovex
Atsushi Ishikawa

OTHER

Ben Greenwood
Collin Harrington
Jeff House
Robert Teritehau
Antoine Albeau
Teiva Joyeux
Thomas Traversa
Victor Fernandez
Roberto Mocellin
Rotelli

LEGENDS

Titus Kinimaka
Christian Hosoi
Robby Naish
Simon Anderson
Mark Richards
Tom Carroll
Wayne Lynch
Raimana Van Bastolaer
Martin Potter
Mel Pu'u
Omar Hassan
Ross Clarke Jones
Jeff Hakman
Dave Kalama
Peter Mel

Roxy

SURF

Lisa Andersen
Sofia Mulanovich
Chelsea Georgeson
Kassia Meador
Carissa Moore
Megan Abubo
Veronica Kay
Malia Manuel
Kula Barbieto
Crystal Dzigas
Aimee Vogelgesang
Lindsay Bowman
Shannon McIntyre
Heidi Drazich
Alisha Gonsalves
Lulu Erkeneff
Anneke Barrie
Brooks Wilson
Bruna Schmitz
Caroline Sarran
Alizeé Arnaud
Lee-Ann Curren
Charlotte Caton
Sophie Hellyer
Francisca de Santos
Marloes van Elswijk
Candace O'Donnell
Marie Vigné
Rosanne Hodge
Sally Fitzgibbons
Laura Enever
Darci Egan
Carly Smith
Lisa Hurunui
Jodie Smith
Jemma Lenton
Selby Riddle
Tegan Riddle
Pippi Sopp
Amelia Davies
Jamee Wheatley
Kasey Martin
Miku Uemura
Kaori Mayaguchi

SKATE

Ianire Elorriaga
Martina Carra
Lois Pendlebury
Alex White

SNOW

Erin Comstock
Amber Stackhouse
Alexis Waite
Jessica Dalpiaz
Jessica Cumming
Kjersti Buaas
Stine Brun Kjeldaas
Tina Birbaum
Lisa Wiik
Lesley McKenna
Cuca Aranda
Anna Olofsson
Camille de Faucomprer
Margot Roziers
Aline Bock
Tania Detomas
Mello Imai
Mille Windfeidtl
Vanessa Coletta
Torah Bright
Andrea Binning
Kendal Brown

OTHER

Daida Moreno
Iballa Moreno
Anne-Marie Reichman
Caroline Barbeau

DCShoes

SKATE

Danny Way
Colin McKay
Rob Dyrdek
Josh Kalis
Rian Wenning
Ryan Smith
Ryan Gallant
Darrell Stanton
Lindsey Robertson

SURF

Bruce Irons
Dane Reynolds
Ry Craike

SNOW

Travis Parker
Travis Rice
Eddie Wall
Simon Chamberlain
Devun Walsh
Bjorn Leines

MOTOCROSS

Nate Adams
Ricky Carmichael
Adam Jones
Jeremy Mcgrath
Dustin Miller
Travis Pastrana
Davi Millsaps
Brock Hepler

BMX

Corey Bohan
Allan cooke
Chris Doyle
Chad Kagy
Robbie Miranda
Dave Mirra

Rossignol Group

SKI

Kjetil Aamodt
Pierrick Bourgeat
Claudia Bouvier
Rory Bushfield
Sage Cattabriga
Guilbault Colas
Roddy Darragon
Toby Dawson
Didier Defago
Lynsey Dyer
Allison Forsyth
Manu Gaidet
Thomas Grandi
Hugo Harrison
JF Houle
Anaais Karadeu
Bruno Kernen
Lindsey Kildow
Sandra Laoura
Kristi Keskinen
Ted Ligety
Julia Mancuso
Tina Maze
Ian McIntoch
Giulia Monego
Carol Montillex
Maria Jose Rienda
Genevieve Simard
Stephane Tissot
Dan Treadway
Kelly Vanderbeck
Vincent Vittoz
Silvan Zurbriggen
Vincent DeFrasne

SNOWBOARD

Jeremy Jones
Benji Ritchi
Doriane Vidal
Mathieu Crepel
JF Pelchat

AMBASSADOR

Luc Alphan
Alberto Tomba

LibTech

Jamie Lynn
Markku Koski
Jakob Wilhelmson
Martin Cernik
Travis Rice
Mark Landvic
Eric Jackson
Sammy Luebke
Jesse Burtner

GNU

Danny Kass
Zach Leach
Kyle Clancy
Hampus Mosesson
Chris Soreman
Barrett Christy
Temple Cummins
Dennis Buonjourno

Cleveland

Vijay Singh
David Toms
Shawn Micheel
Vaughn Taylor
Rod Pampling
David Howell
Bart Bryant

Fidra

Aaron Oberholser
Jerry Kelly
Michael Putnam
Kevin Stadler

Acknowledgments

The author/editor would like to acknowledge first and foremost the guiding light and consistent support of Bob McKnight over two long, hard years. Bob said from the outset that he was going to be hands-on with this project, and he was. I would also like to thank the other people in the Quiksilver chain of management, past and present, who contributed time, insight and advice, particularly Alan Green, John Law, Bruce Raymond, Jeff Hakman, Harry Hodge, Norm Innis, Michael Owen, Charlie Exon, Bernard Mariette, Tom Holbrook and Randy Hild.

Many of the best surf writers and photographers from the past 30 years or so are represented within these pages, and I would like to acknowledge their contributions, which are credited elsewhere. In some cases, however, when using archival material, we have tried and failed to identify the author of a particular image. For this, please accept my apologies and contact me so that we can rectify this in future editions.

Pulling together so much wonderful but diverse material and making graphic sense of it has not been an easy task, so I am deeply indebted to Jeff Girard, whose design work at *Surfer Magazine* and *The Surfer's Journal* was the perfect background, but who I am sure never expected to devote so much time and creativity to making this baby happen.

Finally, this project has frequently seemed to me like a one-man-band, with so much to do, so little time etc., etc. But, of course, there have been many, many people behind the scenes who have contributed in ways both large and small. I have tried to list as many of these unsung heroes as possible (starting with my wife—I may be slow but I am not stupid!) but apologies for any omissions.　　—Phil Jarratt, *Laguna Beach, June 2006.*

Jackie Jarratt	Gina Scrivani	Todd Kline	Yasmin Maksut	Virginie Azpeitia	Robbie Bell
Paul Holmes	Jodi Beck	Stephen Bell	Kyle Hufford	Lucy Reimer	Ken Banks
Kiku Terasaki	Matt Carr	Jasper Sanders	Tim Richardson	Jennifer Songe	Peter Levshin
PT and Leila	Tom Adler	Ann Mollet	Jackie Culmer	Andrea Grabham	Bobby Tan
Rob Colby	Jeff Hall	Simon Wootton	Jacquie Allen	Bobby Tang	Philip Hu
Anna Sherwood	Jeff Divine	Alex Ekstrund	Deb Kelly	Darin Ball	Gladys Chong

© 2006, Quiksilver Entertainment, Inc.

No part of this book may be reproduced, stored in a retrieval system, or transmitted in a form, by any means, including mechanical, electronic, photocopying, recording or otherwise, without prior written permission.

Published by Quiksilver Entertainment, Inc.

15202 Graham St., Huntington Beach, CA 92649

Library of Congress CIP number applied for.

ISBN 0-9786674-0-9

First edition: 2006

CEO/Guiding Light: Bob McKnight
Project Manager/Author/Editor: Phil Jarratt
Design/Production: Jeff Girard
Design Assistant: Daniel Little

Cover image: Art Brewer

Manufactured in China

The following photographers contributed invaluably to Quiksilver's History of Firsts (pages 26 to 31):

Aaron Chang	Gary Benzel (*artist*)	Rick Rievteld (*artist*)
Aitionn (Hugh McCleod)	Hank photo	Robert Beck
	Hoole McCoy	Robert Brown
Anna Sherwood	Jack McCoy	Scott Needman
Art Brewer	Jeff Divine	Sharon Marshall
Barrett Tester (*art*)	Jeff Ellis	Shirley Rogers
Bernie Baker	Jeff Hornbaker	Steve Cooney
Bob Barbour	Jim Russi	Steve Sherman
Brian Bielmann	Lance Trout	Stephen Zeigler
Chris Ortiz	Larry Moore (Flame)	Sylvain Cazenave
Chris Owen	Mark Oblow	Tim Zimmerman
Chris Van Lennup	Michael Vitti	Tom Adler (*art*)
Craig Fineman	Mike Balzer	Tom Servais
Dan Merkel	Mike Blayback	Warren Bolster
Dewey Nicks	Mike Moir	Wolfgang Bloch (*artist*)
Don James	Mo Daddy	
Don King	Pete Frieden	Christa Renee
Fernando Aguerre	Peter Crawford	James Cassimus